"If you're looking to make a real impact in the world and build a brand that reflects your values and vision, this book is a must-read. Rory is not only a master at his craft and has helped myself and my team so much, he is also a great friend and truly authentic. Rory and AJ's book offers real, practical, actionable insights on how to craft a brand that resonates with others and how to make a meaningful difference in the world. The strategies laid out are clear, empowering, and designed to help you turn your passion into purpose. This isn't just about building a brand—it's about creating a legacy that aligns with your deeper mission. I wholeheartedly endorse this book for anyone who wants to leave a lasting, positive mark on the world."

—**Dr. Caroline Leaf**, clinical and research
neuroscientist and bestselling author

"Rory and AJ Vaden have written a book that is as inspiring as it is practical. *Wealthy and Well-Known* is a masterclass in building a personal brand that aligns with your purpose and serves others at the highest level. Their knowledge that is beautifully translated into this book has been essential in helping bring my own message to the world. I feel lucky to have learned so much from them and am thrilled that you can too. Their frameworks, like 'You are most powerfully positioned to serve the person you once were,' resonate deeply with my own mission of helping people live stronger, healthier lives. This book is a must-read for anyone ready to step into their calling and make a meaningful impact."

—**Dr. Gabrielle Lyon**, founder of the Center for MUSCLE-CENTRIC
MEDICINE® and *New York Times* bestselling author of *Forever Strong*

"In a world where so many people are chasing fame, Rory and AJ Vaden remind us that true success comes from serving others. *Wealthy and Well-Known* is a powerful guide for anyone who wants to build a brand that not only creates wealth but also leaves a legacy. Their insights, like 'The best form of marketing in the world is a changed life,' are game-changing. This book will inspire you to focus on the depth of your impact, not just the width of your reach."

—**Trent Shelton**, performance coach and author of *Protect Your Peace*

"Rory and AJ have lived what they teach, rebuilding from the ground up with integrity and resilience. *Wealthy and Well-Known* is more than a book about personal branding—it's a guide to help you discover your purpose, serve with impact, and turn your reputation into lasting influence."

—**John C. Maxwell**, world's #1 leadership expert
and *New York Times* bestselling author

"Rory and AJ Vaden don't just teach personal branding; they embody it. This book is a masterclass in turning your life's purpose into lasting influence and impact. Read it, apply it, and watch your reputation become your greatest asset."

—**Amy Porterfield**, *New York Times* bestselling
author of *Two Weeks Notice*

Endorsements from our Clients

"This book includes a number of frameworks you all taught me years ago that have helped me create a level of financial abundance from my personal brand that I didn't have before. Anyone wanting to create more impact in the world while having less stress should absolutely read *Wealthy and Well-Known*!"

> —**Lewis Howes**, *New York Times* bestselling author
> and host of *The School of Greatness* podcast

"In thirty years, I've never worked with anyone like Rory and AJ before; they are remarkable! In this book, they deliver mastery-level strategies on building a personal brand that aligns with your purpose and creates both wealth and lasting impact."

> —**Ed Mylett**, #1 *Wall Street Journal* bestselling author
> and host of *The Ed Mylett Show*

"When it came to one of the most important projects in my career, I hired Rory and AJ's team, and they single handedly prepared me to succeed. They operate with honesty and integrity, and their blueprints are incredible. Now they've written a masterpiece with *Wealthy and Well-Known* that teaches anyone how to step into their God-given calling of building a personal brand that serves more people."

> —**Eric "ET The Hip-Hop Preacher" Thomas**, PhD, *New York Times*
> bestselling author and world-renowned motivational speaker

"Rory and AJ Vaden have created the ultimate guide for anyone looking t[o] build a personal brand that is both impactful and profitable. *Wealthy and Wel[l] Known* is packed with actionable strategies, heartfelt wisdom, and powerf[ul] frameworks that will help you find your unique voice and turn it into a thrivi[ng] business. As someone who has built a global community of ambitious entrepr[e]neurs, I can confidently say this book is a must-read for anyone ready to st[ep] into their purpose and make a lasting impact."

> —**Natalie Ellis**, founder and CEO of Bossbabe

"Rory and AJ Vaden have created a masterpiece with *Wealthy and Well-Kno[wn]* This book is a must-read for anyone who wants to turn their passion into [pur]pose and their reputation into revenue. Their frameworks are not only pract[ical] but also deeply inspiring, helping you align your personal brand with y[our] divine calling. As someone who has built businesses and platforms to s[erve] others, I can confidently say this book will change lives and empower leade[rs] make a lasting impact."

> —**Dr. Josh Axe**, health entrepreneur, *New York Times*
> bestselling author, and founder of The Health Institute

"Sometimes searching for success, wealth, and notoriety gets masked in doing more, but Rory and AJ taught me it's about pursuing my purpose, first, to achieve meaningful impact. If you want to unlock your fullest potential, *Wealthy and Well-Known* is a fast track to learning how our deepest success lies inside of us, only unleashed when we embrace our uniqueness and serve others at the highest level."

—**Jasmine Star**, speaker, podcaster, and CEO of Social Curator

Endorsements from our Colleagues

"Rory and AJ Vaden have distilled years of wisdom and experience into *Wealthy and Well-Known*. This book is packed with actionable strategies and profound insights that will help you uncover your unique value and monetize it in a way that serves others. Their story of resilience and reinvention is both inspiring and practical, making this a must-have guide for those ready to take their personal brand to the next level."

—**Dan Martell**, *Wall Street Journal* bestselling
author of *Buy Back Your Time*

"This is your wake-up call. *Wealthy and Well-Known* reveals how to stop being the world's best-kept secret and start turning your message into momentum. Rory and AJ don't just teach personal branding—they hand you the playbook for income and influence."

—**Sally Hogshead**, *New York Times* bestselling
author of *Fascinate*

"Building a personal brand isn't about self-promotion—it's about serving others with your expertise. *Wealthy and Well-Known* walks you through the steps to amplify your message and increase your reach, all while staying true to your core values."

—**Michael Hyatt**, *New York Times* bestselling author
and business coach

"Use your gifts and change the world. *Wealthy and Well-Known* is your guide to building a personal brand with real impact. Rory and AJ Vaden break it all down in a way that's clear, actionable, and zero fluff. Whether you're just starting or ready to scale, this book helps you stand out, build trust, and amplify your influence without the burnout."

—**Jenna Kutcher**, entrepreneur, podcaster, *New York Times*
bestselling author of *How Are You, Really?*

WEALTHY
AND
WELL-KNOWN

*Build Your Personal Brand and Turn
Your Reputation into Revenue*

WEALTHY
AND
WELL-KNOWN

*Build Your Personal Brand and Turn
Your Reputation into Revenue*

Rory and AJ Vaden

Published by Mission Driven Press, an imprint of Forefront Books, Nashville, Tennessee.
Distributed by Simon & Schuster.

Library of Congress Control Number: 2025905103
Print ISBN: 978-1-63763-442-4
E-book ISBN: 978-1-63763-443-1

Cover Design by Sami Lane
Interior Design by Interior Design by PerfecType, Nashville, TN

Printed in the United States of America
25 26 27 28 29 30 LSC 10 9 8 7 6 5 4 3 2 1

God, all things are possible with You.
May our lives be a reflection of Your goodness and faithfulness.

To our team at Brand Builders Group,
this book was written to help the world know
of the amazing work you do.

To the many individuals who played a role in our story,
this book was made possible because of you.

To the Mission-Driven Messengers this book is intended for,
may it help you make the world a better place.

CONTENTS

PART 4

Personal Brand Action Plan

INTRODUCTION FROM THE AUTHORS

If you are going to spend the next few hours with us reading this book, then you should know a little bit about who we are and where we come from before you get started. First, we are a married couple who have been in business together since 2006. We met as business partners right out of college, fell in love about a year later, and have been partners in life and in business ever since. We come from wildly different backgrounds and upbringings but share a unique passion for entrepreneurship, personal development, and God.

Quick disclaimer about our faith: We have a deep faith and strong relationship with God, and much of our story shares how we came to that faith and relationship with God. We know not everyone shares the same beliefs we have, and that's okay. This book is not about us convincing you to believe what we believe but about sharing real examples and stories from our own lives that illustrate and define what we believe to be true about finding your purpose and building an influential personal brand.

Now, a quick introduction from each of us.

AJ VADEN

Hi, I am AJ Vaden. My legal name is Amanda, but I have gone by AJ since I was in third grade. I am wife to Rory Vaden, who is my business partner, best friend, and co-author of this book. I am mom to two amazing little men who have taught me more about leadership, life, and patience than I ever thought possible. Being a mom is my favorite thing! I am also CEO and cofounder at Brand Builders Group. That's not my job; that's my professional calling and passion, and I love all the crazy things it brings me on a daily basis.

I am also a daughter, sister, friend, author, speaker, entrepreneur, salesperson, customer service rep, bill payer, chauffeur, cook, cleaner, and party planner. To name a few.

Along with that list I am also bold (some call it opinionated, but I call it passionate). I am a recovering workaholic (making progress daily). I am direct, loyal, and committed. I am imperfect, a lifelong learner, and deeply convicted.

I am many things. As are you.

I could be known for many things. As you could be.

But **what do you actually want to be known for?**

When someone thinks of you, what do you want them to think?

When you leave the table, what do you want them to say in your absence?

When someone introduces you, what do you want them to say?

When you leave this earth, what do you want people to remember?

The problem for most of us is that we have not spent nearly enough time thinking about what we truly want to be known for. We spend more time planning our family vacation than we do the legacy we want to leave. As a result, we end up living a default existence. One that happens "to" us instead of "for" us and for others.

You can either be intentional, proactive, and engaged in this process, or you can let others decide and define who you are. Which route will you go? I imagine if you picked up this book, you already know. You choose the intentional path. Me too! I cannot wait for you to start reading this book, diving into the exercises, and taking the next step into your calling. So glad you are on this journey with us!

RORY VADEN

Hey there! I'm Rory, and there is a good chance that in many ways, I'm just like you. I am an aspiring "Mission-Driven Messenger." I always have been. As you'll read in the coming pages, I developed a passion early in life to speak, teach, write, and inspire others. Through the amazing partnership with my brilliant and beautiful wife, AJ (CEO and cofounder of Brand Builders Group and coauthor of this book), the help of lots of friends and family, and the backing of a powerhouse team, I've been able to accomplish a lot of the things I originally set out to do. I was a two-time World Champion of Public Speaking finalist in my early twenties, became a *New York Times* bestselling author at age twenty-nine, had a TEDx talk go viral, and with AJ built four different multi-seven-figure businesses and two different eight-figure businesses by my early forties.

But it wasn't always that way, and I have made so many mistakes along the way. While I did become one of the youngest people in history to be inducted into the professional speaking Hall of Fame, most of what I remember is spending a couple decades of my life feeling lost and overlooked as one of the "world's best-kept secrets." I struggled with marketing. I struggled with messaging. I struggled to gain the attention of the media and clients. But over the years, AJ and I have figured a few things out about how to reach more people and make a bigger impact (and more income) in the world.

Today, alongside our team of extraordinary humans at Brand Builders Group, we share what we've learned to help other experts, entrepreneurs, and executives become more *Wealthy and Well-Known*. We've helped our clients have a fair bit of success, as dozens of them have:

- become *New York Times* and/or national bestselling authors
- been invited to speak on the biggest stages in the world
- appeared as guest experts on the most popular news media outlets

- built top-ranked podcasts and YouTube channels
- amassed large social followings, email lists, and video views
- grown their revenues hundreds of thousands of dollars—and even millions of dollars—per year through their personal brand.

We've had the privilege of supporting people just starting out with an idea, all the way to working behind-the-scenes directly with some of the biggest personal brands in the world like Lewis Howes, Ed Mylett, Amy Porterfield, Eric "ET Hip Hop Preacher" Thomas, Jasmine Star, John Maxwell, Trent Shelton, Natalie Ellis, and more. We've supported world-renowned healthcare practitioners and mental health professionals like Dr. Gabrielle Lyon, Dr. Henry Cloud, Dr. Caroline Leaf, and Dr. Josh Axe, helping them get their vital messages out to more people. We've worked with former pro athletes, professional service providers, small business owners, authors, speakers, coaches, consultants, C-suite executives, and top-level leaders from direct-sales companies, all to help them build and monetize their personal brand.

While I am definitely a nerd who loves data and systems and strategy and practical tactics, for AJ and me, this isn't just a business; it's a ministry. With so much negativity, indulgence, temptation, and stress-inducing content being promoted around the globe 24/7, we believe there is a spiritual war going on for people's attention. Our goal is to share the best of the expertise we've developed to help "the good guys and gals" win. We're looking to support people who genuinely care about finding solutions that really work for their clients and audiences. We're looking for clients who are on a crusade to make the world a better place. We're looking for people who are willing to dedicate their lives to the service of others. We're looking for *Mission-Driven Messengers*. In other words, we're looking for you!

PART 1

PERSONAL
BRAND
PRINCIPLES

CHAPTER 1

WHAT IS A PERSONAL BRAND?

BY AJ VADEN

May 4, 2018.

"Today is your last day. Your services are no longer needed here."

Hearing those words was like an out-of-body experience. It was a bizarre mixture of shock and relief; an odd combination of peace and disappointment. But in plain and simple terms, I was fired.

This was the ending of an era for me. It was the end of the previous twelve years of my personal and professional life.

You see, I am a recovering workaholic. Let me explain. May 2006 began my personal journey into entrepreneurship, sales, and leadership. Right out of college I got to be part of starting a company with three other guys (one of whom is my now super-handsome hubby). And this was a true start-up. No salary. Performance-only pay. No systems, no processes, and no real idea what we were doing—but lots of grit, lots of hustle, and lots of cold calls. So many cold calls.

I was by far the least experienced of the founding group but firmly believed if these guys could figure it out then I could, too, and eventually I did. By the grace of God and the gift of naivety, we all did. If you were alive in the year 2006, you may remember that the United States was heading into the Great Recession. The lead-up to the deepest recessionary period of the past one hundred years may not have been the best time to start a new business, but we didn't know any other economy or market conditions, so a little blissful ignorance went a long way. Through straight-up sales grit, with a small but determined group of people, we crossed seven figures in revenue that first year. And that seven figures did not come easy. It was a lot of hustle, a lot of twelve-hour days, a lot of learning as you go, and a lot of persevering.

That set the pace for the next decade for me.

Here is what I came to believe about myself: *The more I work, the more worthy I am.* I have to be a top-performing producer to be taken seriously. If I can just outwork and outperform all my colleagues and business partners, *then* I'll be seen as important or valuable. If I just focus solely on work, *then* I will get all that I want in life.

So, I did. I put my full focus, energy, passion, and every hour of my day into work. But it was more than that; I put my full *identity* into my work. I gave it my all—literally all I had. I willingly gave up attending personal events, family gatherings, vacations, birthday parties, wedding showers, baby showers, and time with people I loved all in the name of success. I wore it as a badge of honor that I put the company first. I was completely driven by external validation, and I was consumed with achieving.

About midway through that journey, I knew something was wrong with my relationship to work. There was a "never-enough-ness" of what I was going after. The pressure I invited, the workload I took on, the growing void of friendships or relationships outside of work. I knew I was working too much. I knew this had become unhealthy for me. I knew I should step back. Part of me really wanted to make a change, and the other part just couldn't let go.

I'd tell myself, *Not now. Not with all the team members I'm responsible for, the clients I have made commitments to, the growth of the company, the money I'm making, the accomplishments . . . the pride . . . the ego. I can't leave now.*

So, I didn't. I stayed.

It wasn't until 2017 (eleven years in) that I had a real reckoning with my identity. I became a mom in March of that year. I worked until one week before my due date and took only three weeks of maternity leave before hitting the road doing keynotes again.

Read that again: three *weeks.*

My long-time-coming reckoning hit me on a four-hour drive home late one night in the pouring rain, after my first speaking engagement coming back from maternity leave. I was pumping breast milk while driving *and* calling to check on my baby while navigating the Tennessee highway system. In the distraction of it all, I made a wrong turn and ended up driving back toward Knoxville instead of home to Nashville. I traveled ninety minutes in the wrong direction! (True fact: I am horrendous with directions. Totally awful. Pray to God I never get lost in the wilderness. I will not make it out. You will have to come find me.)

By the time I realized what I had done, it was already approaching midnight. As I was scrambling to figure out what I was going to do, I accidentally knocked my pump off and spilled fresh breast milk all over me and all over my car. I finally pulled over, got out in the pouring rain, and just screamed! I said a few choice words, returned to the car, and started sobbing.

What was I doing? What was wrong with me? Why was I in this car in the middle of nowhere with my newborn at home without me? Why did I say yes to the speaking gig just three weeks after giving birth? Who had I become? And most importantly, **who did I want to become?**

Something had to change. *I* had to change. But I didn't know how. I didn't know what. So, I drove home. I woke up the next day and went right back to work. But something was different. I was different. I knew that I wanted to be different.

Twelve months later I was called into a meeting in which I was asked some pointed questions about the trajectory of the company. I gave my honest, direct, and transparent answers. (Have I yet mentioned I can be very direct?)

Two weeks later, on May 4, 2018, in what I thought was just a routine follow-up to the prior meeting, I was delivered the line that changed my life: "Today is your last day. Your services are no longer needed here." It was a short meeting. Mainly because I was speechless. I had no words. Nothing came out, partly because of shock but mainly because I kept hearing this voice in my head saying, *Keep your mouth shut and let this happen. Keep your mouth shut and let this happen.* That's the bizarre part about the whole thing. That voice was definitely not me talking because I would never instruct myself to "Keep my mouth shut"—not a chance. "Let this happen"—are you insane? But there was this overwhelming and unusual sense of peace and relief at hearing those words, so I listened to that voice; I kept my mouth shut and let it happen.

I picked up my bag, walked down the hallway, and exited the doors. It was over. Just like that. Twelve years of my life—everything I had built—gone. My role in a business I had helped grow from zero to eight figures in annual revenues with almost two hundred people and thousands of customers was, in one single moment—gone. All the relationships I'd built—gone. My team—gone. My income—gone. My known identity—gone. It was all gone. It had ended.

But something else was about to begin.

I don't know your personal story, but I do know this: **Your past prepares you for your future.**

Every event, experience, success, failure, hurt, and victory—every bit of what you have been through—is preparation. Every bit of your life matters because it has made you who you are. It's all part of your story and part of what makes you undeniably unique in the world. **No one else is you, and that is your superpower.**

We grow the most through challenges, not celebrations.

Our character is developed most through losses, not wins.

Our purpose is revealed most through trials, not triumphs.

And people relate more to your personal story than they do to your professional teachings.

Your story matters because it has the power to help someone else. That is part of the responsibility that we all carry, to let our lives be used for good—and what better good is there than helping someone else? In a word, our lives are meant to be used in *the service* of helping others, and that is the largest part of what we should all want to be known for.

REPUTATION

Our definition of reputation is simple: **Reputation is what people think about when they think of you.**

We all have a reputation. Me, you, your significant other, best friend, the next-door neighbor, local high school principal, community church pastor, hairstylist, your child's soccer coach, and everyone else you know.

The concept of reputation is likely not new to you. Most of us have been hearing about its importance since we were kids.

In fact, take a moment and write down the names of real people you know who fit a few of the categories above. This should take less than two minutes. Write down a name, and then next to that name write the first word that comes to mind when you think of the person.

I will do this too.

As an example, I'll pick my kid's soccer coach. The first attribute that comes to my mind when I think of him is "no limit." He runs his practice like he runs his business. Be on time, come prepared, do the work, have a good attitude, play hard, accept the loss, celebrate the win, move on.

I do not know him super well personally, but this is how I view him from my soccer-field interactions and how I would describe him professionally, and now it is how you view him as well. That's the thing about reputation: If you are not intentional in how you build yours, then you will leave it to others to build it for you.

You either do the work to create the reputation you want, or you get one by default.

Now let's make this a little more personal. I want you to write down your own name (just use the margin of this page). But this time, I want you to write what you think people think of when they think of *you*.

Not what you *want* them to think, but what you *actually* think people think of when they think of you.

Now, answer as honestly as possible, "Is that what you *want* them to think of when they think of you?"

There isn't a right or wrong answer; you just need to know where you are starting as you begin your personal brand journey.

When people first learn about our new company, Brand Builders Group, they often come with a misconception of what we do and what a personal brand really is. Most assume that personal branding or a "personal brand" is somehow connected to what you *do*. We hear people mistakenly say that personal brands are only for authors, speakers, coaches, consultants, influencers, podcasters, thought leaders, etc. Or we hear things like, "Your personal brand is all about your brand guidelines (colors, logos, fonts, images), website, social media, podcast, blog, or YouTube channel."

Let me be clear right up front.

A personal brand is NOT:

- A set of brand guidelines, colors, fonts, or logos
- A website, podcast, blog, or YouTube channel
- A social media profile or set of followers
- A business model or revenue stream
- A set of content, thoughts, or ideas (book, articles, blogs, podcasts)
- A short-term project that you are working on for a season of your life

A personal brand is *NOT* what you do.

A personal brand is *WHO* YOU ARE.

It's the consolidation and culmination of your experiences, expertise, beliefs, values, and God-given purpose.

It's the intentional work and effort that shape your reputation to reflect who you are, what you believe, and what you want to be known for.

In fact, a better word for personal brand is simply *reputation*—which, you might recall, means what people think of when they think of you. Personal brand and reputation are synonymous. The term "personal brand" may be new,

Personal Branding is the formalization, digitization, and monetization of your reputation.

but the premise is not because the concept of "reputation" has been around since the beginning of time.

The art and science of intentionally curating and deliberately building your reputation is what is known as "personal branding." Or, more specifically, as we define it, Personal Branding is the formalization, digitization, and monetization of your reputation.

That is what we do at Brand Builders Group. We are a personal brand strategy firm that helps people build and grow their personal brand. In layman's terms, we help people become more *Wealthy and Well-Known*—hence the title of this book.

Why this, out of all the things in the world we could have done after the events of May 4, 2018? I had been fired, and Rory had resigned two weeks later. It was a clean slate. A fresh start. We could have gone in countless directions. Why personal branding?

First, if you are reading this book, it's likely you are already on the journey to finding more meaning in your life. You have a feeling that you are supposed to share a specific message, reach a specific audience, make a bigger impact, give back, or do something more or bigger than what you are doing right now. That feeling is there for a reason: It's a *calling*.

Perhaps you want to do this new thing but don't know where to start. Or maybe you haven't started yet because you can't quite let go of who you used to be so you can become a better version of you. This is why we started Brand Builders Group, and it's why we are writing this book. We have put systems, processes, and a clear methodology in place to help you help others faster.

Work is something you *do*. Work makes up *part* of who you are. But you are more than just your work.

I think what scares us the most about doing something new is that we don't know who we are supposed to be if we start doing something we've never done. For so many of us, our very identity—a core-connected part of our life's purpose and reason for living—is wrapped up in our work. And so, the idea of leaving behind a trade, a profession, a career, or a company makes us *feel* like we are leaving behind *ourselves*. It's almost as if we are left asking, "Who am I if I'm not *this thing I used to do*?"

After I was fired, I had a true identity crisis. My worth was so tied up in my work I could not figure out who I was if I was not that. My old life had to be burned to the ground so I could start fresh. No temptation to turn back. It was my Cortés "burn the boats" moment.[1]

Earlier I shared that I kept hearing a voice in my head saying, *Keep your mouth shut and let this happen*, and by the end of this book, you will know those words were truly impossible coming from my mouth. In the days, weeks, and months to come, it became clear to me who those words were coming from.

Regardless of your religious beliefs or affiliation, I think we could all mostly agree that some things in this world and in our own lives are just beyond us. They are what many would call *supernatural*. That's what this was for me—a supernatural intervention in my life. I knew I should have left that job years earlier, but I just didn't have the courage to do it. So, on May 4, 2018, I believe God stepped in on my behalf and He did it for me. But, because of that, it was going to be on *His* terms, not mine. My part was to listen. To let it end so that something new could begin. One thing that became clear to me in my journey was that **your new life will always cost you your old one.**

The tangible "something new" was Brand Builders Group, but more than that it was the realization that it could all go away; my team, my clients, my income, my social media, my contacts, my security, my friends, my title—all gone, and yet there was one thing that belonged to me and followed me: *my reputation.*

Your personal brand is something that nobody can ever take away from you. You can never be "fired" from your personal brand because it is inherently *you*. You can never "lose" your personal brand because it is your reputation.

That is also why you can't even ask the question, "Do I need a personal brand?" The answer is you already have one. That would be like asking, "Do I need a reputation?" Need one or not, you've got one. And so, we just want to help you make sure it's the one you want.

If you have a good reputation, it will follow you—and it will accelerate and amplify every single thing you do.

If you have a bad reputation, it will follow you—and it will decelerate and diminish every single thing you do.

If you have little to no reputation, few will know about you, and, therefore, your gifts and talents will likely prove to be inconsequential in the lives of others and will fall short of their ultimate potential.

We've gone all in on "personal brands" because we *believe* in their power to transform the world, and because we've personally experienced everything that a great one can do for you. But this is far more than just our *feeling*. Since starting Brand Builders Group, we have invested more than $100,000 and a year of our time into a PhD-led, statistically valid, national research study weighted to the US census and conducted in accordance with traditional academic rigor. It's called *The Trends in Personal Branding National Research Study*.

> *If you'd like to read the entire findings report and
> download our set of infographics at no cost, scan
> the QR code on the front inside cover of this book
> and download the available Research Study.*

Three of the clear data-driven conclusions of that research are that personal branding is:

1. **The Future**
   - Significant generational differences exist when it comes to trust and engagement with individuals who have established personal brands compared to those who do not.
   - With the emergence of AI and technological advancement, it will ultimately be your unique human perspective that differentiates you.
2. **Highly Profitable**
   - Americans are willing to spend more on products and services from individuals with established personal brands.

- 58 percent of Americans would be willing to pay more to receive their services from a professional who does *not* work at a large company but has an established personal brand.
- 63 percent of Americans are more likely to buy from you if you have an established personal brand.
- 67 percent of Americans would be willing to spend more money on products and services from the companies of founders whose personal brand aligns with their personal values.

3. **A Trust Accelerator**
   - Trust is the new competitive advantage, and people trust those they can see, get to know, and learn from on a regular basis.
   - 62 percent of Americans are more likely to accept a job with a company or organization when the founder or executives have an established personal brand.
   - 74 percent of Americans say they are more likely to trust someone who has an established personal brand.
   - 82 percent of Americans agree that companies are more influential if their founder or executives have a personal brand the public knows, trusts, and follows.

REPUTATION FORMULA

If it is so empirically definitive that having an established personal brand and trusted reputation is important, it then begs the question, "Where does a strong reputation really come from?" Ironically, while we regularly hear about the importance

74 percent of Americans say they are more likely to trust someone who has an established personal brand.

of a great reputation, almost no one ever talks about *where* or *how* or *what* a reputation comes from.

For us, reputation boils down to a simple equation we call "The Reputation Formula." It works like this:

Results x Reach = Reputation

A person's reputation is primarily made up of two factors: results and reach.

Results are what you have done or accomplished. They have to do with your experiences, expertise, and education, as well as the *substance* of what you know and your impact on society.

Reach is simply how many people know about you.

Results can be either positive or negative, but Reach can obviously only be greater than zero since you can't have *negative* people who know about you—and counting your family, you should have at least one.

As an illustration, let's use Mother Teresa and apply this formula.

1. Does she have large or small results?
2. Are they largely positive or negative?
3. Does she have large or small reach?

Most likely you would say she has Large Positive Results and Large Reach. Let's now apply this to The Reputation Formula.

Large Results (positive) x Large Reach = Well-Known Positive Reputation

Now, what about someone like Adolf Hitler? I am confident you would say he had Large Negative Results with Large Reach. Adolf Hitler therefore has a huge and well-known *negative* Reputation. Thus, The Reputation Formula can work either positively or negatively.

But here's where it gets super interesting. If I asked you, "Which one matters more—Results or Reach?" chances are, if you are like most of the live audiences we've spoken to, you would say Results. That's what I would've said too. Because that feels like the one that *should* matter more. It seems to me that a person's actual experience and education and track record should be the most important part of their Reputation. But let's examine that a bit more closely using a few other examples.

Have you ever heard the name Michael Phelps? Chances are, you have. Phelps is a former American swimmer and the winningest Olympian of all time. As of his retirement in 2016, he had won twenty-eight Olympic medals, twenty-three of them gold medals.[2] But now let me ask you: Given the context of Michael Phelps, do you recognize the name Katie Ledecky? Think about it for a moment. This is not a trick question. There is a strong contextual connectedness between Katie Ledecky and Michael Phelps. But when I ask you specifically to think of Katie Ledecky, do you know who I am talking about?

If you are like most people who participate in this exercise— *unless you are a huge fan of swimming*—I'm guessing that you do not recognize her name as automatically as you do Michael Phelps. We've asked this in dozens of live trainings with thousands of people from all around the globe, and very few have been able to identify Katie Ledecky as quickly as Michael Phelps. So, who is she? At the time of this writing, she is tied as the winningest female US Olympian of all time with fourteen Olympic medals, nine of which are gold.[3]

When it comes to their Results, they are about nearly as comparable as you can get. In fact, Ledecky has even beaten Phelps's best time in the 800m freestyle—Ledecky's 07:57.42 compared to Phelps's 08:06.70.[4] Two world-class athletes competing on the biggest stage, in the same sport, from the same country, living at the same time, collecting top honors. And yet, when it comes to their Reach, they are vastly different.

Why is that?

I cannot say for sure, as neither of them are clients of ours. However, the comparison helps to underscore a pointed and somewhat sobering truth: Your Reach matters. A lot. It does you no good to be the "world's best-kept secret." That does nothing to serve the people around you. **In order for someone to do business with you, they first have to know about you.**

In today's technology- and media-rich society, there is an unbelievable amount of noise. So much that it's often hard to filter what is real, what is reliable, and what is true. With a million different things competing for your attention, we find that most people simply use Reach as a default filter in determining where to focus their attention and where to spend their money. The most common narrative sounds like this: "If that many people follow them, there must be something to this," or, "With millions of followers all agreeing, this must be true," or, "That many people

> *In order for someone to do business with you, they first have to know about you.*

can't be talking about this or doing this if it doesn't work." It's typical herd mentality—the tendency for one's behavior or beliefs to conform with those of the group to which they belong.

Reach has become just as important as Results when it comes to building your personal brand (reputation), growing your business, and increasing your impact.

And in some cases, you could argue that Reach matters *more* than Results.

You don't have to look very far on the internet to see there are plenty of people with lots of followers who are seemingly making plenty of money without a verified background or expertise in whatever they are talking about or selling. Truth be known, they are quite possibly *less* qualified, *less* educated, and have *less* experience than you do on the same subject matter!

So, why do they make *more* money?

Simple.

Because they have more Reach. They are better *marketers*. They have bigger *followings*.

I'm not saying I think this is how it *should* be, nor do I *like* it, nor do I think it's necessarily *fair*. But I am saying this is how it *is*.

The truth is that many *real Experts,* who actually have years of proven and positive Results, have been spending all their time studying and honing their craft rather than growing their Reach. They have been solely Results focused with minimal or no Reach focus. This most often shows up from a business standpoint with comments like this:

- We've plateaued.
- What worked before isn't working anymore.
- Our customer base has changed.
- There's just too much competition.
- Revenues are down, and we don't know why.

I know way too many incredible individuals with life-changing products and services who feel like they are losing.

And in many ways, they are. They are losing to people who have spent less time getting real Results but way more time learning how to be a great *marketer.*

We live in a world where, unfortunately, the best idea doesn't win. The best marketer wins.

MISSION-DRIVEN MESSENGERS

We want to change that narrative. We don't want to live in a world where the best ideas are never seen simply because they aren't the most polarizing, sensational, or attention-grabbing. It's one of the many reasons we started Brand Builders Group. We want to help return the influence and power to the people who are great thinkers, careful practitioners, and who actually care deeply about making the world a better place.

Our mission is focused on helping the *real* Experts and *true* thought leaders see the value of and learn the principles and tactics required to become a world-class marketer. Some Experts, and historically many Artists, simply underestimate the value and necessity of having to learn to *market*. (We define artist here as anyone who creates something out of nothing.)

There is typically an unspoken, internal limiting belief that says, *My work is so good that people should come find me,* or *As long as I provide great results and a good experience, people will tell everyone they know about me.* Unfortunately, neither is true. Instead, it's just a terribly defeating internal monologue and a horrible business strategy that lessens financial opportunity and guarantees indiscriminate obscurity for the "artist" themselves. On the contrary, the most successful and influential modern-day artists seem to share a different philosophy that **marketing *is* art. There is the art of creating your work, and then there is the art of letting people know that your work exists.**

> *Marketing is art. There is the art of creating your work, and then there is the art of letting people know that your work exists.*

A defining characteristic of a Mission-Driven Messenger is an unrelenting focus on the person you are called to serve and the unique way in which you can serve them best.

Mission-Driven Messengers do not market for the celebration of their own ego, or for the pursuit of vanity metrics, or just to be rich.

They are more interested in making a difference than in making a dollar. They are more passionate about fulfilling their purpose than about making a profit. Consider the following priority statements:

- It's not that you shouldn't care about money; it's okay to want to make money. But put the **mission before the money.**
- It's not that you shouldn't care about income; it's okay to want to grow your income. But let **income come second to impact.**
- It's not that you shouldn't care about revenue; it's okay to want to increase revenues. But make **revenue subservient to reputation.**

In short, let making money—and lots of it—be a byproduct of doing good in the world. You can do both.

And herein lies the connection to your personal brand. Remember, a personal brand is simply the formalization, digitization, and monetization of your reputation. And that formalization includes a strategy to increase your Reach. You don't build your personal brand so you can tell the world how great you are; you do it so your work and your story can reach more people and help make the world great.

Now, I know you may already have a negative perception of the term "personal brand" because you associate it with ego, vanity, or "fake-fluencers" standing in front of borrowed Ferraris and rented private jets.

But that's not what we're talking about when it comes to building your personal brand. We're talking about making the time to access God's divine design of your humanity. We're talking about creating space to explore how your talents could best coalesce in a way that inspires others to be their best selves. We're talking about adding value to the world in a way that builds trust—real trust with everyone who comes in contact with you.

That type of personal brand is not only a service to your fellow citizens and a massively meaningful endeavor bringing purpose to your personal life, but also a lifelong asset that can provide for you and your family. Building a *real* personal brand affords you the kind of security that no one can ever take away—even if you are fired and everything else you've ever known disappears.

Because a personal brand is *your* reputation. It follows *you*. It is not what you do; it is who you are.

WHAT IS A BRAND?

In my former profession I did sales consulting, coaching, and training for all kinds of companies, from pest control to real estate and financial services to direct sales and wholesale manufacturers. I slept, ate, and breathed all things sales, and, I might add, I consider myself a pretty darn good salesperson. It's kind of my jam. The point is, I sold a lot of stuff and taught lots of other people how to do the same thing. But I never really connected the dots of how much all my talking about sales, learning about sales, and doing sales had become ingrained into the way others viewed me. Until the spring of 2021.

Now mind you, we started Brand Builders Group three years prior. I had been CEO for two years, had been married to my husband for eleven years, and had been a mom for more than four years. All those data points are important frames of reference when I tell you this story. Rory and I are at a nonprofit event hosted by a friend of ours. My husband proceeds to introduce me to someone he clearly knows but I have never met. I see them talking across the room, so I walk over to join the conversation, and he quickly begins to introduce me as "the best salesperson I've ever met, the #1 revenue producer at our former company, a million-dollar consultant, and a Fortune 500 sales trainer."

Like, what?! Is this what he thinks of me? Not that these kind words and compliments are bad, but I thought, *Is this what he thinks of when he thinks of me?*

How about CEO of our new company, hardworking mom of our two tiny awesome humans, and a little more on how I am . . . his incredible *wife*?! But those weren't the predominant things that came out of his mouth. Let me also state that this has been corrected, and we no longer have this problem. But what happened that night resulted from more than a decade of unintentional conditioning on my part. Sales was my life. I had unknowingly trained those around me to associate me with *sales* by what I spoke about, where I spent my time, how I invested my money, and what achievements I most proudly celebrated. And although those things had not been a part of my daily life for several years, it was a big part of how my husband introduced me to a stranger in a business setting. "Meet AJ, the best salesperson ever . . ."

This is a real-life lesson in how a "brand" really works. **A brand is simply what other people think of when they think of you.**

What matters to a personal brand is not so much what *you* think you are but much more of what *others* think you are. In that way, you don't actually *control* your personal brand; other people do, because other people choose what to think about when they think of you. However, you can highly *influence* your personal brand by the way you *present* yourself to the world.

> A brand is simply what other people think of when they think of you.

And that's what we are going to talk about in the pages that follow. This book will teach you how to show up in the world in a way that maximizes what you—and only you—can provide for people. And if we do this right, it will not only be fully authentic to who you are but also highly aligned with a monetization strategy that will pay you more than you could've ever possibly imagined, all by just stepping into exactly who you were created to be.

But if a brand is what *other* people think about when they think of you, then it's imperative that you are intentional about choosing *exactly* what you want people to think about when your name pops up in their head or in conversation. Not only that, but to the extent possible, you have to explicitly curate every single touch point that people have with your online and offline reputation. As the old saying goes, "Your reputation precedes you," but the question is, "Do you want yours to?"

One of the simplest but most easily overlooked parts of building a personal brand is to **define what you want to be known for.**

BRAND CHARACTERISTICS

Excellence is never an accident. It starts with intentional, conscious choices about exactly who you want to be and what you want to become. Building a personal brand is no different; you have the choice to decide what you want your life to be about and what you want your personal brand to represent. That can shift as you grow and change. All parts of my past are important and not to be forgotten or dismissed, as they have helped shape me into the person I am today. But some are no longer relevant to who I am and what I feel God calling me to do.

For example, my sales experience is a dominant part of my professional past, and I believe the years I dedicated to that craft prepared and equipped me for the work I do and the business I run today. However, I no longer spend my days teaching sales principles to sales professionals. Much of my audience is likely *in* sales, but none of them are coming to me to learn *about* sales . . . although they may get that as an added bonus. I had to shift the conversation in my content. I had to start appealing to a new audience. Those were choices I made and continue to make each day. That takes intention. Knowing what you want to be known for and who you want to be known by are the first choices you need to make.

To help you get started, let me share one of our favorite exercises to get those creative juices flowing. You are going to create a "Brand Characteristics List." This is a defined set of adjectives that you want people to use to describe you when talking about you personally, your brand, your company, and your work.

Here is the Brand Characteristics List for my personal brand:

- Modern
- Bold
- Inspiring
- Elegant
- Distinctive
- Smart
- Powerful
- Faithful
- Fun
- Personable
- Intentional
- Challenging
- Original
- Insightful
- Thought Provoking
- Compelling
- Relevant

Scan the QR code on the front inside cover of this book to grab an adjectives chart and Brand Characteristics template to complete for yourself.

The Brand Characteristics List speaks to the aspirational direction of your personal brand, but it actually serves a dual purpose.

Functionally speaking, this list is useful as an internal-strategy document to communicate to those who encounter your brand so they understand what *energy* your brand should *emote* for the people who are interacting with all forms of your various content.

If this is done successfully, these words should populate when people experience your digital presence (think website, social media, blog, podcast, content, etc.) as well as your offline presence. These are the words, thoughts, and emotions you are intentionally trying to create as you interact in the world. In fact, take a quick visit to www.ajvaden.com and click through my site to see how the words in my list show up in colors, fonts, imagery, and copy.

A quote that is often attributed to Maya Angelou says, "People will forget what you said, people will forget what you did, but people will never forget how you made them feel." This list will help you get clear on how you want to make people feel when they interact with you.

Your personal brand should move people emotionally. It should make people feel something. It should also move *you* emotionally and make *you* feel something.

Your personal brand should include an entire suite of content and assets that convey a set of ideals and principles that are so important to you that you will dedicate the rest of your life to advancing them in the world. The ideals and principles that you believe in don't even have to matter to those around you. Not everyone will agree with them. That is okay. It's not about being right or wrong, and it's not about trying to convince others to believe what you believe.

This is about you finding and serving other like-minded people who are already aligned with your beliefs, values, and ideals. Some people will be for you, some will not, and that's okay; you are not supposed to be for everyone.

BRAND MANTRA

While a Brand Characteristics List is your intentional design of *how* you want people to describe you and your brand, what we call a

"Brand Mantra" is a way to codify your *why* for building a personal brand in the first place. Although we believe your personal brand does not begin with *why* but rather *who*, we also believe in the incredible value of a well-defined list of the reasons why more formally building a personal brand is important to you.

Don't be one of the many people who vastly underestimate the importance and power of clearly articulating and documenting the *why* behind your endeavor. It's a critical and essential step in the process of succeeding long-term. Building a personal brand will be hard, it will challenge you, and it is work. And on the days you question the effort, energy, and resources it takes to make it all happen, I want you to pull out your Brand Mantra and remember that it's there for a reason. It's there for a purpose. And it's there for a person.

One of my biggest takeaways from Dan Martell's book *Buy Back Your Time* was the revelation that a small business's greatest risk is when the founder simply decides they don't want to do this anymore. That happens when we lose sight of our why, when we forget who we are meant to serve, and when the work starts to outweigh the purpose.

I am not saying that as soon as you do this for yourself you will never have another doubt or feeling of unbelief. You most likely will encounter those thoughts and feelings, and that is even more reason why you need a nonemotional reference point to go back to on a regular basis.

We started Brand Builders Group in June 2018, just one month after I was fired, with a small group of like-minded, underpaid, loyal, committed, and purpose-driven individuals. All of us were going through some sort of unexpected and drastic life change. Each person had left the safety and comfort of reliable income to do something new with a belief we could build something significant. We started in the middle of a crisis, with no money, no database, no website, no online following, and no plan. What we did have was a trusted reputation with the people who knew us.

Early on, we knew we needed to set the stage for why we were doing this if we were to overcome all the adversity we were up against. We had read the book, watched the TED talk, and all agreed with Simon Sinek that a unifying "why" must be established for us to all have clarity and to move forward.[5]

Here is what this small group of people came up with roughly one year into the business:

At Brand Builders Group we exist to empower Mission-Driven Messengers to make the world a better place. We believe that everyone has a story that deserves to be heard because it has the power to help someone else. Our vision is to work with 1,000 messengers who we can know on an intimate level, who we can serve in a meaningful way, and who we can invest in to help them realize their own dream. We will reach that destination because . . .

We are relentlessly dedicated to operating with integrity, doing what we say we're going to do, doing what is right, and always playing the long game.

We never compromise long-term reputation for short-term revenue. We are about mission over money.

We take on clients who we believe in and who we can help to believe in themselves.

We lead by example and teach clients to do the same things that we actually do. We bring practical and creative solutions to real-life problems.

We strive to provide world-class education, unparalleled systems, and straightforward steps that anyone can follow.

We are centered on service. We go out of our way to provide value to everyone we engage with—whether they are a customer or not. We help people know that they are truly important to us, and we make sure everyone feels cared for.

We believe that there is an ROI on service without the need to keep score.

We are the best in the world at helping our clients draw out their passion and uniqueness and then giving them a clear path to grow their influence, impact, and income.

We operate with speed, autonomy, accuracy, and disciplined competence. We are known for initiative, innovation, and excellence in all areas of our lives and business.

We are committed to growth and constantly surrounding ourselves with people and education that inspire us to be better. We are always learning, improving, and reinventing.

We do whatever it takes to build a reputation of trust with our teammates, our customers, and our affiliates. We believe that reputation is our best marketing and that if we do our job right, our customer force will become our sales force.

We are a team. We work together with shared expertise. And we operate in our strengths because we know that if everyone is in their uniqueness, we create more opportunity for our entire collective community.

We believe that the calling on one person's heart to share their story is the result of a signal that is being sent out by someone else who is looking for their help. The calling on our heart is to help empower that connection and to facilitate that transference. We are here to serve. We are here because we believe in ourselves and because we believe in our clients' ability to have more impact and make this world a better place.

We read this Brand Mantra aloud at the beginning of every company meeting. Each team member takes a line and we go through it together. It's a standard part of our opening agenda. I hope our team integrates this as a valuable part of our company culture, I hope our team reads it and gets inspired to change the world, and I hope our team comes to believe in all of it, even if only in an aspirational sense. But the truth is, we read this at every company meeting . . . for me. Because I need the reminder (and because I set the meeting agenda!).

I need to be reminded of the things I so easily forget during the busyness of daily to-do lists, scheduled meetings, project deadlines, customer service issues, and financial reviews. This is for me. This is to remind me, and hopefully not *just* me, that what we are doing has far greater potential than I realize. That we have the ability to positively influence lives for the better. That we can reach people who really need what we have to offer. That our work has meaning and purpose. I need to be reminded that our work isn't just work, but that it is about helping people who can help make the world a better place.

I don't know about you, but I need those reminders, and I need them frequently. I can get so caught up in *doing the work* that I forget about *what the work is for*. I can get so obsessed over projects, ini- tiatives, budgets, and deadlines that I forget we are doing a good thing—a great thing. I forget how far we've come in such a short time. I forget how much God has provided and how much we have grown as individuals and as a company. I forget. So, we read this, and it helps me remember. I remember *why* we do what we do, and that gives me the strength, courage, and endurance to keep going.

Our Brand Mantra reminds me not only of *why* we do what we do, but more importantly, of *who* we are doing it for. I need that reminder, and I am almost certainly not alone. You need these reminders too! You need your own Brand Mantra.

You can start by asking yourself the following questions:

- What do I want to be known for?
- What is the goal for my personal brand?
- How do I want others to feel about working with me?
- How do I want people to think of me?
- How do I want to be remembered?
- How will I impact those around me?

- What is different about doing business with me?
- How will I know my job is done?

Scan the QR code on the front inside cover of this book to download the full Brand Mantra questionnaire and template to start your own.

We are very clear on *why* we are in the business we are in. Are you clear on exactly *why* you are in the business you are in? Do you know the *purpose* of your personal brand? Does the team that supports your business or personal brand have clarity as to *why* you do what you do and the *way* you expect to do business?

If you're not yet clear on these things, give yourself some grace. And then get busy on giving yourself, your team, and the world the gift of you knowing *exactly why* you do what you do. This is one of the biggest reasons why personal brands fail. It's the reason well-intentioned people build reputations that they cannot figure out how to turn into revenue. It's the reason why—in spite of your heart being in the right place and your expertise being legitimate—you often get overlooked, passed over, ignored, or surpassed.

It's not a lack of skill.

It's not a lack of desire.

It's not a lack of integrity.

It's not a lack of character.

It is simply a lack of clarity and a lack of focus.

Which is why, by the end of this book, you are going to be clear on each and every single thing you need to be clear on to build one of the greatest and most impactful personal brands the world has ever seen.

You are about to embark on a journey that will be life-changing, for you and for those around you.

Let's go!

CHAPTER 2

WHY DO MOST PERSONAL BRANDS FAIL?

BY RORY VADEN

The very same week AJ got fired in 2018, we got an unexpected phone call from Lewis Howes. We had known Lewis for years, but we had no idea how God was about to divinely intersect our lives at this particular moment.

Shortly after my first book, *Take the Stairs*, hit the *New York Times* bestsellers list in 2012, my publicist cold-pitched me for a new "up and coming podcast" called *The School of Greatness* hosted by Lewis Howes. Lewis agreed to have me on the show because we were both "young" and because we were both fans of Toastmasters International.

After I decided in my early twenties that I wanted to pursue a career as a professional speaker, a mentor told me to join Toastmasters to get practice giving presentations. I learned about a contest they had called "The World Championship of Public Speaking," which featured twenty-five thousand contestants competing from more than ninety countries for a chance to be called World Champion. I was convinced that winning the contest would help launch my speaking career, so I signed up for Toastmasters and began the process of competing at speech contests.

After countless hours of writing, practicing, implementing feedback, and delivering *hundreds* of free speeches, I made it to the World Championship, where I would compete as one of the top ten speakers in the world—at only twenty-two years old. I lost that first year, but I made it back to the World Championship the next year and in 2007 became the World Champion of Public Speaking First Runner-Up. Not bad! While it didn't launch my speaking career in the way I expected, it did catch enough attention for Lewis to have me on his show. Looking back now, I would count that as one of the biggest life-changing moments of my professional career.

After meeting Lewis, it was obvious he was not only incredibly intelligent but that he genuinely cared about making the world a better place. I encouraged him to write his own book someday, and he told me he had already begun the process. Since I had just gone through the process of writing and launching my first book, I offered to share what we had learned along the way. No formal service offering, no money exchange—just the simple process of teaching what I knew to someone who could benefit from the information.

Lewis launched his first book, *The School of Greatness*, in 2015, and he did indeed hit the *New York Times* bestsellers list! Our friendship was bonded by that experience together.

As you are reading this, I bet you know something that could greatly benefit someone else. Are you sharing that knowledge? Are you offering to help others—with no expectation of anything in return? Most great ideas start by trying to solve your own problems, and in my opinion, the best content comes from simply teaching what you know.

Fast-forward a couple of years. Lewis and I stayed in touch casually, catching up here and there, but didn't have a lot of touchpoints—at least not enough to make logical sense of what happened next.

Right around when AJ was fired, Lewis called me out of the blue and said, "My podcast has grown a ton"—from eight million downloads when I first met him to thirty million—"and I'm generating multimillion dollars of revenue, but I'm not keeping as much of it as I would like. I'm paying all the money to a bunch of people to help me keep everything running. I'm working like crazy. I don't have much margin, I have too much stress, and I have a barrage of different opportunities coming at me every single day."

He shared he was lacking clarity on the long-term strategy of his business and the direction of his personal brand. And then he said, "I don't know why, but I felt a very clear prompt to call you to have you help me." Because AJ had just been terminated and I had subsequently resigned from our former business, our calendars were suddenly and completely wide open.

And so it began. This was the genesis of Brand Builders Group—no business plan in place, no planned service offerings, no clue as to what was coming next. The timing was just astounding and unexplainable. Who would have ever thought that AJ getting fired from a business we had poured twelve years of our lives into would be the catalyst for giving us the space to build a company that would later impact millions of lives? We had gone from running an eight-figure business with thousands of coaching clients and hundreds of team members one day to having *absolutely nothing* the next. Both of our incomes had just gone straight to zero at the exact same time. We were terrified, frozen, silenced, and completely unsure of what we were going to do. We had no idea that we were about to create something that would forever change our lives and the lives of so many people around us. God knew, but we did not. God pushed us off the edge of a cliff and then days later gave us Lewis as a parachute.

You may be in a situation right now where you feel like things aren't going your way. If you are, I want you to hear what I'm about to say: If you feel like life is being unfair to you, don't get mad; get better. Instead of wondering, *Why did this happen?* ask yourself, *What do I need to learn?* There is purpose in all of it, and one day you will be able to look back and see how all the pieces fit together. It's just like putting together a puzzle. You start confused, disoriented, and struggling to see how it's all going to work out. There are moments of frustration, but then you also have moments of victory when you find two pieces that go together. Eventually, if you stick with it, the whole thing comes together, and a beautiful picture emerges. That is how life works. That is how business works. That is also how huge brands are built. Because not only was God putting Lewis in our life to help us; He had put us in Lewis's life to help him.

> *If you feel like life is being unfair to you, don't get mad; get better.*

After that divinely orchestrated call from Lewis, I agreed to help. Shortly thereafter, he flew to Nashville and we all spent two days in the basement of our house talking, brainstorming, and strategizing about the future of his personal brand. We had no formal process, no organized content, and no agenda. We simply said, "We can teach you what we know from what we've experienced." So, we did.

DILUTED FOCUS

As Lewis was describing his situation, we noticed he did indeed have "a lot" going on, including courses, a mastermind, a membership site, speaking, live events, a newly released book, and perhaps a new coaching offer on the horizon. In the midst of the conversation, he also casually mentioned his podcast had sort of "taken off" with relatively little attention and effort.

We listened and made a list on the wall of all his revenue streams. He wrote out every single one. Turns out his small team was managing *seventeen* different streams!

How many revenue streams are you managing? If you are like me, you've probably heard people talk about the value and importance of "multiple streams of income." And if you are managing many different streams of income, there is a chance that you even wear that like a badge of honor. But there's a problem with this concept—a big one. The concept of having multiple streams of income is *a complete myth*!

In chapter 7, we will dive deep into Monetization Strategy and explain why. For now, you just need to know that—especially if you are a small business—pursuing "multiple streams of income" is one of the most dangerous and destructive causes of why businesses fail economically. Consider Lewis's situation as an example.

Next to each of his revenue streams, we asked Lewis to score the following areas:

- How many years have you've been building this revenue stream?
- How stressful is it for you?
- How life-giving is it for you?
- How scalable is it for you?
- How aligned is it for your skills and the skills of your team?

We've since operationalized this exercise into our formal curriculum at Brand Builders Group as "The Revenue Streams Assessment."

Scan the QR code on the front inside cover of this book to complete your free Revenue Streams Assessment.

As we simply analyzed Lewis's list and the corresponding scores of each revenue stream, something jumped off the page for me. I told him, "It looks like this podcast thing you're doing is where all the natural momentum is. And it seems like you treat it, think of it, and talk about it as an ancillary part of your business more than like the core of your business."

You see, at the time, according to his revenue, Lewis was really a course-creation company. He had been making the most money from selling courses on how to be successful on LinkedIn and how to sell using webinars, and he had not formally recognized how much natural momentum there was for his podcast. Prior to this exercise, it wasn't obvious to Lewis and his team *what* was really working in his business because they were all scrambling to keep so many *different things* working in his business.

Lewis's situation was the perfect real-life example of one of the key concepts from my first book, *Take the Stairs*:

If you have diluted focus, you will get diluted results.

Let me explain. Let's pretend that you, as a human being, have 10 units of resource. A unit of resource can be money, time, attention, prayer, family, team, etc. But if you spread those 10 units of resource across 10 different initiatives, then each different initiative only gets 1 unit of resource. That's what most people in the world do—they spread themselves too thin. As a result, they produce marginal levels of quality and output with each of their initiatives.

If you have diluted focus, you will get diluted results.

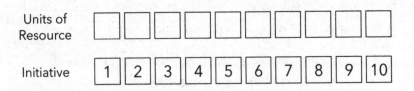

However, if you take those 10 units of resource and allocate all of them to just one initiative, that changes everything. It exponentially increases, to a factor of at least 10, the likelihood of that one initiative being successful. Not only that, but in a world where most businesses and brands put out quality reflective of around 1 to 2 units of resource per initiative, imagine how much faster you'll stand out among the crowd, and how much further you'll go, if you put all 10 units of resource on just one of your initiatives!

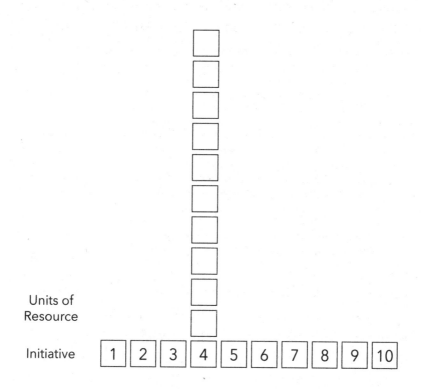

As we applied this concept to Lewis's brand, I asked him one simple question that would end up changing both of our lives: **"What do you think would happen if you stopped doing all of this other stuff and instead just went 'all in' on the podcast?"**

At the time, my question was genuinely meant to be more rhetorical than literal, but something "clicked." This was the clarity Lewis had been looking for, and it started a chain reaction that has set us both on a trajectory we never could have imagined.

A STAR IS BORN

By the end of our two days together, Lewis, his business partner Matt, AJ, and I had all collaboratively decided that the best course of strategic action for Lewis going forward would be to systematically *reduce* the number of things he was doing. This included cutting the different ways that he was earning revenue. The decision was to focus. Much to Lewis's credit, he had the courage and will to *stop* doing many of the things he had been doing.

Lewis decided that—for at least the next few years—he would *not*:

- Do one-on-one coaching.
- Accept new speaking engagements.
- Write any new books.
- Build any new funnels.
- Launch any new courses.
- Do any more consulting.
- Take on any more side projects.

Instead, he would say no to pretty much everything and put *all* his time, energy, and resources into growing his podcast.

I was even there by his side, in the front of the room, weeks later when Lewis announced to his most elite, high-profile, top-spending customers that he was going to shut down his private mastermind. These were people who were each investing tens of thousands of dollars per year to be in this group led by Lewis—which added up to *millions* in revenue for him. He'd decided to shut the entire thing down the night before based on a conversation he, Matt, and I had in the hotel lobby. To be clear, Lewis didn't just walk away from millions of dollars over the course of time; he walked away from millions of dollars in a single *instant*!

Lewis had the discipline, courage, humility, and faith to walk away from *multiple millions* of dollars to instead pursue something he believed could make an even greater impact in the world. Now, what about you?

What do you need to stop doing to create more focus?

What distractions do you need to eliminate?

What is the #1 most important goal you want to pursue?

Where do you need focus?

Success does not happen by accident; success happens with intention. That can be success with anything—your business, marriage, finances, faith, family, friendships, health, and the list goes on. To be successful at anything requires focused time, attention, and intention.

Today, a new breed of personal brand has emerged, and we first saw it in Lewis. The personal brands dominating the game today are the ones chasing *purpose* more than *profit*. They chase making a difference more than making a dollar. They care more about making the world a better place than about gaining attention for themselves. That is what we call a Mission-Driven Messenger.

> *The personal brands dominating the game today are the ones chasing* **purpose** *more than* **profit**.

Up until that point in 2018, it had taken Lewis more than five years to get his first thirty million downloads. But in the next two and a half years, with relentless focus, The School of Greatness podcast grew from thirty million to more than five hundred million total downloads!

What's wild is that we never taught Lewis anything about how to grow a podcast, nor about how to find guests or be a great interviewer. He and his team did that all by themselves.

Yet, when Lewis was featured on the cover of *Entrepreneur* magazine in March of 2023, he had a multipage spread sharing the story of how he built his personal brand. In that article, he gave an incredibly gracious and generous shoutout to Brand Builders Group.

Why?

Was it because we taught him the technical strategy to grow his followers? Nope.

Was it because we shared secrets to hacking social media, Google, or podcast algorithms? Definitely not.

Was it because we helped him understand the technology or digital assets needed to pull all the elements of a personal brand together? No way.

It was because we shared a legitimate business *strategy* that can be applied to any enterprise or personal brand. It has become our most central, emphatic, celebrated, proven, and time-tested strategy of all:

When you have diluted focus, you get diluted results.

SHEAHAN'S WALL

One of our central frameworks for helping personal brands understand what it takes to become well-known is called Sheahan's Wall. We named this framework after Peter Sheahan, who created the essence of the original concept in his book *Making It Happen: Turning Good Ideas into Great Results*.[6] Peter is a legendary corporate consultant and one of the most brilliant business minds on the planet. I heard him speak about a different iteration of this framework many years ago, and we have since adapted it to be more specific to our audience of personal brands, but we named it after him since that is where the concept originated.

In any industry, vertical, or geographic market, there are two main groups of people: those that are "Unknown" and those that are "Well-known."

Sheahan's Wall

UNKNOWN (Obscurity)		WELL-KNOWN (Notoriety)
Topics		
Audiences		
Profiles		
Business Models		
Jobs		
Ideas		

People in the Unknown category are struggling with obscurity. In addition to being unknown, they are often unclear and untrusted. They aren't recognizable. They don't have influence. They don't stand out among competitors or other industry leaders.

The other group of people are Well-known. Instead of obscurity, they have notoriety. These people are very "recognizable." They could be celebrities like The Rock, Bono, or Oprah. Or they could be people that are more recognizable in their "space." For example, Tony Robbins, Brené Brown, Gary Vaynerchuk, Dave Ramsey, and Mel Robbins are some of the more recognizable personal brands in the thought leader space at the time of this writing.

Between these two categories of people—the Unknowns and the Well-knowns—is this huge invisible barrier that we refer to as Sheahan's Wall, a figurative wall that any personal brand must break through in order to gain notoriety in their company, community, industry, or nation.

The challenge stems from the fact that most people who are Unknown look to those who are Well-known and they try to emulate what they are doing right now.

A newer speaker may look at Tony Robbins and think, *Tony has multiple presentations and different live events on all sorts of topics like motivation, relationships, business, health, and money. I need to speak on a variety of topics to appeal to the masses like Tony does.*

Or a lesser-known content creator may look at Gary Vaynerchuk and see that Gary shares expert ideas on social media trends, entrepreneurship, personal character, investing, sports, music, and wine. So, they think, *I have lots of different expertise, just like Gary Vee. Let me talk about all of it!*

Similarly, a newer entrepreneur may look at The Rock and think, *Look at all the ways this guy makes money! He's an actor, entrepreneur, rapper, and wrestler. He owns an energy drink, a clothing line, an ice cream company, a tequila brand, a skincare line, a production company, and a football league. To be successful, I need multiple streams of revenue as well.*

This is compounded every time we go online, when we see someone promoting a new *business model* with an advertisement for:

- How to get rich doing online courses.
- How to make six figures as a personal coach.
- Why you should launch a mastermind.
- How to make money selling tickets to your own live events.
- How to build passive income as an affiliate.
- How to host high-end destination retreats.
- How to create recurring revenue through a membership site.
- How to get rich by self-publishing a book.
- How to become an influencer and do brand deals.
- How to become a highly paid keynote speaker.
- How to launch a podcast and make millions from ads.
- How to get rich being the next YouTube star.

Sound familiar?

It gets even more challenging when you have lots of different *audiences* you have to address or appeal to based on the variety of your topics or content.

Multiply that by trying to grow a following and post consistent content on all the different online *platforms*, such as:

1. Meta (Facebook)
2. X (Twitter)
3. Instagram
4. YouTube
5. Snapchat
6. Podcast
7. [Insert whatever the trendy tool of the day happens to be]

Now you are juggling lots of topics, multiple audiences, and a growing list of online platforms. Good luck with that. I am overwhelmed just by writing it.

So, here you are, well-intentioned Mission-Driven Messenger, trying to build your personal brand by talking about too many *topics*, addressing too many *audiences*, spending time on too many *platforms*, trying to make money with too many *revenue streams*, all while you have too many new *ideas* and you're doing too many different *jobs*.

And guess what happens to small business owners when they try to do all those things?

You got it. They *bounce* off the wall. This is the most common reason why personal brands fail: They are talking about too many different topics to too many different audiences on too many different platforms trying to sell too many different business models.

It's the same issue Lewis had; it's the same issue AJ and I have had with our personal brands; and it's the same issue that all two-thousand-plus of our clients at Brand Builders Group have had. That is why this one principle reigns supreme. I'll say it again: "When you have diluted focus, you get diluted results."

This begs the question, "How do you break through the wall?"

That leads us to the single greatest piece of personal branding advice I've ever received. I heard it early in my career and from that very moment, something intuitively told me it was absolutely true.

BREAKING THROUGH THE WALL

While I wish I could take credit for this quote, I cannot. I heard it from a multi–New York Times bestselling author and Hall of Fame speaker named Larry Winget, who said:

> **"The goal of a personal brand is to simply find your uniqueness and exploit it in the service of others."**

That's it. Larry summarized it all in one sentence. The way you break through the wall is to "find your uniqueness and exploit it in the service of others."

Another way of saying that might be, "Find the one thing you can do as well—or better—than anyone else in the world, and do it again and again to the point where everyone benefits and takes notice."

Imagine with me for a moment that Sheahan's Wall is literally a concrete wall looming right in front of you. In your hands you hold a sledgehammer, and your goal is to use it to break through the wall as fast as you can. Think through the different approaches with me.

If you randomly swing the sledgehammer and smack multiple places on the wall, nothing is likely to happen. You would just expend a lot of energy and get frustrated because you wouldn't make any progress.

But what if you take a different tack? What if you hit the same spot on the wall over and over again?

You'll be frustrated at first. You won't feel like you are making any progress. Despite all your backbreaking work, the wall will look as solid and impenetrable as ever. You might consider quitting. You might think, *None of this is making a difference.* But then, right on the verge of giving up, you bring the sledgehammer down on the wall once more and notice a tiny crack—the first evidence that something is happening inside the wall, away from your view.

Energized, you keep hammering away, sending blow after blow into the same spot on the wall. But now, you're beginning to see changes. There's a dent where you've been hammering. Chips of concrete explode off the wall with each blow. The sound of the sledgehammer's impact seems different. And then, finally, after much longer than you anticipated, you finally see it: daylight breaking through a tiny hole in the wall. Two blows later, the head of your sledgehammer disappears through the wall and emerges on the other side. From that point forward, the wall quickly starts to fall apart and come crashing down.

You then walk through the opening, look around, and realize you're all alone. All your competitors gave up long before you broke through. They believed the voices that said the task was impossible. But not you. You've done what very few ever will. You've broken through the wall. Not out of great skill or talent or tools or technique so much as from sheer focus and consistency and commitment.

It's true that if you have diluted focus, you get diluted results. But that also means **where there is focus, there is power.**

Now that you know how to break through Sheahan's Wall, let's go back and analyze some of the celebrity personal brands we mentioned earlier. This is where it gets fascinating.

People often use Gary Vaynerchuk as a counter example to the strategy of focusing on one single uniqueness by pointing to his vast array of topics. But actually, Gary Vaynerchuk is the *perfect* example of how to break through Sheahan's Wall using the very strategies that we're talking about.

I will admit that *today* Gary has a vast breadth of topics on his various platforms—it would be hard to deny that. However, in the *beginning*, how did Gary Vaynerchuk *become* Gary Vaynerchuk? If you know much about his story, then you know he talked about only *one* topic in the very beginning: wine. And not only did he primarily talk about one topic in the very early days, but he also primarily operated on only one platform: YouTube. Gary first broke through the wall not for his opinion on lots of different things but for his expert opinion on *one* thing, which he called WineLibrary.TV. One topic, one audience, one platform.

What about Dwayne "The Rock" Johnson? As I shared earlier, he has *so many* different revenue streams. Isn't he a counterexample to focusing on one uniqueness? No way! Why? Because, in the *beginning,* The Rock was known for *one* thing: being a pro wrestler.

One business model, one audience, one platform.

Tony Robbins definitely speaks and writes about many different subjects today, but how did he *first* get famous, and what did he get famous for? Anyone who was alive at the time will tell you that a huge part of what made Robbins popular was the infamous "fire walk" where he had his event participants immediately apply the mental-toughness principles he was teaching by walking across a bed of burning coals. Even now—to our knowledge—Tony hosts *Unleash the Power Within* events where people *still* do the "fire walk."

One event, one audience, one platform.

How about Brené Brown? Does her career arc and notoriety model the proposed strategy here of finding one uniqueness and focusing on that in the service of others? You betcha! I don't know Brené personally, but from what I've read, she never set out to become the world-renowned speaker and thought leader she is today. Quite the contrary! Instead, she spent more than two decades studying *one* topic: shame. She became the world's leading authority on that one subject, and that's how she originally broke through the wall.

One research topic, one audience, one platform.

Oprah is another classic example of someone who became famous for one thing—being an inspirational talk show host.

One business model, one audience, one platform.

We could go on. If you apply the concept of Sheahan's Wall to the most recognizable celebrities in the world today, you will see an almost irrefutably consistent pattern: **People who have become famous first became famous for one, and only one, thing**. Then *later*, once they broke through the wall, they started expanding into other things.

Even Amazon.com is a great example of Sheahan's Wall. Yes, it's undeniably true that today Amazon sells almost anything you can possibly think of, *but* in the very beginning, they became known first for selling one thing: books.

> *People who have become famous first became famous for one, and only one, thing.*

Using our brick wall analogy, all these well-known people *became* well-known by hitting the same spot over and over and over—until they finally broke through. Only *then* did they expand into all the other things we now know them for.

Sheahan's Wall

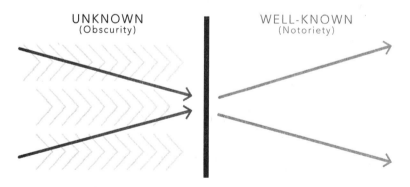

UNKNOWN
(Obscurity)

WELL-KNOWN
(Notoriety)

This is why trying to emulate the career arc of celebrities or anyone who is well established in their industry, community, or business is deceptive. You cannot compare the start of your journey to the end of someone else's. They didn't start where they are today. Neither should you.

You can't look at what someone else is doing now; you must instead look at what they did *back then* in order to break through in the first place.

You can't do what they are *doing now* to get where they are; you have to do what they *did* to get where they are.

HOW TO BREAK THROUGH THE WALL

By now you might be thinking, *I get it, Rory. I'm tracking with you. If I have diluted focus, I will get diluted results. And to paraphrase and personalize Larry Winget, "I must find my uniqueness and exploit it in the service of others." But how exactly do I do this?*

How do you find your uniqueness? How do you figure out your one thing? How do you know which "spot" to hit on Sheahan's Wall over and over, again and again?

If you are thinking that, then you are right where you are supposed to be. The truth is that while the strategy of "finding your uniqueness" is *simple*, it's not at all *easy*. In fact, it can be an incredibly difficult and frustrating process—especially if you try to do it alone.

This is why our company Brand Builders Group exists, and it's part of why we wrote this book. We want to help Mission-Driven Messengers, experts, entrepreneurs, and executives find their one uniqueness, narrow down their audience, strategically select their platform, and simplify their business model. In the process of doing that, you can make a massive impact in the lives of the people you are meant to serve.

Our personal brand methodology consists of four distinct phases of the Brand Builder Journey where each phase is broken down into three topical areas.

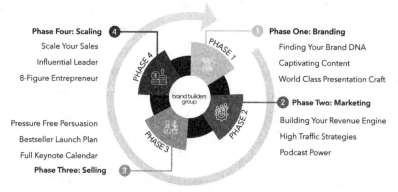

Phase 1: Branding—This is about finding your uniqueness and clarifying what you have to offer to the world that no one else can. Half of the battle of personal branding is separating yourself from the crowd with original content, true thought leadership, and compelling delivery of your message in a way that moves people to action.

Phase 2: Marketing—This is all about nurture and growth. This is your chance to build a perpetually growing, digital ecosystem around your personal brand that serves your audience 24/7/365. Learn about offer structure, copy that converts, funnels, webinars, podcasts, email strategy, social media, and how to create your online infrastructure.

Phase 3: Selling—This is where you learn all you need to know to drive warm, inbound, pre-qualified leads right to the front door of your business. You'll also learn how to generate unlimited referrals, have offline sales conversations, and sell high-dollar offers with zero pressure. Plus, this is where you'll discover how to truly "break through the wall" by launching a bestselling book and becoming a sought-after speaker in your industry.

Phase 4: Scaling—This is about turning your personal brand into an enterprise business. Learn about driving predictable revenue, scaling your sales force, running efficient operations, and leading an organization as you build key team members. You'll also learn financial strategies for having healthy cash flow and increased profits. Plus, you'll focus on creating more margin in your life by learning to more effectively automate and delegate throughout your organization.

If you are wondering where you fall in our process as you read this book, you are currently in Phase 1: Branding. Our first curriculum, Finding Your Brand DNA, is the primary focus of the following chapters because that's where *everyone* starts. This book is dedicated to helping *you* find your uniqueness. We're about to walk you through the entire process of this fundamental and most foundational step of figuring out exactly what you were created to do.

If, at any point while reading the book, you get stuck in trying to find your uniqueness, you can request a free strategy call with our team by scanning the QR code on the front inside cover of this book and clicking on the "Free Call" link on our website. If you do, one of our expert strategists will talk through some tips as well as share an overview of the various ways we work with people at all experience and investment levels (from newbie to celebrity).

But after taking thousands of people through the process you're about to experience reading this book, we've learned what you are probably thinking right now: *What's the shortcut?*

THE SHORTCUT TO UNIQUENESS

We have identified a repeating pattern that appears in about 95 percent of the clients we work with.

We did not know this when we started the company, but after seeing the same pattern time and time again, we finally realized it was not just a coincidence but an everlasting truth that applies to all personal brands.

What we discovered is that, for all of us, **you are most powerfully positioned to serve the person you once were.**

That's the secret. That's the shortcut. That's the pattern.

That's the hidden formula and powerful truth of the world's most successful and recognizable personal brands, and that's how most of them eventually find their uniqueness.

That is part of how we helped Lewis find his uniqueness and focus his business model strategy on the podcast. Beyond monetary conversations around his revenue streams were deeply personal and intimate discussions about exactly *who* Lewis was talking to—which then edified *where* and *how* he should talk to them.

You are most powerfully positioned to serve the person you once were.

If you aren't familiar with Lewis's personal story, his dream was to play in the NFL. After becoming an all-American collegiate athlete, Lewis landed a spot playing professionally for an arena football team called the Tennessee Valley Vipers. However, in the second game of his pro career, Lewis crashed into a wall while making a diving catch and broke his wrist. In one play, his entire lifelong dream and the countless hours spent training for it were gone.

After his football career ended, Lewis struggled to find direction with the next chapter of his life. All he had ever thought about was playing football, and once that vision evaporated, he didn't have a plan.

He had moved to LA and was living on his sister's couch when it dawned on him that he needed a mentor, or coach, or some sort of school he could attend to teach him what to do in a situation like this. He started to wonder why there wasn't a more accessible way for everyday, ordinary people to learn the principles of success. Why wasn't there a *School of Greatness*?

That was the impetus that led Lewis to start his podcast, *The School of Greatness*. He didn't start it from a place of being the guru; he started it from the place of being the student! He wanted to interview successful people about the lessons they had learned on their path to the top. And that's how the show was born.

You see, "finding your uniqueness" is more than just narrowing in on one platform or business model; it's also about zeroing in on exactly *who* and *what* type of person your personal brand is going to serve.

Let's refer back to some of biggest personal brands in the world and how they got there. Brené Brown has dedicated her life to studying and solving the issue of *shame*. Dave Ramsey has built a nine-figure business by focusing primarily—for more than thirty years—on helping people get out of *debt*. Tony Robbins has said that a big part of his life's purpose was to help people break free from *pain*.

We then posed the question to Lewis, What problem are *you* going to solve for the world?

After hours of back-and-forth dialoguing with Lewis and hearing about his own personal struggles, he eventually blurted out, "I guess I've spent a huge part of my life learning how to overcome *self-doubt*, and now I want to spend the rest of my life teaching people how to do the same!"

Boom.

There it was.

Self-doubt.

Self-doubt is the problem Lewis solves for others because it is the problem he struggled with himself. It was the journey that he had been on his entire life. It was the path he had personally walked down. It was the mountain he had climbed. And remember, *you are most powerfully positioned to serve the person you once were*.

Now, it's your turn. What problem are *you* going to solve for the world?

To help you quickly find the answer to that question, ask yourself the following questions:

- *What challenge have I conquered?*
- *What setback have I survived?*
- *What obstacle have I overcome?*
- *What tragedy have I triumphed over?*

The answers to those questions reveal the shortest, most direct path to a person's *uniqueness*. They guide you to the topic and message and content that you are *uniquely* equipped to talk about because you have personally experienced the heartbreak of being on that journey.

This personal experience provides a level of credibility that no degree and no number of research hours can ever touch. It also provides a level of purpose for a person that will never be extinguished.

YOUR LENS TO THE WORLD

Nothing is as powerful for a personal brand than when an individual becomes clear on what the unique problem is that they are supposed to solve for the world. Once you grasp that, the purpose and intent of your personal brand come into focus. You have a reason to go out and share with the world everything you know. And this is about far more than money; it's about elevating humanity.

Take podcasting, for example. As the host, you have the unique opportunity to select most if not all the questions you'll ask your guests. If you are super clear on *what* problem you solve for the world and *who* you solve it for, you have the ability to tailor all conversations through the lens of your uniqueness for your listeners.

Case in point: Rush Limbaugh (love him or hate him) was the king of news radio talk shows. He had one of the most popular daily broadcasts for decades between 1984 and when he died in 2021. At one point his show aired on 650 radio stations and reached over 15 million listeners each week.[7] But no one listened to *The Rush Limbaugh Show* just to get the news. They could've gotten that from a variety of other sources. People listened to Rush for *his take* on the news. Most people tuned in because they fully agreed with him . . . or because they passionately *disagreed* with him and rage-listened to the show. Either way, nobody listened just to get information. They wanted his perspective (aka *lens*) on the news. He was clear on his stance, he was authentic to his uniqueness, and he knew his audience.

That's a big part of the role for any personal brand. You are a conduit of the message. You are a container for the content. You are the steward of a very specific message and for a very specific type of person in the world.

BRAND BUILDERS GROUP IS BORN

The day before AJ was fired, I would've gotten our former company's logo tattooed on my rear. Although we were married and business partners, our individual experiences and relationships to our former business were very different. AJ had felt overworked and out of alignment for a really long time. Plus, even though she had been there since day one, she had always felt like a bit of an outsider.

It never fully dawned on me until years later just how taxing the whole journey had been for her—down to her soul level. I know she endured years of massive high-intensity work largely just to help my dreams come true. In fact, one of our wedding vows was "to make your dreams my dreams," and that she did, because she was lending all her talents and brilliance to support me in everything I did, both personally and professionally. And, from an objective standpoint, the company was also benefiting.

But from my perspective at the time, we were crushing it. Our team had rallied together to help me become a *New York Times* bestselling author when I was just twenty-nine years old. My 2015 TED talk, "How to Multiply Your Time," had gone viral with millions of views; my second book had just launched; and the speaking career that I had been working so hard to develop since I was seventeen was finally operating in full force. Plus, my podcast was getting millions of downloads and, although I was late to social media, my following was growing. Things were great!

We had also grown our former company to eight figures from scratch. We had gone from making cold calls out of the Yellow Pages to being invited into seven-figure consulting deals with some of the world's most recognizable corporate brands. Our team was making money. Our clients were making money. The company was making money. We were making money. Things were great!

We had recruited some of the coolest and sharpest people I had ever worked with. We were traveling the world for speaking and consulting assignments and taking our team to exotic locations for incentive trips. AJ and I had just built our dream home, and I was invited to be on the board of directors for our parent company. While we were definitely working like crazy, we were doing meaningful professional work that was making a difference for our clients. Again, things were great!

And then in a single split second, it was all gone.

Our income went to zero. Our calendar was cleared. "Our" customers and "our" team were no longer ours. And here we were starting over with a new house, a newborn baby (our first), and no plan whatsoever.

When people ask me if I think it was God's divine timing that we got a completely unsolicited phone call from Lewis Howes asking for my help right after this all went down, it should be no surprise that my answer is, "You better believe it! Only God could coordinate such a dramatic turn of events." Nothing else even makes sense.

Even after Lewis called, we weren't thinking that we would somehow make a business out of the things we were sharing with him.

We were just helping a friend and teaching what we knew. It was actually Lewis who told us, "This is what you were born to do." We didn't even realize that what we were teaching could become a whole new business. It was his confidence and support that helped us believe.

We all need a person like Lewis in our lives. Someone who appreciates the knowledge and experience we take for granted. Someone who can see past all the stuff we don't have and focus on what we can provide. This is a good time to let you know we started Brand Builders Group with no contacts, no social media profiles, no website, no marketing assets, no podcast, no YouTube. Nothing. Nada. Zilch. And yes, we were starting a personal brand strategy firm without all those assets. We very much recognize the irony.

But do you know who did have those things? Lewis Howes. He had built a growing and loyal audience of trusted fans and clients. And because he had built that trust with his audience and we had built that trust with Lewis, his audience trusted us as well. That is the power of a personal brand.

We landed our first two paying clients at his mastermind. Our first landing page was built to go live for his audience, and our first public interview introducing Brand Builders Group to the world was on his podcast. Like I said, everyone needs a friend like Lewis!

Everywhere you look, all you see are people trying to convince you that digital marketing and social media is the fastest way to grow your business. Well, I'm here to tell you we are living proof that the fastest way to grow your business is not marketing your services to strangers on the internet; it is investing time into real human relationships. Helping people. Supporting each other. Building trust. Because one trusted relationship can change everything.

Since 2018 we have been abundantly blessed in so many ways. The love and care of our team is unmatched. We have forty-plus team members that simply crush it. Together, we have built more than a great team; we have built a family. That family has rebuilt everything we once had—and we've done it starting out with much less and in half the time.

We've also had the honor of working directly with several of the biggest and most influential personal brands in the world. These clients—who have also become family—are topping the podcast charts, appearing frequently on the bestseller lists, dominating social media feeds, and showing up as speakers on the biggest stages in the world. But most of all, our clients are changing the lives of the people they are reaching, and we get to be a small part of it.

We have learned a lifetime of lessons and information from working alongside so many personal brands since we first started. And we have now spent years compiling, condensing, and organizing that information into this book to help you build your own personal brand.

Why?

Because we know what it's like to be the new kid.

We know what it's like to have to start over.

We know what it's like to be the underdog.

And we know what it's like to so desperately want to leverage our own expertise to improve the lives of others and make the world a better place but to also simultaneously feel completely overlooked, unseen, and unknown. We know what it's like to feel as if you're the world's "best-kept secret."

But we also now know exactly what it takes for a Mission-Driven Messenger to build a reputation and a personal brand that breaks through Sheahan's Wall and into a life of impact.

The rest of the book is going to show you exactly how to do the same thing.

CHAPTER 3

WHO ARE YOU?

BY AJ VADEN

In order to know where you're going, you need to pause and notice where you are and remember how you got here.

Before we delve into the nitty-gritty details of building your personal brand, I want to encourage you to take some time to reflect. After reading this chapter and before you start the next, create some white space in your calendar and carve out some time to just appreciate all the things you've been through and all the people you've encountered. All the wins, losses, successes, and failures. Remember the things you've overcome that you didn't think you'd survive. Take time to note the events in your life that challenged and grew you the most, and give credit to how far you've come.

If you take the time to do this, the following chapters will make a lot more sense. The dots will connect faster and the heart behind your efforts will be filled with purpose. I mentioned in chapter 1 that a personal brand is not *what you do* but *who you are*. It's the culmination of all your life's stories, experiences, trials, lessons, and victories packaged and put together in a way that carries the ability to help someone else. The rest of this journey is about determining who that someone else is, what they need help with, how you can help them, and how you can build a profitable and impactful business doing that over and over again. But this chapter is the precursor to all that. This is the time to get clear on who you are.

Let's start with a simple question: If you and I were to meet for the first time at a dinner party, how would you introduce yourself?

Perhaps you'd keep it simple and only give me your name, prompting me to ask the next most popular question, "So, what do you do for a living?" What would you say?

What if I then said, "Tell me about who you are"? What would you share?

My guess is that you have some sort of standard response for the *what you do* question, but I feel 99.9 percent sure you have no standard response for the *who you are* question—most likely because you've never been asked and also because you've not spent nearly enough time thinking about it.

> **Who you are *is not* What do you.**

So, let's think about it right now. Who are you?

And remember, *who you are* is not *what do you*. Don't get these two things confused. Who you are is not a title, role, or label. It's not tied to accomplishments or achievements . . . or a perceived lack thereof. It's less tied to "doing" and a lot more connected to your "being."

WHY IDENTITY MATTERS

Our identity isn't a label. It's not a job title or a social media handle. Identity is the foundation on which everything else in your life is built. It's the silent partner in every decision you make, every relationship you have, and every goal you set. When you know who you are, you create a solid foundation that strengthens every aspect of your life. Without that clarity, though, we're often left chasing validation through professional accolades, people-pleasing, and living according to others' expectations.

Because of that, we often end up in jobs we don't love, doing things that lack fulfillment, hanging out in crowds that aren't good for us, and feeling more and more lost as time goes on. Nobody wakes up one day and just *has* a midlife crisis. These types of moments are the culmination of years and years of making unguided and unintentional decisions that leave you on the doorstep of asking "How did I get here?" and "Who have I become?"

Our identity shapes how we see ourselves, how we allow others to treat us, and what we believe we're capable of achieving. It's the difference between saying "I can't" and "I'm working on it." Your identity is both who you are today and who you're growing into tomorrow. It's also a reflection of where you came from. If you haven't defined it, you'll find yourself pulled in a thousand directions, reacting to the demands, expectations, and opinions of the world around you. This can happen both over the course of time and in an instant.

Two days after my seventh birthday, my family loaded into my dad's Cadillac to hit the road on a short trip from my hometown of Dalton, Georgia, to a doctor's appointment in Chattanooga, Tennessee, which was normally only a thirty-minute drive up I-75. Being the only girl and the middle child, I usually found myself sitting in the middle seat to split up my two quarreling brothers (ages five and ten at the time). About fifteen minutes into our drive, we abruptly came to a halt as we hit standstill traffic on the interstate. We were at the end of a very long line of idling cars when, out of nowhere, a semitruck going 75 mph smashed into the back of our car. In an instant my life, and my family's life, changed.

We were the first car in a devasting thirteen-car pileup. My dad, although injured, was able to escape from the driver's side window. As he assessed the total devastation around him, he realized I was

conscious but trapped in the back seat. He was able to clear a big
enough space through all the broken glass to pull me out of the
wreckage and rescue me through the back seat window. I don't recall
much of this experience, but I remember playing with a doll in the
middle seat in one moment and then sitting on the side of the road
in the next. As I sat there, I watched countless strangers rush out of
their cars to try and help. People we'd never met risked their safety for
my family, not to mention all the people trapped in cars ahead of us.
Many families were impacted and many individuals injured that day.
Some recovered, and some did not.

What felt like hours to me was an unbelievable and insanely
fast response time for rescue vehicles to arrive on the scene. As my
dad recalls, they showed up in record time, as if they were somehow
on standby. There is no doubt if it had not been for this miraculous
timing, many would not have survived. Police cars, ambulances, and
fire trucks all arrived within minutes, although it took hours before
they were able to peel back the metal of our Cadillac to rescue the rest
of my family.

Both of my brothers were pronounced dead on the scene. They
were taken by Air Evac to the closest hospital while both my parents were taken by ambulance. I sat in the back of a police car
watching everything unfold. My mom and dad both sustained
multiple injuries, none of which were life threatening but all of
which were life altering.

My ten-year-old brother was revived en route to the hospital. He
sustained multiple injuries, the most critical being the collapse of the
entire right side of his facial skeleton. It was crushed due to the unbelievable impact when the semitruck demolished our car and how he
was sitting when he made contact with the right side of the car frame.

Medics were eventually able to sustain a faint heartbeat in my
five-year-old brother during transport. He'd suffered an immense
brain injury as he was slammed between the back seat and front seat

of our car with such force that it cracked his skull. He remained in a brain-damage-related coma in the ICU for months, given less than a 10 percent chance of survival and a virtually 0 percent chance of a "normal" life if he were ever to wake up.

Then there was me. I eventually arrived at the ER by police car, where the medical team examined me and confirmed there were no serious injuries despite the amount of blood that covered my body. No broken bones, no internal bleeding or unseen injury, no concussion, not even a single scratch on my body.

I will pause here and fast-forward a bit. My parents moved into long-term living quarters near the hospital to be close to my brothers. I lived with friends and family while spending weekends with my parents. There's much I don't remember about this time, but here is what was permanently etched into my brain: My brothers were "miracles."

You see, shortly after my older brother was admitted to the hospital, there were plans to try to reshape his face surgically using metal plates. Then one day the doctor approached my parents to notify them they wouldn't be able to do the surgery. I remember a sense of panic and a lot of questions. Now, as a parent of two boys myself, I can only imagine the helplessness and devastation my mom and dad must have felt. But amid all the tears, the doctor was trying to explain why they couldn't perform the operation.

With no medical explanation, my brother's facial bones had started to heal on their own. They were somehow reattaching and rejoining. The surgery could not be done because he was healing on his own. He didn't need the operation. It was a "miracle" they could not explain. But my mom could, as she had started a prayer chain that spread all over the country. We are a family of faith, and strong believers in the power of Jesus, and we were witnessing His healing hand front and center.

Then there was my younger brother. Week after week the hospital chaplain would meet with my parents and discuss options, what the future would hold, and if removing life support was the best course. It was always a hard *no*. We would sit and wait for another miracle. My parents were steadfast in this decision, so we waited. The doctors were clear that if my brother were to wake up, he would have permanent brain damage. He would most likely not be able to walk, talk, or even feed himself.

Then one day, out of nowhere, about three months into his ICU stay, he suddenly awoke asking for Rice Krispies! You read that right. Not only did he wake up; he woke up asking for cereal. He was alert. He was talking. The exact things the doctors had told us repeatedly could not and would not happen—were happening. There was no scientific explanation and no medical reasoning. It was a "miracle." *He* was a miracle.

And our friends, family, church, hospital staff, and prayer warriors were not the only ones to think so. The story of our car accident and my brothers' miraculous recovery was spreading. In fact, my younger brother was the Children's Miracle Network poster child in 1990, and we participated as a family in telethon fundraising events for years telling the story of my brothers and their miracle story.

I spent years listening to people tell stories, ask questions, praise, and celebrate the miracle we experienced. The personal challenge for me was that I was never included in that story. I came to believe not only that my brothers were saved because they had a unique purpose (which I do believe) but that since my story was not their story, I didn't have the same kind of purpose they did. I believed they were miracles and therefore had a more special place in our family. I believed that because they got the attention and the spotlight, they were more important than me. I became accustomed to being overlooked and somewhat unnoticed. I began believing that I was *less than*. I was no miracle, after all. I felt unimportant, unseen, undervalued, and that I had to *do something* to be seen, noticed, or valued.

No one set out to make me feel this way. No one told me these things. These are things I told myself. These are conclusions I came to on my own. These are lies I believed. These are still the same lies I struggle to fight off when I question or doubt *who I am*. We all have a set of lies that creep into our lives when we don't have authority over our identity and a strong set of beliefs about what is true.

I didn't have the words for it as a child, but looking back, I can articulate exactly how and why I took on a *less than* view of myself—and it is just as easy for you today as it was for me back then: If you don't define your identity yourself, you will by default allow the world to do it. That is, if you don't tell people who you are, then *they'll* tell *you* who you are.

So, what is true about who you are?

First, if you are not already firm in this belief, let me be the first to tell you:

> *Your identity is what you choose to believe about yourself.*

You are chosen. You are loved. You are worthy. You are good. You have purpose. You are a child of the Most High God, and He created you, just the way you are, to do a task that only you can do, for a time such as this.

You are not who the world says you are. You are not who people say you are. You are not your past or future mistakes.

Your identity is what you choose to believe about yourself. But that is a choice you have to make consciously. If you don't make this choice consciously, the natural default is to adopt the things other people say, or even don't say, about you as your identity.

WHAT YOU SAY ABOUT YOURSELF

You have likely heard of the concept of positive affirmations. An affirmation is

1. the action or process of affirming something, and
2. the assertion that something exists or is true.

I was fortunate to learn and buy into the idea of writing out positive affirmations about myself early in my professional career. I would write things like, "I am strong," "I am powerful," and "I am capable" on sticky notes and put them within sight on my bathroom mirror or desk. Later I would jot sayings like this down in a notebook during annual goal setting sessions. But for some reason, over time, I stopped doing this. I forgot how powerful words are and how important they are to my overall sense of self-worth—especially the words I say to myself.

After years of neglecting this valuable practice, I decided to make it a permanent practice in my life to remind me of what I believe about myself and what God says about me . . . and others. So, while on a family trip, I walked into a beachside tattoo shop and got the words "I am" tattooed on my wrist. There's no forgetting now. "I am worthy," "I am chosen," "I am loved," "I am forgiven." I am . . . what are you?

In order to stand firm in *who you are*, you have to first get clear on *what you believe*. I know that what we believe can often be traced back to some of the biggest pains we have experienced. I also know our biggest pains often lead to the biggest breakthroughs, and our biggest breakthroughs lead to a greater purpose. It's a chosen perspective shift to see and believe that **your pain is preparation for your purpose**.

Let me introduce you to what I will refer to as the Perspective Pendulum. A *pendulum* is defined as "something that alternates between opposites."[8] We often hear the phrase "the pendulum has swung too far" in reference to a drastic change. We use this phrase because in true pendulum form there is a center of gravity, a point where things are evenly balanced and supported, which helps us understand or predict how an object will behave when it's moved.

We as human beings need more than a physical center of gravity; we need an emotional center of gravity to balance and support who we were created to be. That means we need to set and determine what we believe to be true and call out what is a lie. By having an emotional center of gravity, we simultaneously create a stronger sense of purpose in our lives.

So, I want you to imagine a large pendulum. Every big pain you have experienced is represented as the weight on that pendulum (*see the irony here?*). The weight sits at the end of the suspension string, and it is what swings back and forth from the pivot point. You are the pivot point. You are the pivot point because you get to decide what you believe. This is a choice in perspective. It's a declaration of truth in your life.

Now, everything to the left of that weight (your pain) is a lie. These are the things that people have told you or said about you (as it relates to this pain) that are untrue. There are also things you have told yourself or said about yourself that are untrue (shown on the right side of the pendulum). These are lies. Write them down. Call them out of the shadows and declare them as lies in your life. Because they are. They are not true. Each pain we carry has the opportunity to speak life or death over us. The only thing standing between those two realities is what you allow yourself to believe.

When we allow untruths to become truth in our life, we allow death into our life—the death of our hopes, dreams, goals, relationships, happiness, future, and so much more. So, how do we stop that? We call it out for what it is. We become aware of the lies so when we hear them, we can recognize them for what they are. But then we have to overcome them with truth.

So, underneath the center point of that weight (your pain), I want you to counter every lie with a truth. We have to call it out before we can claim it, and we have to claim it before we can proclaim it.

Call out the lie. Claim the truth. Then proclaim it for the rest of your life.

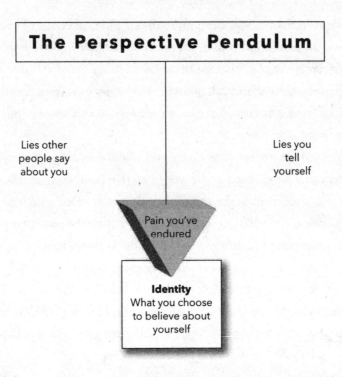

You can do this exercise with every significant pain you have experienced in your life to help you see the purpose behind every pain. The purpose is there, but it's up to you to do the work to redefine and reshape those pains. It took me a long time to figure out the purpose behind the pain I felt after our family's car accident. I carried those lies with me through middle school, high school, and well into college. Because of those lies, I made lots of really poor and potentially dangerous choices on who I spent time with, what I did for attention, what positions I put myself in, and how I viewed my self-worth. It wasn't until I was twenty years old that I began to hear whispers of truth over my story.

I was attending my sorority's parents weekend dinner, seated at a table with a sorority sister and her family. My sorority sister, Katie, casually introduced me to her mom, who happened to be a doctor of some kind. Suddenly Katie blurted out, "You should tell my mom your story!" I knew what she meant. She wanted me to tell her doctor-mom the story of our accident and how my brothers miraculously survived and recovered. I knew the drill; I could tell the story in my sleep.

So, I gave Katie's mom my normal story recap. At the end she stopped eating, grabbed my hand, and said, "AJ, my goodness! *You* are the miracle in this story!"

I literally interrupted her and said, "No, sorry, you must have misheard me. It was my brothers; they are the miracle."

She replied, "No, I heard you. You said you escaped a thirteen-car pileup with no injuries? Not even a scratch on you? Do you know how unbelievable that is? You are a true miracle!"

I was so stunned by what she said, I'm not even sure of how I responded. But I clearly remember driving back to campus that night thinking about that statement for the first time.

Was *I* also a miracle?

Did God save *me* that day too?

Could I have been protected for a reason?

Did I have some greater purpose?

Was I . . . important?

The answer was and is, "Yes!" Yes, I was a miracle. God did save me that day. I was protected for a reason. I do have a greater purpose. I am important. It took thirteen *years*, a decade of self-doubt, countless tears, and one person willing to speak life over me for me to start looking for the truth instead of believing the lies.

OWNING YOUR STORY

Comparison diminishes the power of your story. **Do not be afraid to share the challenges, shortcomings, failures, or any other low points you have experienced along the way. People find connection in the valley as much as, if not more than, they do on the mountaintop.**

Comparison diminishes the power of your story.

However, if you are anything like me, you might share the tendency to want to hide the hard parts of your story—you know, the parts that don't make you look so great, the unfiltered embarrassing parts that keep you humble, and then the really hard parts that you wish you could forget. Yup, those are the ones. I am telling you to share those parts!

Part of discovering who you are is learning to own your story—your *entire* story, not just the highlight reel but every moment, every lesson, every challenge. You may think, *but AJ, there are things in my past that don't align with who I want to be.*

And to that I say, of course there are. Undoubtedly, we all have countless things in our pasts that do not align with who we are today or who we want to be.

The things of your past don't *define* who you are today, but they've *shaped* who you've become. Those are the parts that most resonate with the people around you. The hard parts of your story are what connect you to other people. It's what helps them see beyond any facades, assumptions, or straight-up misconceptions about you. It's also what helps people relate to you because now they know you've been there, and you truly do get it.

Owning your story is about embracing your journey. It's about understanding that every experience, both the good and the bad, has contributed to the person you are today.

I challenge you to write down your story—not the one you tell on social media or at a networking event, but the real story. Include the struggles, the

> **When you accept your past, it loses its power over you.**

fears, and the moments of uncertainty. Because here's the beautiful thing about owning your story: When you accept your past, it loses its power over you. You take the reins, and that's when you start moving forward with purpose. And every new experience, every challenge, every lesson is adding to your story.

But it's important that it's your story. Not someone else's.

Scan the QR code on the front inside cover of this book to grab our story template and complete your own Life Story exercise.

THE POWER OF PURPOSE

Knowing who you are isn't a destination; it's a journey. And on this journey, you're going to have moments of clarity and moments of confusion. There will be times when you feel completely aligned and times when you question everything. That's okay. That's normal. Every step, every question, every moment of uncertainty is part of the process. Clarifying what is uncertain is the first step toward becoming certain.

When you discover who you are, you open the door to understanding your purpose. Purpose isn't something we achieve; it's something we live. We live it best when we're authentically ourselves. When you know who you are, you start aligning your actions, relationships, and work with that truth. Purpose flows naturally from authenticity.

When you start to realize your identity is much more tied to *who you are* than *what you do*, everything else becomes clearer. You stop saying yes to things that drain you, and you start pursuing the things that energize you. You become more intentional, more aligned, and more fulfilled. And that's what I want for you: to be able to look in the mirror and love the person looking back—not just for what you've done but for simply who you are.

Discovering who you are isn't about following a path someone else has set for you. It's about creating your own path, guided by your values, your purpose, and your vision. You are more than a label, more than a title, and more than what others say about you. You are your own story, and only you have the power to tell it.

So, own it.

Embrace it.

Let it be the foundation on which you build everything else.

Doing this will not only change your life; it will also impact the lives of everyone around you—your family, your friends, your community, and maybe . . . just maybe . . . the world.

PART 2

HOW TO BUILD A PERSONAL BRAND

CHAPTER 4

IDENTIFYING YOUR WHO

BY RORY VADEN

The day I became an actual "writer" was a day I'll never forget. You see, there is a big difference between "someone who writes" and someone who is a true "writer"—a lesson I learned from an unexpected source: my brother.

If you aren't aware, my first book was called *Take the Stairs,* and we often tell the semi-miraculous story of how I (really "we," because it was only with AJ and our entire team's help) became a *New York Times* bestselling author. However, the real story is the story of what happened to get the book deal in the first place and everything that went into creating the book long before it appeared on any shelves or bestseller lists.

One day when I was about twenty-four years old, I was walking through an airport when I stepped into a bookstore. While perusing the business shelf I noticed that a few of the books had this beautiful blurb that said "*New York Times* bestselling author." And that was the first time I remember thinking, *I wonder what it takes for someone to become a* New York Times *bestselling author?*

A few weeks later, I went to a local bookstore and pulled several books off the shelf that all included a *"New York Times* bestseller" mark. I sat with the pile of books around me trying to identify any consistent patterns of what they had in common. As I was flipping through the Acknowledgments sections of these books, I kept noticing that several of the authors referenced the same woman's name, even though they were different books!

I looked this woman up online and saw that she was a literary agent. She was apparently a very successful one, as she had represented several of the world's best-known personal development and business authors: Tony Robbins, Dr. Stephen Covey, Dr. Phil, Denise Austin, and many more. Immediately I decided, *This is the agent for me! I must meet her!* In my mind, I thought she would be so excited to meet an aspiring young author with big hopes and dreams of changing the world, that she would quickly see the potential in me and want to work together. In reality, right on her website it said, "Not accepting new author submissions at this time."

That didn't stop me; I filled out the form on her site. But I didn't hear anything back. A few days later, I sent them an email. Again, I didn't hear back. Then I called them . . . and still didn't hear anything back. For about six weeks I engaged a rhythm of calling and leaving a voicemail followed a few days later by an email. I kept telling them I was a new author and was excited to meet with her to share my book idea.

This woman and her team were so unresponsive that at one point I decided to send a *fax* just to see if I could get her attention! That did not work either. Naively, however, I was still convinced she would want to work with me if she would just get to know me. So, naturally, I decided the only way to ever meet her was to find out where she was and visit her in person. Her business address was right on the website, and thus I decided to buy a plane ticket and fly to her office! True story.

I knew she was super influential and super busy, so I realized that if she were already in the office by the time I arrived, I would likely get screened by the receptionist and never get to see her. Based on that assumption, I determined that my best chance was while she was first walking *into* the office from the parking lot. That meant I had to get to her building early so I could be absolutely certain I was there before she was.

That's how I ended up sitting inside her building hallway on the floor, in my best suit, at 4:30 a.m., in a random office park in Dallas, Texas. I had a printed copy of my first book proposal in hand and nothing but a prayer and a dream in my heart. This was my chance. This was my shot. This was my one opportunity to meet her and impress upon her my vision for this book and why she needed to work with me.

But there was one thing I didn't plan for. . . .

The day I was there, she was out of town! Go figure. However, not all hope was lost because the woman who showed up early that morning to open the office would change my life forever. Her name was Nena.

Nena was intelligent, sharp, savvy, and super knowledgeable. She was also very direct and to the point—which may have been amplified by the fact that some unknown man was sitting on the floor outside her office door. But like me, Nena was young. I could tell that she was a dreamer and a go-getter, so as quickly as I could fumble the words together, I tried to tell her what I was doing and why I was there.

I think out of pure shock that I had flown across the country on the "hope" of a random meeting, she took a few minutes to listen to me and my book idea. She was gracious and kind but also honest. She politely said, "Rory, you seem so great. You're going to do big things in the world. However, we could never work with someone like you. Your platform"—it would take me years to even figure out what the word meant: *the direct audience that you have access to*—"just isn't big enough. We work with celebrities, TV stars, professional athletes, politicians, and titans of industry. We help them get book deals with major publishers not just based on the quality of their ideas but also largely based on how many books they can sell. As someone just starting out, you just don't have enough reach to be a prospect for us to work with. I'm sorry, but we can't help you. Oh, and please stop calling."

My heart sank. It felt like in one breath my dream had been dashed to pieces. I didn't even fully understand at the time what she was saying. But the part that was very clear to me was that while I wanted *them*, they didn't want *me*. I was devastated, and I know I had tears welling up in my eyes. I barely held it together long enough to blurt out, "Please, Nena, just tell me what to do! I'll do anything. Tell me what to do, and I promise I'll do it. If you tell me what steps I need to take, I promise I will do exactly what you say!"

She replied, "I'll make you a deal. Because I do like you, and I can see that you care deeply about this, I'll tell you what: I will promise to read through your book proposal, and I will give you feedback on it—but you have to promise to stop calling us after that."

"Deal!" I said enthusiastically. Nena gave me her card, I gave her my proposal, and the meeting was over. I never even made it inside their office! This whole encounter happened in the hallway. In her defense, she was probably nervous about me hanging around outside of her door. But in that moment, I couldn't help but think about Jim Carrey's voice in the old movie *Dumb and Dumber*: "So you're tellin' me there's a chance? Yah!"

It was 2006 when I walked into the airport bookstore and first had the thought of one day becoming a *New York Times* bestselling author. I had started reaching out to this literary agency firm in 2007. I had bought a book on how to write a book proposal in early

2008. That meeting with Nena in the hallway was around the fall of 2008. And after that meeting, I heard . . . nothing. More silence. More unresponsiveness. I continued to "gently pester" Nena every couple of weeks to see if she had looked at my proposal. I didn't hear a "get lost" or "never contact us again" or anything. It was just silence. For months.

Then, one night in February of 2009, I got an email at around 9:45 p.m. It was from Nena! She wrote one line: "Rory, do you still want my feedback on your proposal?" I immediately responded, and we hopped on a phone call. I was so excited! But then she tore my proposal apart. She was very constructive and very honest. She critiqued my writing, my frameworks, my title, the layout of the proposal, and, most of all, the marketing plan.

She was so helpful, but the honesty of her feedback felt so *hurtful*. The part that was heartbreaking was realizing just how professional she was and what kind of level she was operating on—and how far away I was from that. Before meeting her, I had no strategy, no coaching, and no plan. I was just blindly and naively stumbling in the general direction of a dream. Nonetheless, at this point, it felt like a dream that was never going to come true.

I was so incredibly grateful for Nena. Not just because she followed through on what she said she would do but because she didn't blow me off. She lent me the respect of giving me her honest feedback. She had the courage to tell me the truth. And she invested her time in someone that she was likely never to get a return on. That made me so, so thankful for her. But it didn't change the fact that she ended the conversation by saying, "I really like you, Rory, but we could simply never work with someone like you. I hope that you find this feedback useful and that it helps you in your journey, but please stop contacting us."

With that, I was back to the drawing board. I didn't know where I would end up with this manuscript, but I did have absolute clarity on what my next steps were; I had to incorporate all of her feed-back. I hired an editor and writing coach, read a few more books on book proposals, attended as many free online trainings as I could about becoming an author (I was "broke as a joke" and in full start-up mode, so *free* is all I could afford), and worked hard in the evenings and on weekends to try and tighten up the proposal. Most of all, I was trying to learn how to be a *writer*.

Six months later, my proposal was ready. It was the best that I could possibly make it. I had incorporated every single thing Nena had told me. My writing coach had signed off on it. And I had done my very best to apply everything I had learned from various online training programs. So, it was time to go back to Nena.

The process began all over again. Email, no response. Phone call, no response. More emails, more phone calls, another Hail Mary fax message. No luck. It appeared Nena was nonverbally communicating that she had followed through on her commitment to read my pro-posal, and now she wanted me to follow through on my commitment to leave her alone. But then AJ had a brilliant idea!

She took me to the grocery store, where she picked out a wide selection of *instant* goods. Instant oatmeal, instant Jell-O, instant popcorn, instant pudding, instant gravy, Minute Rice, etc. When we got home, AJ packed all those items in a nicely wrapped basket. She had me print my most up-to-date book proposal, and she tucked it into the basket as well. She then had me include a hand-written note that said, "Dear Nena, hopefully by using these prod-ucts, you'll find a few extra minutes in your schedule to review my revised book proposal!"

And we sent it off.

A few days later, Nena emailed me! "Dear Rory and AJ, that was super creative. Thanks for the basket. I'll spend a few minutes reviewing your proposal and be back with another round of feedback soon." Per her continued integrity, Nena did review the proposal, and we spoke by phone again soon after.

On the one hand, the feedback was encouraging, as she said, "Rory, your writing is so much better. Your ideas are clearer and sharper and more unique." But on the other hand, it was more of the same: "You know how much I respect you and want to encourage you, Rory. You are on a good path, but your 'Platform' is simply nowhere near big enough. We could just never work with someone like you. But keep going and one day I know you'll make a big impact in the world."

For a third time, she had spoken the painful words aloud to me, "We will never be able to work with someone like you." Out of everything she said, for some reason that was the thought my mind had most grabbed onto and kept repeating.

"We will never be able to work with someone like you."

"We will never be able to work with someone like you."

"We will never be able to work with someone like you."

Somehow, though, I just *felt* like this wasn't over. We all need to be prepared for these kinds of moments. No matter how hard you work, how good you are, who you know, or how much you care, at some point in your journey you are going to fail. You are going to be told "no." You are going to come face-to-face with rejection.

In fact, you're not going to face rejection just once, you're going to face it again and again and again. The world may tell you that your ideas aren't good enough, or that you're not smart enough, or that someone is already out there doing the thing you want to do. But when push comes to shove, you have to decide deep down whether you feel a true calling on your life.

And if you feel that calling—if you *truly* feel compelled that you are supposed to share your story or your message or your expertise with the world—then you simply have to *decide* right now that you will not be stopped. **You have to resolve that the purpose of your**

life and the divine calling over your life is simply going to overpower whatever amount of rejection you encounter. You must flat out commit and declare that you will keep going. No matter what.

It doesn't matter if it's the voices of naysayers in the marketplace, the voices of trolls online, or the voices in your own head. You have to become dedicated and determined to listen only to the voices that push you toward your dream—and block out all the rest.

While it felt as though perhaps my time with Nena had come to an end and the road through her wasn't the right one, the message mattered too much to me to let it go. So, for the next year, we just kept building.

Building the company.

Building the audience.

Building relationships.

Building trust.

We were also building my speaking career. Remember, I had come in second at the World Championship of Public Speaking in 2007, and now, a couple of years later, my speaking calendar was gathering momentum. One night in August of 2010, I was keynoting an event in Nashville, Tennessee, when a man named Robert walked up to me afterward.

He said, "Rory, I really loved your presentation. I think you have what it takes to make it in this industry, and I would like to help you."

Blown away, I replied, "Thank you so much! That means a lot to me. What exactly do you do?"

You have to resolve that the purpose of your life and the divine calling over your life is simply going to overpower whatever amount of rejection you encounter.

Robert said, "I'm the business manager for a speaker named Andy Andrews. Have you heard of him?"

In my mind, I start freaking out thinking, *Have I heard of Andy Andrews?! You mean the Andy Andrews who is one of the most hilarious and inspiring speakers of our time? You mean the* New York Times *bestselling author? You mean the author of some of my favorite books ever,* The Traveler's Gift *and* The Noticer? *That Andy Andrews? Of course I have!*

What I actually said calmly was, "Oh yeah. I think I've heard of Andy Andrews."

Robert then gave me the gift of a lifetime when he said, "Well, I've worked with Andy his entire career. I'd like to invite you over to our office, and we will show you anything and everything you want to know. When do you want to come by?"

The next week, I was sitting in Robert's house learning all about the insider secrets of how the world of writing and speaking works. When I shared with Robert that I had been working on this book proposal for a couple years, he said, "Oh, book proposals? Yeah, that's easy. Let me show you what we just used to get a seven-figure advance."

Again, in my mind I was freaking out going, *Did he just say seven figures?! Does he really mean that they got paid more than one* million *dollars to write a book?* In fact, that's exactly what he meant, and it blew my mind. But what was even more powerful was when he *showed* me the proposal.

In an instant, I could see a massive difference between his proposal and mine. So many things were different and better, most of which had to do with the layout, which I knew I could emulate. But there was something more that I couldn't quite put my finger on. And then Robert shared one line of advice and one secret that would change the trajectory of my life.

He said, **"Rory, the real secret to writing a great book proposal is not to write an outline for a book. Instead, write a business plan for all the things you're going to do to *sell* that book."**

Just like that, it "clicked" for me. There was something about the way he said it that made me "get it." I had learned everything I needed to learn, and I had seen everything I needed to see to get to the next level. I immediately went home and started crushing through the revisions of my book proposal. Not only was I implementing the format and layout from Robert and Andy's proposal, but more importantly, I changed mine to reflect the *thinking* that supported it.

Two weeks later, I sent my new book proposal to Robert. He gave me a few key pointers. I made the revisions and sent them back to him. He then gave me his sign-off. "Okay. Now you're ready."

After having Robert's counsel, I felt more confident than ever. I showed it to AJ, said a prayer, and emailed my new and completely revised book proposal to Nena. The next day, she called me on the phone.

On the line with her was another woman, Jan—the one who had been listed in all the Acknowledgments sections of those books I had looked at years earlier! The date was November 16, 2010—approximately three and a half *years* after I had first contacted them—that Nena and Jan finally said the words, "Rory, we'd like to sign you!"

Within weeks, several of the biggest publishing companies in the world had reviewed my book proposal. We sold it to Penguin, and I was officially becoming a traditionally published author.

AN AUTHOR, BUT NOT YET A WRITER

If someone had told me at that point—nearly four years into pursuing my dream of becoming a bestselling author—that I was only 10 percent of the way there, I likely would have not only cried, but I would've quit.

While the one seemingly impossible mountain of getting an A-list literary agent and a traditional publishing deal with one of the most reputable houses in the industry had been climbed, several more peaks were looming just ahead. Namely, there was this issue of actually having to *write* the manuscript.

As you may have deduced from my story about Nena, I had been so focused on getting the book deal and coming up with a plan for how I would *sell* the book once we had it, over the course of that multi-year journey, that I had all but lost sight of another key part: *writing* the book. As I was reading back through my signed agreement, something finally jumped out at me that I had literally not thought about: The manuscript was due in three months!

I remember thinking, *Three months?! Wait! How can I write a book in three months? I'm not even a writer. I've never done this before. How does this process even work? Where do you start? Isn't there some kind of training for outlining a book? Isn't there a secret-handshake society where the other writers all get together and tell you exactly what to do now?*

Nope.

All I got was a contract and a deadline—one I had committed to hitting.

Panic set in . . . and something else with it. I had a new foe that showed up on the scene: imposter syndrome. The voice inside my head switched from *We could never work with you* to *Now look what you did, dummy. Look what you've gotten yourself into. You convinced all these people you were the "next big thing" and that you were going to become a bestselling author, and you don't even know how to write! Now everyone is going to see right through you. They're going to see the real you. You're no author. You don't even deserve to be in this position, and you're about to be exposed to everyone.*

Yikes.

It wasn't super uplifting or encouraging, I know. Needless to say, given that I was writing a book about the psychology of overcoming procrastination (that's the topic of *Take the Stairs*), I knew I just had to start. So, that's what I did: I sat down and started dumping words on the page.

It's not so much that my writing was *bad*; it's just that it wasn't very *good*. I never really liked English class all that much, I don't have a robust vocabulary (*robust* is stretching it for me), and to this day I have never had any formal training as a writer. I tried to take the pressure off myself and just "put the pen to page" to build some momentum.

My ideas were good. The content was good, and I knew it "worked," but the problem was that the writing wasn't powerful. It was blasé. Just generic words after generic words all pushed together into a pile of logical but not emotionally moving blocks of text.

I was wrestling with this fine-but-not-great writing situation when my brother called.

My brother Randy is truly my *big* brother. He's not only five and a half years older than me, but since we were raised together by a single mom, he was in many ways more like my dad for the early part of my life. We have different biological fathers, which helps explain why he's always been much larger than me physically. Growing up, Randy was an athlete and a competitor. He's the one who taught me how to be tough, resilient, and disciplined—mostly from beating the crap out of me when we were younger. But I *love* my brother.

I credit Randy's influence for many of my favorite character traits about myself. That's why I was so bothered by what was going on in his life around 2011 when I was working on my first manuscript.

On top of being an all-pro athlete in high school and a beast in the gym during his adolescent years, my brother went into the United States Navy to serve our country in his twenties. I'd always had so much respect for him and, having been on the receiving end of a few hard hits in our roughhousing as kids, I also had a healthy amount of fear of him. This is what created the dilemma when, after he got out of the military, he gained weight—a lot of weight.

In his peak physical condition in his twenties, my brother weighed around 195 pounds, which meant, at five-foot-eight, he was "stacked." Years later, however, after coming out of the military, he slowly but steadily gained weight. At his worst, he had lost all his muscle and, at 280 pounds, was over 50 percent body fat.

This bothered me.

Sure, I was worried about his health, but there was something more to it. I wasn't just concerned; I was actually mad about it—mainly because it was just so different from who I knew him to be. When we were young, he had a habit of working out and competed as a fighter. As we got older, though, his habits changed. He was always talking about the "new program" or the "new diet" or the "new thing" he was trying. He would start strong and begin to see improvement and results. But then, he would inevitably revert to unhealthy ways.

That's exactly what had happened at the time of our phone call that night in 2011. By that point in our careers, we were both busy, and he was raising a family, so we didn't talk often. But on this particular night, we took time to catch up. Sure enough, he started telling me about some new gym he'd joined and how he was finally turning things around. I wondered, though—even by the way he was talking—if this was likely just another fad that would come and go for him. It didn't seem like any real change in his psyche had taken place. It pissed me off because I just felt like he wasn't going to follow through.

Do you think I shared that with him?

Absolutely not! Did I mention how much bigger he is than me and how afraid of him I am?

No, I didn't share it with him—not because I didn't care but because I didn't have the courage to tell him what I was really thinking and how I was really feeling. Instead, I did something else. I wrote. I wrote *at* him. Only I didn't do it in a letter or an email; I did it in my manuscript.

Because I happened to be in the midst of this writing project, I got off the phone and, in somewhat of an unapologetic fit of light rage, I wrote fully emotionally charged words *at* him and *to* him.

For a few hours, I lost sight of the fact that I was writing a book for the public, and I allowed myself to become consumed with just writing *to my brother that I love*. I wrote everything to him that I so desperately wanted to say to his face but that I was too much of a coward to speak up about. I allowed myself to disappear into the writing, letting go of how it sounded, what people might think, or even what I was trying to say.

I only focused on one thing: trying to change my brother's life through the words I was typing on the page. I wanted to get through to *him*—no one else. I only cared about talking to *him*—and not to anyone else that might ever read it.

Later, I went back and read what I had written. It was so incredibly powerful, so different from all the writing I had done up until that point. It was so much more poignant and impactful. The chapter I wrote that night went on to become chapter 2 in *Take the Stairs*, "The Buy-In Principle of Commitment." *That* was the day I became a real *writer*, because I learned an important principle that has stayed with me every day since: **Most messengers communicate to the world; but Mission-Driven Messengers communicate to a person.**

Did my writing change my brother's life? Well, unfortunately not. I'm honestly not sure if he ever even read it—and I'm still a bit scared to share this story with him.

> *Most messengers communicate to the world; but Mission-Driven Messengers communicate to a person.*

The good news is that my brother eventually managed to figure out how to change his own life. Over the years, he became a legendary competitive girls' fast-pitch softball coach. He realized that he couldn't ask his girls to do things he wasn't willing to do. He got back on track, lost over eighty pounds, and cut his body fat from over 50 percent to under 5 percent. He ultimately did enter a fitness competition for which he weighed in at 199, took home first place in two categories, qualified for Nationals, and earned the overall Masters title. Way to go, big bro!

However, the whole phone encounter with my brother *did* make *me* a much better writer. I've since written multiple books and hundreds of articles. And the lesson of writing to a *person* instead of to the world at large not only shaped my career but the lives of many of our clients.

WHO IS YOUR *WHO*?

The idea of targeting your communication to a single person isn't just a good tip; it's a foundational principle. Ironically, one of the greatest challenges that personal brands have—and one of the biggest reasons they fail—is that they are trying to talk to too many different people.

Remember the tenet from chapter 2, "If you have diluted focus, you will get diluted results"? That applies not only to your business model, and not only to the message you're trying to convey, but also to the audience you select. For example, we see this a lot with clients who are struggling to grow on social media. They may complain about "the algorithm" or the "competition" in their space. However, we can almost always (and quickly) identify one of the biggest challenges with their profile: It's not crystal clear *who* their content is targeted toward.

We'll commonly find that their content is a random smattering of topics that span personal and professional realms. One day, a picture of their cat. The next, a funny internet meme. Then an inspirational video . . . a beautiful sunset . . . some family portraits. They might mix in a random quote or Bible verse. While it's never "wrong" to post whatever you want on a platform that is inherently designed to be "social," that is a terrible content strategy if you want to actually use social media to grow your business and the reach of your personal brand.

But it can be tricky, right? We totally empathize with the challenge of trying to serve multiple audiences. If you're like most people who come to us, you're torn because there are potentially many types of viewers of your feed. You might have:

- Your colleagues at work
- Your friends from high school
- Some of your customers
- Prospects you're trying to attract
- Grandma
- Other people who share the same hobbies as you
- A group of people who are interested in the "new" business thing you're interested in

And, of course, you'll have all sorts of other audiences you are trying to talk to and serve. The great irony is that **the more audiences you try to serve, the more likely you are to fail at serving any of them well**.

What's the secret? In short, it's focusing solely on supporting *one* audience and being okay if the others fall off. It's a decision you have to make.

To gain attention early on, in the beginning, you have to choose your *who*. In fact, this is one of the first (if not *the* first) and most (if not *the* most) important decisions that a personal brand must make if you want to grow.

One of my favorite leadership authors is Simon Sinek. I think he is legitimately one of the best writers, speakers, and *thinkers* of our time. I love the way that he strikes the perfect, delicate blend of intellectual capacity and emotional humanity. Simon, of course, broke through "the wall" and became famous when his viral TED Talk and bestselling book popularized his flagship phrase, *Start With Why*.

> *You should in fact not "start with why" but instead start with who.*

I believe in Simon's message and am a huge fan of his; however, I think that phrase is actually wrong when it comes to personal brands. Simon's message in *Start With Why* is geared more toward what makes great companies, and that is incredibly different from what makes a great personal brand.

For personal brands, I am strongly convicted and utterly convinced that **you should in fact *not* "start with why" but instead start with *who*.** Strategically, tactically, and emotionally, the first decision that a personal brand needs to make is exactly *who* they are talking to. The moment you become clear on your who, every single other downstream decision becomes clearer.

For example, once you know precisely what type of person you are trying to reach with your message, you automatically can answer so many other questions about your personal brand, such as:

- What are the best online platforms for me?
- Where do I spend my time offline?
- What type of content do I need to create?
- What types of problems do I need to solve and what questions do I need to answer in order to be useful?
- What products or services could I build that would be attractive and enticing?
- How much should I charge?

In turn, being clear on those answers will make it easier to find clarity on so many other things, including:

- What type of team do I need to build?
- Where should I be advertising?
- What is the right technology for me to utilize?
- Which platforms are the most important to create content on?

- How long do my free and paid programs need to be?
- When can I expect to make a profit from this venture?

Once you are clear about your who, you are clear on the *type* of person you are trying reach. Once you are clear on the *type* of person you are trying to reach, you can suddenly know so much more about them and, thereby, extrapolate so many logical and obvious business decisions that need to be made.

Contrast that, however, with someone who is *not* clear on their "who." If you don't know exactly who you are trying to reach, then you don't know:

- Where to show up
- What type of content to create
- What type of offers to make
- How much they can afford to pay

You will also sell hardly anything because none of your programs— and certainly none of your marketing—will speak directly to their *specific* problems or their *specific* desired outcomes. **By not being specific in who you are targeting, you become generic in what you are producing.**

This creates the most ironic result, which again is that by trying to reach everyone, you effectively reach no one, because nothing you create or produce "connects" with your audience in a deep or meaningful way. Instead, your content and your personal brand as a whole become part of the very same sea of noise that you're trying to escape! Instead of separating *from* the noise, the opposite happens and you become a contributor *to* the noise.

Think of this like being at a cocktail party. There is a blanket murmur among the crowd of people. They are all talking about some mishmash of topics around whatever is happening in their own little worlds. It's all indistinct noise. Nothing stands out. Nothing is truly noticeable. It all just blends together into a consistent, ambiguous buzz.

Now imagine that right then someone from across the room says your name. Do you hear it? You do, don't you? The sound of your name cuts through the noise. It rips through that ambivalent murmur and somehow leaps up and grabs you! The sound of your name is enough to yank your attention right out of the middle of one conversation and pull you over to being fully attentive to another.

Why?

How?

It has everything to do with a message and a signal being sent out that is *hyper* customized *just* for you. Because of the precise focus of the message, it travels on a wavelength that is dialed directly into your frequency. When someone calls your name, you intuitively, biologically, and automatically recognize the distinctiveness of that signal—and you *immediately* tune into it and respond to it.

Notice that it's not the *volume* of the signal nor its *intensity* that really captures you. No. Instead, it's the *specificity* of the signal that interrupts your attention. That's exactly what we're talking about here. Specificity—not intensity—provides the power of the signal.

This metaphor applies *perfectly* to your personal brand. When you are trying to create content that is generally for "everyone" or even for just one large group, your messages get dampened and muffled and pushed down amid the murmur of the crowd. Your signal comes in as a loosely connected wave that bounces off Sheahan's Wall and is absorbed back into the noise.

But when you speak with specificity, it's like a tight stream of energy that pierces a hole right through the wall. **Your message gets through the barrier not because of its brilliance or its strength, but simply because of the message's uniqueness and hyper-relevance to the recipient.**

One key difference with the messaging of your personal brand is even more powerful than using a person's name. When you use a person's name, you *only* capture the attention of that person. But when you speak the specific language of the type of person your brand is dedicated to reaching, you reach *every single person* who is operating on that frequency. This again points to the power and accuracy of Sheahan's Wall:

Sheahan's Wall

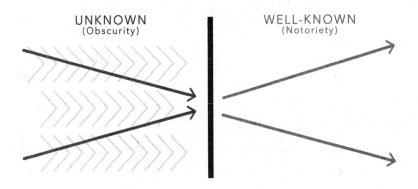

UNKNOWN
(Obscurity)

WELL-KNOWN
(Notoriety)

It is this completely ironic and counterintuitive result that by trying to reach a lot of people, you connect with very few people. Yet paradoxically, by trying to speak deeply, specifically, and intensely to only *one* person, you end up reaching masses of people!

While I didn't know it at the time, this is exactly what happened in my writing style when I was writing to my brother. Before my phone call with him that night, I was writing to everyone. As a result, my material wasn't deeply moving or connecting with anyone. But when I wrote *to him* and *at him,* it spoke powerfully to everyone who could relate.

This concept is vaguely remnant of The Pain Paradox principle that I wrote about in *Take the Stairs.* Simply put, the Pain Paradox principle states: *Easy short-term choices lead to difficult long-term consequences. Meanwhile, difficult short-term choices lead to easy long-term consequences.* That same discipline is required for a personal brand to consciously and proactively choose to focus on a narrower audience. But choosing a *narrower* audience doesn't mean you'll reach a *smaller* one; quite the contrary, it means you will very likely reach a much *larger* one!

HOW TO FIND YOUR WHO

Once you are sold on the power of this principle, the next question becomes, *"How* do I find my *who?"* Conceptually you already know the answer, because we wrote about it in chapter 2 when we shared that "You are most powerfully positioned to serve the person you once were."

You may be thinking, *On a practical level, what are the actual activities and exercises I can do to find my who?* I'm glad you asked. We have a process for this, and it starts with some basic thinking about demographics.

I like *Investopedia's* definition of demographics: "statistics that describe populations and their characteristics."[9] However, we've created our own acronym for these, which doubles as an exercise as you simply answer each of the following:

- **D**.ependents?
- **E**.ducation?
- **M**.arital status?
- **O**.ccupation?
- **G**.ender?
- **R**.eligion?
- **A**.ge?
- **P**.osition? (job title)
- **H**.ometown?
- **I**.ncome?
- **C**.ulture?

While some of these probably technically fall outside the lines of what academically make up a person's set of demographics, this list has worked really well for us. It's a checklist of what we consider "objective" and/or "measurable" data points about a person. (Plus, we love acronyms!) Whenever someone is starting on the journey to narrow down who their audience is, we find that discussing and listing out of some of the most likely D.E.M.O.G.R.A.P.H.I.C.s or demographic ranges is super helpful.

Demographics get us going in the right direction, but they are not nearly as important as *psychographics*. For psychographics, I like Oxford's definition: "the study and classification of people according to their attitudes and aspirations."[10] When we talk about psychographics, what we're really asking is, "What is going on inside the *mind* of the person we're trying to reach?"

The better you are at understanding, knowing, and predicting what dialogue they are having in their head, the more skilled you become at articulating the words that attract and convert them.

Now, how in the world is it possible to know what is going on inside someone's head that is not your own? The answer is to be super specific about the type of person you are trying to reach. That secret shortcut is to know that person well on the front end, because that person used to be you! (Serve the person you once were, remember?) This is yet another example that underscores and edifies what I wrote about earlier in this chapter: The sooner you are clear about your *who*, the clearer every single other downstream decision becomes, including knowing what words to use in all your collateral.

After you finish the demographic questions, the next step is to go through and answer each of the following questions about your audience's *psychographics*:

- What does this person care most about?
- What does this person want or need?

- What is this person searching for?
- What are this person's passions and interests?
- What is this person's biggest life mission or goal?
- What are this person's limiting beliefs?
- What questions does this person need answered?
- What is holding this person back?
- How is this person feeling?
- What keeps this person up at night?

What you are looking for is what we call "thematic overlap." You want to identify intersections between your personal story and the answers your hypothetical avatar—or ideal target prospect—is looking for. We know that your uniqueness lies somewhere near the intersection and overlap of those two data sets.

Scan the QR code on the front inside cover of this book to request a free brand strategy call with our team.

DIALING IT IN

Once you've completed the broad level brainstorming on the demographics and psychographics of the person you're trying to reach, we want you to take one more step in narrowing down your avatar. Create a list of real-life people you know who best "fit" or "model" your avatar based on the details you have already mapped out.

If you've been in business a while, one of the fastest ways to do this is to simply ask yourself, *Which of my existing clients would I consider to be my "ideal" or "perfect" client?*

To put it another way, you might think, *I wish all my clients were just like* _____.

We started broad and now we're continuing to narrow it down. We're trying to get "locked in" as tightly as possibly on who your perfect person is and what characterizes them.

If you are newer in your business or personal brand journey, then think of people you know in real life who represent the type of person you are trying to reach.

When doing anything related to your personal brand, **it's always best to isolate the face of one single real-life person you know who serves as a representative of the type of person you are creating content for**. For example—and this is something I still do, even though I've been writing for more than a decade—before I write the first word of a blog post, I'll write the name of a person I know in real life at the top of the page. *That* is the person I'm writing that specific blog to, just like I wrote my first book to my brother (see chapter 2). I know the more pointed I am about talking to that one person, the more impactful the message will be to everyone who reads it.

The next step in the process is to coalesce the high-level demographic and psychographic traits with the specificity of the real-life representative into an "Avatar Story." Here, you are going to write a fictitious backstory that codifies your "Avatar" as if they were a real-life person. This is important because going forward, this Avatar will represent the most clearly defined and specific individual that your entire brand, message, content, and all related assets are created *for* and catered *toward*.

This is "your person," and the more closely you nail the description of this "person," the more powerful your content will be, the clearer your strategy will be, and the more likely you'll be to "break through the wall."

Here is a sample of what one might look like:

Anthony Dunn is a forty-year-old, late millennial and former college athlete who has had the grit, perseverance, ability, and opportunity to create a great business and life for himself and his family.

He has been happily married, but not without ups and downs, to his college sweetheart for more than fifteen years. He has two grade-school-aged girls who keep him very busy learning about dolls, dance, and all things pink. They are both daddy's girls and love doing everything with him, including watching SEC football, reading books, traveling to the beach, and visiting the zoo.

After graduating from the University of Georgia (go Dawgs!), Anthony was thrilled to accept the job offer of a "lifetime" with a company that was all about creating products that could help people live a happier and healthier life. So, he went to work for a healthcare organization where he could climb the corporate ladder, make great money, and do something that matters. Ten years into that company, he realized that it was not all that it originally seemed. Quotas kept growing, new leaders came and went through a revolving door, and more and more limitations were placed on his once well-rounded and evolving role. With the support of his wife, he resigned, decided to go all in on his dream, and started his own company.

With the same work ethic and propensity for mentorship he had as a collegiate athlete, Anthony got to work. A lot of work. With a whole new industry to learn, a business structure to set up, pricing to set, new clients to acquire, and operations to manage, he was soon overwhelmed, overworking, and wondering why he was doing this.

However, Anthony knew deep down this could be some-thing special and that he had an opportunity to change his life and many others. He dreamed of helping people overcome their limiting beliefs around leadership; he wanted to travel the world with his family and speak on global stages; and he had a desire to write books that could help leaders become better and make a bigger impact while also earning a bigger income. He knew he could do all this, but he also realized he needed help. Just like back in college, he needed a team—a community

*of people who could share tips, ideas, and best practices. He
needed a coach, someone to identify his blind spots and point
him in the right direction.*

*Anthony has a vision, he knows his purpose, and he has the
means to do something about it. So, he does.*

Look at how specific this is. Do you know someone like Anthony?
I bet most of us do. You should feel the emotion behind this even if it's
not you or your Avatar. But if it *is* you or your Avatar, the description
should resonate at a soul level. This is more than some generic exercise; this is tapping into the emotional state and psyche of the person
who needs you in their life.

Once you get the story just right, we recommend you try to find a
stock image or AI-generated photograph that matches what you think
the Avatar could look like in real life. Once you find that picture,
print it out and tape it near your computer so you never forget who
you are writing to, who you are creating content for, and why you are
doing the work to build your personal brand. It's for a person!

*Scan the QR code on the front inside cover of this book to complete
your Avatar Story exercise using our free story template.*

FINDING YOUR WHY

Hopefully by now you can see the power and importance of getting
specific about your *who*. Further, you can see how having a clear *who*
makes it so much easier to make practical decisions in your business
about how to market, where to market, who to hire, how to structure
your business, and a long list of other key tactical decisions. Yet, after
everything we've learned, I've concluded that *none* of those is the most
significant reason why you need to clarify who you are addressing.
There is actually a much bigger and deeper reason at play.

The truest truth about why you must find your *who* is this: **For most people, our *why* is a *who*!**

A true Mission-Driven Messenger pursues the path of building a personal brand because what they care about most is *impact*—and impact requires a *who*.

Mission-Driven Messengers care about making the world a better place. They want to help *people*. They want to make a difference in the lives of other humans. The reason they do what they do is not because they need it themselves but because they have an irresistible calling to share something with others.

Their *why* is always connected to a *who*. They are trying to reach someone.

> For most people, our *why* is a who!

They are trying to teach someone. They are trying to help someone. They are trying to make a difference for someone. **They aren't trying to achieve a *thing*; they are surrendered to serving a *person*!**

Most people would say that the reason they work so hard is to provide for their kids, or maybe to make their grandparents proud, or maybe to pay forward something they feel they owe to a mentor. Perhaps they want to serve someone in need, or maybe they even consider it their spiritual duty to be all they can be to honor their creator.

In all of these instances, our *why*—our reason for working so diligently at doing the thing we're doing—is actually for a *who*! The cause and the purpose of our life is to serve others. And that's not just what makes a powerful personal brand; that's what gives purpose to our humanity. Our lives have meaning in the context of helping others, and, as we've seen, we are most powerfully positioned to serve the person we once were.

If you have read this far into this book, you're aware that **we know what it's like to *be you*, because we *are you*!** We've lived through the heartache and frustrations and setbacks and confusion and rejections and failures. But we're here because we also know the thrill of building a thriving business that does good in the world. We know the deep joy that comes from hiring a team of amazing people who buy into your mission and help you deploy it into the market in a bigger way.

That's why we're here. We're here because we believe that for each of us, **our highest self is to be our highest value to other people.** We are here to serve the people we once were. We are here for you in the exact same way that we know you are here for someone else who is out there in the world who needs you right now.

Our highest self is to be our highest value to other people.

We're fully committed to helping you find your uniqueness, so that you will find your person, so that *you* will help that person—in the unique way that only you can—to solve their problem.

Now that you know *who* your *who* is, let's talk about how you can go find them!

CHAPTER 5

CLARIFYING YOUR PROBLEM AND CAUSE

BY RORY VADEN

At seventeen years old, I woke up in the middle of the night with a clear and vivid message on my heart. The message was one small word:

Discipline.

It's hard to describe the way I received that message, but I distinctly recall being convicted that I was to go out and share this message of discipline with the world.

The first time I ever saw a professional speaker was in sixth grade at Platt Middle School. Sitting in the gymnasium, I heard this guy in his twenties tell the story of his drug addiction that began in high school. After graduation, he started selling drugs, got caught, and went to prison. He shared the tragic tale of his brother's murder and then story after sobering story of his friends who had lost their freedoms, their families, and their lives due to poor choices. Yet, somehow through this awful narrative, the guy was hilarious, entertaining, and truly inspiring. While I don't even remember his name, I do remember his story and the way he told it, and his story *impacted* me.

Here's what I remember thinking. First, *If instead of making* bad *choices and then later trying to course correct, where would someone end up if they actually made* good *choices their whole life?* I can't say I have never made a bad choice, but because of that speech I can say I have never touched drugs nor been in a position that could potentially lead to jail or death. All because of his story.

Second, *I wonder how you get the job of getting to hold the micro-phone to entertain and inspire a room full of people?* My dream of one day becoming a speaker started in that sixth-grade gym.

Several years later, during my sophomore year of high school, I was on student council, which controlled the budget for hiring one or two "motivational speakers" for the school year. I remember being on the committee to approve a fee of $1,000 for someone to come speak at our school. This blew my mind! You mean to tell me these people get paid to come and talk to students?! Now, for a second time, my dream to become a professional speaker had been stirred.

My brain struggled to believe that someone would get paid one *thousand* dollars to hold a microphone, tell some stories, make people laugh, and teach a couple of useful tips. It was at that moment that I decided, "This is the career for me!" I then started to attend leadership conferences and continued to see more and more great speakers. I was hooked! I knew that one day I had to speak, but I kept processing the question, *What might be the thing that I could go around talking about that people would pay money to hear?*

Then, in the wee hours of that definitive fall day of my senior year, I had my answer: *discipline*. I somehow intuitively *knew* that I was supposed to go out and share the message of discipline with the world. So, I did. I launched my very first company, Discipline Dynamic. My dad built the website, I had a low-cost designer create the business card, and, as fast as that, I was "official."

I started out mostly speaking in high schools, for youth leadership groups, college student organizations, and a few nonprofits, predominantly all for free. For years, I struggled to find anyone to pay me because I didn't understand anything about sales, marketing, or positioning. I realized there was much more to learn to actually make the "paid" part of my dream a reality.

During college, I joined a direct sales company that taught students how to sell door-to-door during the summer. It was a way to make money and learn sales, and my primary motivator was the incentive that the top sales students every year were invited to speak on stage at the next year's annual event. It was at one of those events that I heard a speaker named Eric Chester.

Eric was phenomenal! He was next level compared to any speaker I had ever heard. He was hilarious, thought-provoking, insightful, and deeply inspiring with his personal stories. One of those stories included his son who was attending the University of Colorado in Boulder—a campus I was recruiting at for this company!

After his speech, I went up to Mr. Chester, introduced myself, and told him, "My dream is to one day do what you just did. But right now, I'd like your son's phone number!" Turns out I was learning sales after all. I ended up recruiting his son with a dual commitment I made with Eric. He asked that I promise to mentor and watch out for his son throughout the summer, and in return, when it was all done, he would mentor me. Deal of a lifetime. Easy yes.

Eric quickly saw that I needed a lot of help on my branding and positioning, so he introduced me to his good friend and fellow speaker David Avrin. The introduction was great, but I couldn't afford to pay Dave anything. I was just wrapping up grad school and every penny was spoken for. But I was lucky. Blessed. Fortunate. Dave saw something in me that he felt inspired to help cultivate. Let this be a reminder to us all about the importance of paying it forward, helping the up-and-comers, and giving not just our money but our time to those around us. If not for the time Dave poured into me, you would likely not be reading this book. For years, he would just sit with me—for hours at a time—so I could pick his brain on how to build my brand.

While it was exceptional to have someone like David Avrin pouring into me, it's important to note that people will *want* to help you if:

- You are respectful of their time.
- You are humble enough to listen to their advice.
- You show your gratitude for their contribution to you.
- You give back to them however you can.
- And most of all . . . you take action to implement the things they spend time teaching you!

People want to help winners, but they don't want to help whiners. Don't be someone who seeks "mentorship" as a way to avoid actually doing the work that moves you toward your dream. Be the person who does the hard work of doing the hard things they tell you to do.

People want to help winners, but they don't want to help whiners.

Even though David was encouraging to me, he had some tough truths to deliver. "Rory, there is a really big issue with your personal brand. You are very clear on the solution, discipline. But you are totally unclear on the problem you're solving for people. You're out there telling everyone they need more discipline, but no one knows why."

Clarifying even further, he continued, "The problem you solve needs to be marketed as clearly as the solution. You see, 'discipline' is your answer, but to what question? 'Discipline' is your solution, but to what problem?"

People buy solutions to *problems*. They buy answers to *questions*. But in order to get them to buy, don't market or advertise the *solution*; instead, promote the *problem*. Don't market or advertise the *answer*; instead, advertise the *question*.

Imagine that you are a plumber who discovers the world's most amazing sealant for bathroom pipes that never crack and never leak under any circumstance. And imagine that you are such a passionate plumber who cares so deeply about your craft that you are absolutely ecstatic about this revolutionary new breakthrough method in your trade. Next, imagine that you then go on a marketing rampage telling the whole world about how awesome this sealant is. Guess who would pay attention? Correct: only other plumbers. The rest of us do not care about what the sealant is made of, who makes it, or *how* it works. We just care *that* it works.

But now imagine you are a plumber whose marketing says, "Have a leaky faucet? Call us and we'll fix it forever!" Now who is going to pay attention? Everyone in the world who has a leaky faucet, which is exactly what you want! By promoting the *problem*, you get the right people to pay attention—the people with that problem. By marketing the *question*, you attract the right people who have that same question.

Therefore, the power is in promoting the *problem*. The influence comes from raising awareness of the *issue*. The conversions result from causing people to think about a *question*.

When you are trying to get someone's attention, you have to first give them a reason to care. The job of a marketing professional is to create the context and to place people in a perspective that makes them want to pay attention. That happens most effectively and most efficiently by talking about problems.

People understand problems. They know when they have them. They can easily see and identify when something has gone wrong. But contrary to what you might think, people often don't understand solutions all that well. If they did understand solutions, they probably would already be using the solution and wouldn't have the problem in the first place.

Perhaps a clearer way to say it is people don't buy solutions as much as they buy the disappearance of problems. They often don't even care to know much about *how* the solution works as long as it works.

Now the question is, *What problem do you solve for your audience?*

If you are like most individuals, you have *no idea* what problem you actually solve for people! If that is not a question

> **People don't buy solutions as much as they buy the disappearance of problems.**

you have asked yourself or have spent much time thinking about, or if it's a question that has never been asked of you, then that presents a devastating marketing challenge for your personal brand.

If we are not crystal clear on the problem we solve, there is no *way* our prospective customers will be either!

I was so frustrated when I couldn't answer a simple question that David proposed to me again and again, every time we would meet: "Rory, what problem do you solve in one word?"

This question stumped me for *months*! How could that possibly be? How could such a simple question be *so* hard to answer? "What problem do you solve in one word?" I was plagued and dumbfounded and annoyed and angry and discouraged. I just could *not* wrap my head around it. "What problem do you solve in (only) one word?"

Why was it so difficult to answer that dang question?!

David explained to me, "People buy luxuries if and when they have excess money. In everyday reality, what people *really* spend their money on is solving problems. People will always spend money to make their problems go away."

> **People might *find* money to buy luxuries, but they will always *find* money to solve problems.**

This made sense to me. If you're hungry (problem), you will spend money on food. If your kid gets sick (problem,) you will find the money to see a doctor. If you blow out a tire (problem), you will spend the money to get new tires. If the water heater breaks (problem), you will find the money to get it repaired. People *might* find money to buy luxuries, but they will *always* find money to solve problems. You need to position your personal brand as a solution to a problem. If you do that, you will always have customers in any economy or any geographic territory.

The job of marketing is to communicate the problem and promote the end result. It is *not* to tell them *how* you will resolve the issue.

After months of ideating on my one-word problem, it finally hit us: *procrastination.*

Discipline is the antidote to procrastination. Discipline was the answer; procrastination was the question. Discipline was the solution; procrastination was the problem.

Once we landed on my one-word problem of procrastination, everything started to change.

THOUGHT LEADERSHIP EMERGES

After we narrowed down the Problem I solve to just one word, I suddenly had tremendous focus and power—because now I not only spent my time teaching people the solution; I also started studying the Problem. From where I stand now, I believe that *studying* the Problem is one of the most essential parts of what it means to be a thought leader.

You're not just providing answers. You're helping your entire audience to better understand the Problem. You are exploring the intricate nuances and all the various complex circumstances in which that Problem shows up in the world. That makes your work of building a personal brand exciting, original, innovative, and deep.

As I started studying procrastination, I started focusing more on the Problem, I started thinking more about the Problem, I started asking more people about the Problem, I started interviewing people about the Problem. Even in casual conversations just as I would meet someone, I would question how and why and when they have this Problem in their life. It was in the midst of doing that deep, focused work that I started to create original thought leadership on the subject matter.

This wasn't because I was "smarter" than everyone else but simply because I was dedicating more time to a very narrow niche area of study.

Clients often come to Brand Builders Group and want us to give them a shortcut. But we don't sugarcoat it or offer false hope with "tricks" or "gimmicks" that make them feel like they're making progress when they aren't. That's not what we do. But there is one real "hack" for becoming one of the world's leading thought leaders:

You think about that subject more than anyone else!

The "hack" is to dedicate your life to the service of others by isolating one issue, one area, and one zone that you think you might be able to develop further in a way that makes the world a better place. You spend time reading about it, learning about it, talking about it, and pontificating about it.

It's not a hack or a gimmick at all; it takes real work. But it's not that complicated or difficult either. In fact, most people spend more time chasing "hacks," "gaming the system," or "tricking the algorithm" than they would if they actually just did the work of selecting an area of focus and became entrenched in the subject matter. When you have a deep level of focus, a series of small, marginal discoveries start to emerge that eventually add up to be a significant contribution.

Do that long enough, and one day you'll look up and people will be calling you "one of the world's leading experts on _____."

That's all a thought leader does: They forward the thinking on what's already been said or done in one particular area.

That is what happened to me. Once I started talking more publicly about procrastination and its impact on teams, organizations, top-line revenue, and bottom-line profits, companies started calling to hire me to come speak to their people. They felt the pain of the Problem I was talking about.

The Problem is what makes people wake up and sign up. The Problem is what makes them *engage* and interact. The Problem is what makes them pay attention, and pay money!

FINDING YOUR ONE-WORD PROBLEM

Hopefully by now, you've already been thinking about this cornerstone question, "What Problem do I solve in one word?" because it's time to dig in and find the answer to that question for you.

We are about to start taking you through a six-part framework called the Brand DNA Helix. Each part of the framework is a different question that you're going to answer, but the questions operate in tandem sets, like a chromosome pair. The answers from those question sets help determine a foundational element of your personal brand called your *Brand Positioning Statement,* which consists of five core components:

1. **Uniqueness:** a one-word distillation of your Message that captures the core essence of your proposed solution to the Problem.

2. **Message:** a one-sentence solution-oriented through line statement that distills your entire body of work into a single actionable command, instruction, or order.

3. **Problem:** A one-word identification of the core issue you are going to solve for your audience.

4. **Cause:** A one-word clarification of the underlying root issue that is responsible for creating the Problem.

5. **Avatar Persona:** A one-phrase description of the audience you are going to serve.

You will learn much more about the Brand Positioning Statement in the following chapters as we deep dive into each of its components. For now, you just need to know two things about it. First, we generally construct it from the bottom up starting with Avatar (previous chapter), then working on Problem and Cause in tandem (this chapter), and then working on Uniqueness and Message together (next chapter). The second thing you need to know is that your Brand Positioning Statement is the most critical and essential foundational asset of your personal brand, because it is a collection of strategic conclusions that will ultimately direct and guide nearly all of your future decisions once it is established.

If your Brand Positioning Statement is clear and aligned, your influence, impact, and income are likely to grow. If it is not, you are likely to struggle. Thus, helping you clarify yours is the primary objective and tactical outcome we hope this book will generate. You can have confidence that your personalized Brand Positioning Statement will reveal itself as you move through each of the forthcoming questions and exercises presented by each step in the Brand DNA Helix.

The first question in the Brand DNA Helix is the big question we've already been discussing in this chapter: "What problem do you solve?"

While we ultimately want to distill the answer to that question down to a single word, we'll start the process by creating a "Problem Cloud." First, you'll brainstorm any and all *possible* one-word answers (or even semi-related words) that help you strike at the essence of what your Problem might be. Later, we will narrow down the options based on the academic rules, characteristics, and principles our firm has discovered to be true about what qualifies as a "Problem."

Scan the QR code on the front inside cover of this book to complete your Problem Cloud using our free template.

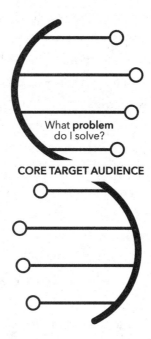

As you start developing potential options in your Problem Cloud, I also want to share with you some examples of influential personal brands that are *not* clients of ours. This is to help you see the application and validation of these concepts outside the realm of this book.

Dr. Brené Brown started as a research professor at the University of Houston. But then in 2010 she gave a TED talk that has gone on to be viewed more than sixty million times. She has written six #1 *New York Times* bestselling books and has created TV specials for both *Netflix* and *HBO*. She has not only become one of the most influential "personal brands" in the expert space, but she has transcended that to become one of the most influential voices in the world. How did she do it?

Brené Brown studies *shame*. In fact, she has made an entire career of exploring and understanding the topic of shame. And as a researcher, writer, and lecturer, she *owns* the topic of shame. You cannot talk about the issue of shame without having someone mention her name. Why?

Because she dedicated more than two decades of her life to a hyper-specific problem that few people before her had ever talked about in the mainstream. Dr. Brown "broke through the wall" by becoming the world's leading authority on one very specific problem.

Dave Ramsey has also become one of *the* biggest personal brands in the world. He has more than one thousand employees, and more than seventeen million people listen to him on the radio every week. His company has had one billion—that's *billion* with a *b*—podcast downloads. That all adds up to a *multi*-nine-figure (hundreds of millions of dollars) business each and every year.

Dave has built *all* of that by owning a one-word problem: *debt.* He has been saying nearly the exact *same* thing on the radio for three hours every single day. Over and over and over and over again . . . for *thirty* years!

Dave Ramsey *owns* the topic of debt. You cannot talk about debt without talking about him. In fact, you hear the clarity of his brand positioning right in the opening of his radio show: "Welcome to *The Dave Ramsey Show*, where *debt* is dumb, cash is king, and the paid-off home mortgage has taken the place of the BMW as the status symbol of choice!"[11] He then goes on to share with callers his Seven Baby Steps to help people solve his one-word Problem of debt. Through focus, clarity, and consistency, he has helped millions of people become debt free—all without making many substantial changes to what he actually teaches.

Tony Robbins is another example. Tony is without a doubt one of our generation's biggest expert personal brands. His events sell out entire arenas of tens of thousands of people. He's been featured on the cover of *Fortune* and *SUCCESS* magazines, has been called a "top business guru" by Harvard Business Press, is a multi-#1 *New York Times* bestselling author, is one of the highest-paid professional speakers in the world, and has been regularly featured on the biggest national morning television shows. He has also been the personal coach to billionaires, celebrities, and top performers in multiple industries, people like Hugh Jackman, Serena Williams, and Conor McGregor.

If you learn about Tony's personal story, you'll see that he grew up in a home suffering from the pain of food insecurity. Even to this day, if you hear him speak live, he talks about how he has dedicated his life to helping people live free from *pain*. According to Tony, his one-word Problem is pain. Thus he has researched and studied and investigated a wide array of models and constructs to help people experience less pain in any and all areas of their life.

Of course, this lesson of focus and dedication to solving a singular problem extends beyond business.

Mother Teresa, for example, dedicated her life to serving people in *poverty*. Trying to help resolve this issue of poverty was how she spent every single moment of her adulthood—and she broke through the "wall" and became known worldwide. Why? Obviously because she was a beloved minister to those in need, but also because she spoke out on an issue. She brought attention and awareness to poverty, and she took a stand for eradicating it from the world.

Dr. Martin Luther King Jr. did something similar. He *literally* gave his life toward the cause of ridding the world of a problem: *inequality*. People celebrate him for that work because he was adamant and resolute in his dedication and fortitude that we should live in a world without racism. He took a stand on the issue. He fought for the issue. He brought attention and awareness to the issue. He also *wrote* and *spoke* about the issue. Ultimately, he was killed because of how influential a voice he had become on such a necessary movement in the United States. He had such strength of purpose and such clarity of focus. He reshaped the future trajectory of all civilization because he so selflessly devoted his life to a singular cause.

Have you devoted your life to a singular cause?

Would you devote your life to a singular cause?

Fortunately, you can be tremendously successful without having to dedicate every single waking moment of your life to just one thing, but that is the general direction you should go. And so, it begs the question, "What Problem exists in the world that I would literally *dedicate my life* to solving?"

That's how you become well-known. You become known for *something.* You become known for *a thing.* You become known for doing something really big in one specific area.

CHARACTERISTICS OF A PROBLEM

In one word, what Problem do you solve?

If you're not there yet, don't worry! As we dive into helping you figure this out, let me share with you some characteristics of a clear Problem.

First, the Problem must be a noun. It's an issue or obstacle that is standing in the Avatar's way of achieving their desired outcome. The Problem has to be something your Avatar would say is "blocking them." In fact, one of the best ways to identify your Problem is to think of all the answers that your Avatar might give to the question, "What is standing in your way?"

One of the most common mistakes we see Mission-Driven Messengers make when they first attempt the Problem Cloud exercise is that they come up with adjectives instead of nouns. They'll say things like "frustrated" or "overwhelmed." While those can be helpful in a brainstorm, they can't be the final answer because they are not nouns. Plus, when identifying your official Problem, we're looking for *an issue someone is having,* not *a feeling they are experiencing.*

Second, your Problem must be a true negative. It must be a challenge or issue that someone needs to overcome. Using my early career as an example, "discipline" could not qualify as my Problem because discipline is not a problem. The *lack* of discipline or the *absence* of discipline is a problem.

As another example, the Problem we solve at Brand Builders Group is *obscurity*. We define *obscurity* as being unclear, untrusted, or unknown. We know the perfect Avatar for our brand wants to be more well-known so they can make a bigger impact, but our Avatar is *struggling with obscurity* because the client is failing to be noticed, recognized, or trusted in the way their expertise deserves.

This leads to the third important characteristic of your Problem: Your Avatar must be *aware* they are struggling with this specific problem. Thinking back to my early career, people who are procrastinating typically *know* they are procrastinating. People suffering from debt (Dave Ramsey) or shame (Brené Brown) or pain (Tony Robbins) are typically aware—or at least can be made aware—that it's an issue in their life. The same is true with us at Brand Builders Group.

Our perfect client knows they are struggling to gain more awareness and trust for their personal brand. They also know and believe if they had more awareness and trust, they would attract more customers. Further, they believe they deserve those customers because of their genuine expertise that can help people improve their lives. Our clients don't need help with their expertise; they need help expanding their notoriety so they can help more people. That's what it means to be unknown.

A companion dynamic that obscurity speaks to is not just being *unknown* but also being *unclear* or *untrusted*. Our Avatar struggles with obscurity but simultaneously struggles to succinctly articulate the value they provide.

An additional feature of a well-defined Problem is that your Avatar is *willing to admit to the problem*. That's important for two reasons. First, your marketing will focus on the Problem, and the

Problem is what makes your Avatar pay attention. But for your Avatar to pay attention, they must first be willing and able to admit they have the Problem. Second, nobody will buy from you if they can't admit they struggle with the Problem you solve.

> Nobody will buy from you if they can't admit they struggle with the Problem you solve.

These concepts are not only theoretical and conceptual; they are biological. If you understand the basics of neuroscience, you will better comprehend that every day, all around you, at every moment, is a massive amount of stimuli. Thus, one of the key functions of the human brain is to determine what stimuli are relevant and to filter out all stimuli that is irrelevant.

Think of your own everyday office environment, and you'll start to see what I mean. If your brain was fully present to everything happening in your physical environment, you would be paying *conscious* attention to:

- The exact temperature in the room
- The loose hinge on the chair you're sitting in and its impending breakdown
- The clicking of a keyboard, HVAC sounds, and every noise from outside
- Every smell from the coffee to snacks in the breakroom to candles burning next door
- And so much more . . .

That level of conscious effort, attention, and focus would quickly render anyone unable to function. Thus, one of the brain's primary jobs is to eliminate irrelevant information so we can focus on what keeps us safe.

A specific section of the human brain function called the RAS—Reticular Activating System—is responsible for this. The RAS is a network of neurons and a bundle of nerves located in the brain stem that connect to the hypothalamus to mediate behavior.[12] This helps us block out irrelevant stimuli while triggering us to notice relevant stimuli.

It is precisely this area of your brain that makes you notice every single other person driving the same car as yours right after you buy it. Of course, what's wild about that experience is you never once before noticed how many people drive that particular car until after you bought it—and then it seems like *everyone* is driving it! Obviously, that's not true. There are the same number of those cars on the road as there were before. The difference is that your RAS had blocked all of those out as irrelevant stimuli. But now your RAS notices all of them because they're the same as yours, and your brain is triggering you to be alert and aware of your own car.

Why are we having this mini lesson on neuroscience in the middle of a personal branding book? It's so you understand that the brain is literally signaling to people what they should pay conscious attention to and what they should unconsciously ignore.

If your Avatar isn't willing to admit they are struggling with the issue you solve (i.e., your Problem), their brain is biologically pro-grammed to ignore you at the subconscious level—before you ever have a chance to win them over. That is exactly why so many of our efforts go *unnoticed* and *ignored*. It's not a credibility problem or an expertise problem; it's a marketing problem, because your Problem is what makes people pay attention. When you clearly identify your Avatar's problem and articulate it in a way that they admit to having it, their brain *automatically* notices you and engages with you and pays attention to you. But until that day comes, you will just be ignored.

That's why you need to do the work of narrowing down the Problem you solve to one word. When you get the word right, that word becomes a glaring, unavoidable signal with an inescapable grav-itational pull that automatically draws your perfect audience to you.

That is why we often say, when it comes to communicating your Problem, the more specific, the more terrific!

Here are some prompts to help you find your Problem:

- What is blocking your Avatar from getting what they want?
- What issue is standing in their way?
- What problem does your audience knowingly admit to having?

An advanced tip is to think of your own life. Remember that you are most powerfully positioned to serve the person you once were. So, there is something *you've* overcome in your past to get where you are today. Spend time thinking about:

- What obstacle have you overcome?
- What setback have you survived?
- What challenge have you conquered?
- What tragedy have you triumphed over?

Think specifically about the person you once were. That is the most common way you can identify the Problem accurately, quickly, and most powerfully. Remember, your goal is to complete this sentence with one simple word (noun): The Problem I solve for people is _____.

THE CAUSE

Related to the concept of identifying the Problem is identifying your "Cause." The Cause comes from the second question in the Brand DNA helix: "What am I passionate about?"

As the visual suggests, the way to build an influential personal brand is to build from the inside out. These first two questions work in tandem to help you do that. A key part of us finding your Uniqueness comes from understanding what you are most passionate about.

Your Uniqueness should make you *emotional*.

Let me introduce you to a quick emotional test to help you discover your Cause; it's called The Goosies test. In my opinion, one of the greatest television shows of all time was *World of Dance*. The show was produced by Jennifer Lopez, who also doubled as a judge along with Derek Hough and Ne-Yo. This competition show had the most incredible dancers I've ever seen, from all different genres, doing flips and dips and tricks. It was truly a wholesome, inspiring, and uplifting show. But the biggest marketing lessons came from watching J.Lo critique the teams.

Every once in a while, J.Lo would see an act so powerful and so moving she would simply look at them and say, "I got *goosies!*" Of course, she was referring to a physical reaction in her body that science refers to as horripilation, or the pilomotor reflex where bumps appear on your arms—most commonly known as "goose bumps."[13] Yet, what she was actually communicating was something much more profound.

What J.Lo was saying without saying it was, "Your performance was *transcendent*. There was an unexplainable magic to what you just did. You defied the laws of reason and logic and commonplace tactics. You delivered a gift to those of us watching that wasn't just skillfully technical; it was emotionally divine."

Those moments were the equivalent of dancers operating in what we call your Uniqueness. We believe in this so much that we have legitimately operationalized "Goosies" as a formal part of our internal training for our team of strategists. We teach them to pay attention to the moments in a conversation when one of our clients is talking and we get Goosies—the physiological signal that something magical and meaningful has just happened.

We want to pay attention to those moments because they are hints and alerts that we are near the epicenter of a person's Uniqueness. And it's that type of energy and power we want to build someone's personal brand around. That is where the concept of the Cause comes into play.

In Brand Builders Group official lexicon and vernacular, the Cause is another one of the foundational components that will make up your Brand Positioning Statement (which we will explain more fully in the next chapter). We deliberately chose the term "Cause" for its dual meaning, as it is both a technical concept and an emotional one.

The technical description of your Cause is that it's the root source of the one-word Problem you solve for people. The Cause is the actual cause of the Problem. It's the reason *why* your customer is experiencing their Problem. The Cause is the *underlying* issue; it's the problem behind the Problem.

Remember that your Avatar is aware of the Problem because they know they have an issue. But your Avatar is likely to be unaware of the Cause of the Problem—because if they were aware of that, they would most likely address it themselves and the Problem would go away. For now, you can think of the Problem as a symptom of the Cause.

The critical reason why a personal brand must make a defining distinction between the Problem and the Cause is this: You address the Problem when you are *marketing,* but you address the Cause when you are *teaching.*

You address the Problem when you are marketing, but you address the Cause when you are teaching.

You don't actually treat the Problem for people. You treat the Cause, and the Problem goes away as a byproduct. However, you don't market the Cause, because your prospects are unaware of this underlying issue. As you learned earlier in this chapter, if they are unaware of it, they won't pay attention to it. If they don't pay attention to it, then they will never buy from you.

Thus, one of the biggest business mistakes Mission-Driven Messengers make is to spend too much time teaching and not enough time marketing early in the customer journey. As a result, they may be giving away a lot of information to try and help people, not realizing that if they are speaking to issues that are too deep or underlying (the Cause), they are inadvertently compelling the market to overlook them.

This happens partly because they passionately want to help people and partly because they don't have clarity on the difference between a Problem and a Cause, and thus don't understand when to utilize each of them. As a result, they are actively causing people to ignore them—the very same people they are desperately trying to reach.

The emotional description, which is perhaps even more important, is that the Cause is also the *reason* why your personal brand exists. The

Cause is a core part of why you would dedicate your life to this pursuit. Another way of describing it is that the Cause is connected to the very *purpose* of your life.

To refer back to some of our earlier examples, Brené Brown isn't just studying shame for the sake of research. Helping people break free from shame is a very part of Brené's existence.

The same is true with Dave Ramsey. Understanding the academic and logical causes of why or how people get trapped in personal debt is useful and important, but that isn't the dynamic that makes Dave Ramsey so great. It's his fire and passion and commitment to spending his life doing everything in his power to make sure other people never have to go through what he went through in getting overleveraged in a way that led him to bankruptcy.

Lewis Howes doesn't work just for money and lifestyle. He has literally dedicated his life to reaching people who are experiencing the same self-doubt that he had to overcome and providing tools for them to move through that.

The most influential personal brands all have one thing in common: a Cause. They are truly on a *mission*. They are on a crusade. They are working to eradicate something from the world to make things better for other people. It is that Cause that enables them to "break through the wall" long after other people would have given up.

As we work to identify your Cause, let's look at the clues given to us by the academic criteria while also exploring the question, "What are you truly most passionate about?"

Here are some prompts to help you find your Cause:

- What lights you up?
- What do you love learning about?
- What do you care about?
- What gives you joy?

- What fills your cup?
- What could you spend all your time talking about?

Those are questions that are related to your passion. Your answers give us clues to your Uniqueness and your Cause.

Passion does not have to be centered around positive energy, though. Passion can also be found by considering:

- What makes you mad?
- What pisses you off?
- What makes you sad?
- What breaks your heart?
- What makes you cry?
- What do you believe needs to be eradicated in the world?

We want to know, "What is the thing that you look at in the world and say to yourself, *I'm not okay with that! I'm not comfortable with that! I won't accept that! I'm not going to allow that on my watch!?*"

That is God's divine design of your humanity. Whatever it is that breaks your heart, breaks your heart for a reason. We believe the reason certain things break your heart is because you were purposefully and specifically *created* to do something about those problems. It's as if those issues are supernaturally *assigned* to you and that you're being spiritually guided and directly called to use your unique talents and gifts to resolve and settle them. In order to create a truly trusted personal brand, we need to find that emotionally laden center, because wherever that emotional headquarters is, that is where we will find your Cause.

PROBLEM VS. CAUSE

We are often asked how to delineate between the Problem and the Cause. Here are some key distinctions:

1. The Problem is what your Avatar is struggling with. The Cause is why they are struggling with it.

Let's use the Brand Positioning Statement for Brand Builders Group as an example.

The Problem we solve is obscurity.

The Cause is distraction.

The Problem or issue our clients have is that they are living in some level of obscurity; not enough people know about them—or not as many as they would like. What most of our clients don't realize, however, is that the real reason (i.e., Cause) *why* they are living in obscurity is distraction. They often *think* they are in obscurity because they just haven't had a lucky break yet or any number of other factors. But we *know* that it's actually because when you have diluted focus, you get diluted results. Our Avatar is most commonly talking about too many topics, trying to serve too many audiences, on too many different platforms, hoping to monetize too many revenue streams. They are diluted and distracted.

2. The Avatar is aware of the Problem. They are unaware of The Cause.

Again using our business as an example, most of our perfect prospects are aware of the fact that they are not yet well-known. They can look around at various criteria in their life and reach the conclusion that they are not as known as they'd like to be. They *know* they have the Problem of obscurity.

Contrast that with our company's Cause. While our prospects are easily able to self-identify as struggling with obscurity, chances are they have no real idea of *why* they have that issue or how to break free from it. They don't realize that the reason they're dealing with obscurity is not because it's in their destiny or fate to remain anonymous. It's not because their mission isn't important. It's not because they're ignorant or unqualified. It's not because other people have advantages that they don't. The real reason they're struggling is simply because they're distracted. Perhaps the most powerful thing you can do for your clients is help them see something they didn't see before, the Cause.

3. The Problem is what you address in your marketing. The Cause is what you address in your teaching.

We mentioned earlier that marketing and teaching are very different. Marketing is something you do to attract people. Teaching is something you do to change people.

In your marketing, you want to highlight the Problem, describing the issues you help people resolve. You want to demonstrate you know exactly what it looks like to live a day in the life of a prospect who is dealing with things you can help them break free from.

In your marketing you introduce the Problem, explain the Problem, describe the Problem, quantify the Problem, and share common mistakes that people make when they are trying to resolve the Problem on their own. It's only in your teaching that you detail the specific steps on how to solve the Problem. This coincides with another principle we mentioned earlier: You don't treat the Problem; you treat the Cause, and the Problem goes away as a byproduct.

> *Scan the QR code on the front inside cover of this book and click the "Free Call" link on our website to learn more about working with one of our strategists to help you delineate between your Problem and your Cause.*

One of the most common mistakes we see is people trying to "teach" in their marketing copy and sales collateral. Again, that's a terrible strategy that will not only reduce your sales but lower the number of lives you could positively impact. It doesn't work because you're trying to make two sales at once.

First, you're trying to "sell" the customer on understanding their Problem and seeing your product or service as a solution. This is exactly what you should do in your marketing. But then, you start trying to make the second sale, "selling" *how* you're going to help solve the Problem by overcommunicating what the Cause is. That part is unnecessary and less effective because it means they have to agree to both "sales" in order to move forward with you. Instead, save the "how" part for *after* they have purchased from you. You don't have to convince people *how* you're going to change their life in order for them to buy; you just have to convince them *that* you can change their life in order for them to buy.

You don't treat the Problem; you treat the Cause, and the Problem goes away as a byproduct.

Here are examples of Problems and corresponding Causes:

Problem	Cause
Obesity	Poor Diet and Exercise
Obscurity	Dilution
Procrastination	Distraction
Overwhelm	Ambiguity
Poverty	Ignorance
Loneliness	Low Self Confidence, Lack of Intimacy
Stress	Unhealthy Lifestyle, Toxic Environment
Fatigue	Poor Nutrition, Not Enough Sleep
Shame	Trauma, Guilt
Underperformance	Inconsistency

This matters from an *internal* personal brand strategy perspective because this is how you niche down. This is how you become the world's leading thought leader on _____. It's by choosing a Problem and then studying, researching, exploring, testing, and owning it.

It also helps you identify the divine design for your life, access your life purpose, and tune in to your specific calling. Once you get clear on your Problem and your Cause, you will feel more "activated" and "focused" and "committed."

From an *external* marketing perspective, if you do this right, it will also help you make more money! To call back to some of the examples we've used so far, Brené Brown, Dave Ramsey, Tony Robbins, Lewis Howes, Gary Vaynerchuk, and The Rock have changed the world in many positive ways—and they've also all gotten rich!

We've had some similar success by applying these principles in our own life. We built our first eight-figure business in part by associating my personal brand with being an expert on procrastination. We have since built a second eight-figure business by AJ and I redefining our personal brands to become known for having solutions to obscurity. Several of our clients have also been able to replicate significant financial results in their businesses by applying the same principles.

And now, that's what we want *you* to do! We want you to pick a problem and *own* the problem.

We *also* want to teach you how to make money from it. Part of how you make money from it is by learning how to *promote* it. Smart marketers know that you have to learn to sell the Problem more than you sell the solution. You need to promote the Problem. You need to draw attention to and raise awareness of the Problem. In general, you need to become *the ambassador* of your Problem.

The more your personal brand becomes associated with a specific Problem, the more money people will pay you to help them solve it. And the more clearly you are able to define the Problem, the more likely you will be to solve it in an original way—which is exactly what we're going to talk about next.

CHAPTER 6

FINDING YOUR UNIQUENESS

BY RORY VADEN

The problem with most speakers is that they can teach, inspire, and entertain for an hour, but when the speech ends the audience is not super clear on exactly what to *do* when they leave the room. The challenge lies in being able to answer this question: "What is the *one thing* you want your audience to do when you're done?"

The same is true for most authors. They can write an entire book yet cannot answer "What is the *one thing* you want your reader to *do* once they read your book?"

The same is true for most businesses too. Do you know what you want your customer to do, learn, think, act, or believe as a result of your products or services?

I struggled with this same issue. As a speaker, content creator, author, podcaster, business owner, and entrepreneur, I was not clear on what I wanted my audience to "do" as a result of consuming my content.

I was missing a clear **Message**. A Message is a solution-oriented one-sentence through line statement that distills your entire body of work into a single actionable command, instruction, or order. Having a clear Message is more than just a "good idea" or an arbitrary academic exercise for you to do with your content; it's a critical imperative of driving revenue. That's because delivering a clear message is how you change someone's life, and the best form of marketing in the world is a changed life.

The best form of marketing in the world is a changed life.

A changed life is one that creates pragmatic results in the lives of your fans, readers, and/or subscribers. Those results are the residual byproducts of those people making decidedly different choices and taking deliberate actions as the result of engaging with your thought leadership.

Nothing is more powerful for finding and converting new customers in your business than when past clients can specifically point to a tangible result they experienced that can be traced back to you. In fact, according to our PhD-led *Trends in Personal Branding National Research Study*, testimonials from clients are the single most important marketing asset a personal brand can have when it comes to convincing people to spend money with you.

If you don't or can't concisely communicate a clear instruction, it's unlikely your audience will know how to take action. And if they never take action, they will likely never get results. While no one should be allowed to complain about the results they didn't get from the work they didn't do, they also shouldn't be held accountable for actions they never took because the directives were never clear.

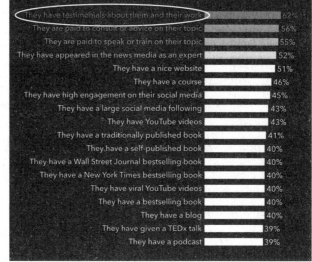

Having **testimonials** about themselves and their work is also **the most important factor** for Americans when it comes to paying someone for a product or service.

Q: How important are each of the following when it comes to paying someone more for a product or a service?

They have testimonials about them and their work	62%
They are paid to consult or advice on their topic	56%
They are paid to speak or train on their topic	55%
They have appeared in the news media as an expert	52%
They have a nice website	51%
They have a course	46%
They have high engagement on their social media	45%
They have a large social media following	43%
They have YouTube videos	43%
They have a traditionally published book	41%
They have a self-published book	40%
They have a Wall Street Journal bestselling book	40%
They have a New York Times bestselling book	40%
They have viral YouTube videos	40%
They have a bestselling book	40%
They have a blog	40%
They have given a TEDx talk	39%
They have a podcast	39%

Scan the QR code on the front inside cover of this book to download a free copy of this study.

YOUR MESSAGE

Do you know what your message is? What is the *one* thing you want people to *do*?

Could you tell it to me in a single sentence if we were in a room together right now?

My guess is that you can't. That's okay because it's really hard to do. It's not easy to boil your entire life's work, your full body of knowledge, and the comprehensive analysis of all your research down to just one sentence. It's not easy, but if you want to change lives, it's necessary.

This is a huge part of what separates you from the crowd because most people can't do it, don't know how to do it, or simply won't do it.

A mentor of mine, Eric Chester, said it best when he told me early in my career, "Most people say a little about a lot; if you want to stand out, you need to discipline yourself to instead say a lot about a little." Remember, breaking through Sheahan's Wall is about consolidating your focus. In the same way that everyone hears a high-pitched clink of a wine glass in a crowded room, so too do you want your message to have such a strong and clear frequency that it cuts through the noise.

> *"Most people say a little about a lot; if you want to stand out, you need to discipline yourself to instead say a lot about a little."*

To help you arrive at finding your one-sentence Message—what we sometimes call the *command statement*—let's introduce the next corresponding set of questions from our Brand DNA helix:

- What do you research?
- What do you have results in?

What do I **research?**

What **problem** do I solve?

CORE TARGET AUDIENCE

What am I **passionate** about?

What do I have **results** in?

We use these two questions to help us find your Message (and Uniqueness, which is coming next). These questions work because they help us learn the story of what you've learned in your life about how to solve the Problem. Remember, the Message of this entire book is to **"teach what you know to the person you once were."** That is our advice, consolidated into just one sentence, about exactly what it takes to build a breakthrough personal brand. It's based upon our core premise that "you are most powerfully positioned to serve the person you once were."

The fastest way to find *your* Message is to understand your unique method of how you have learned to solve the Problem in your own life. As noted above, there are two areas of your journey we have found the richest to explore in helping us arrive at that conclusion. Again:

- What have you Researched?
- What do you have Results in?

The Research question helps tap into your education on the subject. It looks at the things you've studied and spent time learning, reading, discussing, brainstorming, pondering, and questioning. This confirms and narrows where you have academic head knowledge and is an important factor in choosing an area of focus for your thought leadership.

The Results question is completely different because it looks at what you have actually *done*. Research helps us understand your *education*, but Results helps us understand your *experience*. Your Results speak to what you have accomplished and the measurable outcomes you have created for yourself and other people around you.

While someone can always challenge your Research, question your academic method, or critique the value of your education, nobody can debate your experience. Your Results are powerful because they speak for themselves. We can point to the Results you've created and verify that they are either real or not. Both Research and Results are important because we—and the marketplace in general—place a high value on academic rigor, for obvious reasons. But your Results is where we get insight into your Uniqueness.

If your personal brand is trying to move people down a path that helps them solve a specific Problem, then what is most powerful and useful is hearing the practical methods for *how you* actually solved the problem. There may be many people who solve the same or similar Problem, but if you follow this process properly, no one in the world will be able to solve the Problem in the same *way* that you do. That is where the magic is, and that's

> *No one in the world will be able to solve the Problem in the same way that you do.*

what we want to bottle up and package for the whole world. We want to help you show and teach people how to do exactly what *you* have done.

In Brand Builders Group nomenclature, here are the essential and key characteristics of selecting a proper Message:

- It must be an action or command statement that tells people exactly what to do. It is an instruction and an order.
- It is a singular through line that summarizes the essence of your advice. It must be only one thing. It can never be multiple things.
- It is the truth about what will change the Avatar's life. It should directly address the Cause and thereby solve the Problem as a byproduct if executed properly.
- It is primarily for strategic internal alignment and clarity of communication. It's not to be used for external marketing.
- Its language should be extremely fundamental and easy to understand. It is not a slogan or a catchphrase. It should not include fancy words or jargon.
- It should be literal, explicit, actionable, and practical. It can never be ethereal, abstract, or nebulous.

- It's always an affirmative. It is never a negative. It is a "do," never a "don't do."
- It is something you've done and/or tested and that you fully believe in as responsible for success that you've created in your life and/or in the lives of others.

I know that is a simple checklist, but having taken thousands of clients through the Finding Your Brand DNA process, I can tell you it is usually *quite* difficult to lock in someone's Message. Ironically, it's so much harder to narrow down what you want to say into just a few words than it is to explain it with a lot of words. I'm reminded of a famous quote from Woodrow Wilson, "If I am to speak ten minutes, I need a week for preparation; if fifteen minutes, three days; if half an hour, two days; if an hour, I am ready now."[14]

Let's use my three books (including this one) as relevant case studies for what we mean by a Message.

- *Take the Stairs* = "Do things you don't want to do."
- *Procrastinate on Purpose* = "Spend time on things today that create more time tomorrow."
- *Wealthy and Well-Known* = "Teach what you know to the person you once were."

You might initially look at this and think, *Why would such simple ideas make such a big impact?* To which I would contend, the idea works not in spite of the fact that it's simple but *because* of the fact that it's simple! The hardest work is not in writing the book; the hardest work is in writing one sentence that explains the entire book!

As you start to think about codifying your personal brand's Message, notice again some of the features of the three Messages listed above.

First of all, they are command statements. Each of them is *doable*; they are telling you an actual action to take. Notice also that they are practical and explicit. They have no "high-brow" vocabulary words, no jargon, nothing obscure, and nothing that needs more definition.

They are not slogans or cute phrases that you would print on a T-shirt or post on your website. Instead, they are powerful principles that you would teach to someone if you truly wanted to change their life.

They are each *singular*; they invite you to focus on one core idea. They are also *affirmatives*—meaning things to do. Contrast that to an ineffective Message about what you *should not do*. If it was telling you something *not* to do, then it would leave open an infinite number of possibilities of things that you *should* do—and that's not helpful.

Perhaps the most important feature of each book's Message above is one that is not visible to the naked eye. The most essential and necessary criteria of a Message is that you need *proof* of it actually working. In other words, it has to be the *true* answer to what has changed your life and helped you and/or others successfully overcome the Problem. It's not important that the Message be *the* truth because that is usually debatable. But an uncompromising mandate of a Message is that it has to be *your* truth—something you can emphatically assert as a solution that has worked in your own life. Your life has to be a case study of an experimental demonstration that has proven the basis for your premise, predicated upon the results you've personally experienced.

Your Message needs to be unique to you. That doesn't mean you're the only person who has ever said anything like it. It means it has to embody and encapsulate *your* unique *way* of doing things. Part of what makes it irrefutable is that you are the only source of proof that matters.

Scan the QR code on the front inside cover of this book to access additional tools and exercises to help you narrow down your Message.

UNIQUENESS

As we have already hinted at, there is a strong symbiotic and direct connection between your Message and your Uniqueness. We define

Uniqueness as "the one-word distillation of your Message that captures the core essence of your proposed solution to the Problem."

Remember Larry Winget's quote, "Find your uniqueness and exploit it in the service of others." We've actually taken that statement to a level of pragmatism that forces you to once again do the work of capturing your Uniqueness in one word.

When we use the term Uniqueness, we don't try to establish Uniqueness on anything external or temporal, because we don't believe that you find your Uniqueness by looking at what everyone else is doing and then trying to differentiate yourself from them. In our experience, that method yields answers that are often superficial, circumstantial, and almost always unsustainable.

Rather, we look to establish a person's Uniqueness by working from the inside out. Your real Uniqueness is found simply by clarifying and celebrating more of who you already are. This concept is reminiscent of something Sally Hogshead, our good friend and *New York Times* bestselling author of *Fascinate*, wrote: "To become more fascinating, you don't have to change who you are. You have to become *more* of who you are."[15]

Another common misconception is that finding your Uniqueness means you have to say something that's never been said before. You might think you have to come up with revolutionary breakthroughs that are brand-new, never-before-heard, and earth-shattering. But that's not necessary, as that would once again be determining your Uniqueness from the outside in—which is not the direction of our process. That method would mean you're looking at what everyone else has said and just trying to be *different*, but that's not how we approach it.

You don't find your Uniqueness by asking, "What is different about me?" You also don't find your Uniqueness by asking, "What can I say that's never been said before?" Instead, you find your Uniqueness by asking, "What is my unique *way* of solving the Problem?" The power of your Uniqueness is not that it is *new*. The power of your Uniqueness is that it *worked* for *you*.

People can argue about what works and what doesn't. They can contend what is true and what is false. They can challenge what is best and what is marginal. But nobody can discount or yield as inconsequential *your* way of how *you* actually solved *your* own Problems and improved *your own* life! They also cannot replicate it or copy it identically because it is dependent on your unique experiences. It's fundamentally tied to your personal story. It's unequivocally attached to your unique and specific perspective on how to solve the Problem. And it's all of those properties that make your personal brand inherently rare.

Lots of people can talk about the same Problem, but only *you* can share the unique way you learned how to resolve it. In that way, your Uniqueness becomes your uncopiable difference. And if people want your unique perspective and your unique method, they have to get it from *you*! You are the only human in the world who can share it in your unique way. There is no other you! In spite of living on a planet with billions of people—it automatically puts you in a category of one. That is exactly what makes a personal brand—because it is *personal*; it's your unique lens on how the world works related to solving the Problem.

To use my personal brand arc as an example, there is nothing more unoriginal than a message about "hard work." At a high level, it would be easy to critique my *Take the Stairs* book as just one more book that tells you to work hard. Yet *Take the Stairs* was successful because I talk about my unique view on a nuance of hard work, which is self-discipline.

Similarly, there are hundreds of TED Talks on productivity, and tens of thousands of books written on the subject. Yet if you want to learn how to multiply time using The Focus Funnel, you *have* to get it from me. Why? Because it came out of *my* head! I'm the *only* person in the world who can teach productivity with that method—because I created it.

The same is true about Brand Builders Group. There are countless branding firms, brand consultants, personal brand coaches, and experts talking about personal branding. But *no one* in the world teaches it the *way* we teach it. They don't have our stories, frameworks, data, or methodologies. Why not? Because we *created* them! We did the hard work and critical thinking of codifying the specific way in which we do what we do. We *invented* the concepts, which immediately puts us in a category of one.

If you build a brand properly from the inside out and with the power of focus in mind, no one should ever look like you! And even if they try to, they would at best be a copycat that is both inauthentic and ineffective.

Theoretically, then, pinpointing your Uniqueness should be easy. All you have to do is identify the thing that changed your life in one word. You have to summarize your entire philosophy about how to overcome the Problem in one word. And you have to distill your one-sentence Message down to one word.

A strong synonym for the way we use the term Uniqueness would be "solution." Your Uniqueness is more related to your methodology than to your personality. At Brand Builders Group, our Uniqueness is "Service." Our solution, our methodology, our belief, and our experience about how to build a truly *Wealthy and Well-Known* personal brand is a one-word distillation of our message, "Teach what you know to the person you once were." Boiled down to one word, that is Service.

So, what is your proposed one-word solution of how to overcome the Problem or obstacle that your Avatar is facing?

BRAND POSITIONING STATEMENT

A few times thus far in the book we have referenced a concept we call the Brand Positioning Statement. Everything you've read up until this point has been preparing you for the creation of your very own version.

As a reminder, your Brand Positioning Statement is a collection of strategic conclusions that will direct and guide your entire personal brand. The five core components are:

1. **Uniqueness:** a one-word distillation of your Message that captures the core essence of your proposed solution to the Problem.

2. **Message:** a solution-oriented one-sentence through line statement that distills your entire body of work into a single actionable command, instruction, or order.

3. **Problem:** A one-word identification of the core issue you are going to solve for your audience.

4. **Cause:** A one-word clarification of the underlying root issue responsible for creating the Problem.

5. **Avatar Persona:** A one-phrase description of the audience you are going to serve.

While we always list these in the order here (we will explain why in chapter 8), it's important to note that the answers for each of these components are usually discovered by the Messenger in closer to reverse order. In other words, the answers typically come from starting from the bottom and working our way up. In our live strategy sessions, we have determined through lots of trial and error that following the proper sequence often helps us arrive at clarity much faster, so that is how our agenda is structured. Relatedly, you'll also notice that the order of the chapters in this book and the sequence in which we've presented these concepts also more closely follow that general, bottom-up order. We started in chapter 4 with identifying your Avatar

Persona (who), then in chapter 5 we worked on the Problem and the Cause in tandem, and in this chapter we're working on the Message and Uniqueness jointly as well.

As you can tell from the strict word counts we place on each component, your Brand Positioning Statement should easily fit onto one page. In fact, the entire statement is often made up of less than fifteen words. However, for some people it can be an incredibly difficult and frustrating process to land on these fifteen words. It's not because the method is complicated; rather, it's because the method is so simple that it *forces* you to be relentlessly disciplined about narrowing down your focus—and for a distracted mind, that can be excruciating.

> *Scan the QR code on the front inside cover of this book if you get stuck and you want to learn how we can help you personally via a call with our team.*

Your Brand Positioning Statement serves as your North Star, your guiding light, and your calibration point for every functional future decision you will make. The moment your Brand Positioning Statement becomes clear, every single other downstream decision also becomes clear. However, if your Brand Positioning Statement is not clear, your entire personal brand is going to feel splintered, disconnected, and confusing.

A personal brand with a clear Brand Positioning Statement knows exactly *who* they are trying to reach. Because of that, they know much more about *where* they can go to reach that type of person. And, if you are clear about the Problem you solve for that person, you then know precisely *what* to market to them to attract them. Once you convert them as a customer, you know specifically *how* to help them change their life by introducing them to your clear Message and Uniqueness that directly remedies the Cause. That exponentially increases the likelihood that they will actually *do* what you tell them and experience tangible results in their journey.

As your clients experience those positive and noticeable results in their life, everyone around them will take notice. That's what we mean by our philosophy that "the best form of marketing in the world is a changed life." When your customers experience results, those results speak for themselves, and the people around them start asking them what led to their transformation. If your business or personal brand is the answer to that question, then that will automatically lead people back to you, which will be the only marketing you ever need. To say it concisely, if you build your personal brand properly, your customer force will become your sales force.

If you build your personal brand properly, your customer force will become your sales force.

Contrast that, however, with someone who is *unclear*. If they are not clear on their *who*, then right out of the gate they are diluting all their resources across multiple channels. They likely won't have clarity about where to go or the resources to target and optimize their outreach effectively. Even if they do, if they aren't clear on the Problem they solve, nobody will pay attention anyway. And when they do get lucky enough to land a few customers, there won't be clear instruction for what the real Cause is or how to solve the Problem (that is already fuzzy for people in the first place), so the likelihood that many customers will get transformational results is slim.

As customers fail to get results, they not only do not renew or refer business to you, but they likely work against your business's growth. Sometimes customers will be unhappy and communicate their bad experience to others, which will in turn harm your business. The best case in this situation is that they will simply become indifferent about your business and never talk about it or think about it ever again. Either way, your machine is broken, and it's not because you are unqualified as a person or because your sales team isn't doing a good job; it's because you are fundamentally *unclear* on who you are trying to serve and what you are trying to do for them. Because of that, you are likely chasing multiple things without much momentum on any of them. That ultimately leads to failure because, again, when you have diluted focus, you get diluted results.

Don't let that happen to you! Take the time now to get crystal clear on precisely what your personal brand is all about.

TRIANGULATION

We've developed some key tools and techniques to help you figure out your Brand Positioning Statement faster. One of those tools is triangulation. A key feature of each of the components of a Brand Positioning Statement is that they are all "related" to each other in some way. Because of that, we don't necessarily have to arrive at the answers in any sequential order.

Instead, we can start with whichever of the five core components feels most clear and then leverage off that to get clear on the others. That happens by simply knowing and understanding the required criteria that each component must satisfy and by evaluating the interconnected nature of each one.

If you are naturally a "chronic overachiever," "do-gooder," or "type A" personality, chances are you are really going to want to go in order, check a box, and move on. But I invite you to suspend that typical modus operandi for this part of the process. Almost every other step in our four-phase methodology and twelve-topic journey of building a breakthrough personal brand is extremely sequential and orderly. However, what we've learned about Brand Positioning Statements is that they require patience and a bit more of an artistic approach to really get them right.

Rather than thinking of this piece of the process as a series of steps, I want to encourage you to think of it instead as if you were assembling something like a bed frame. If you've ever done that before, you know that the proper way is not to tighten each screw all the way down one at a time. The best way is to put each screw into the frame loosely and tentatively as you make your way around the whole frame. And then once the frame is loosely in place and it feels like everything is lined up properly, you "triangulate" by slowly tightening down each screw a little bit more and then bouncing to the opposite side of the frame to tighten down the next.

You repeat that process again and again, ensuring that each piece stays aligned and in place as you tighten the previous screw a little bit. You want to be careful not to force any one screw too far in and inadvertently create too much torque on any of the other parts by your desire to move faster. You just adjust each screw a little while rotating around and focusing on moving the whole unit to completion. In so doing, you make sure everything stays aligned and all falls in place together. That's a bit what the solidification process looks like for a Brand Positioning Statement.

The other thing to know about this process is that you need to allow it to be "messy." One of the first rules of being a great author is to never edit as you write. You write first and edit later! This is the same way, and it's a good time to be introduced to another one of our mantras: "Say it ugly first!"

Give yourself permission to slot things into a place even if you're not sure it's "right" or in the right place. Put some stuff up on the board and adjust it later. Throw a lot at the wall and see what sticks. Once you put some concepts in place, you can then use the laws of their inter-relationships to pressure-test which fit | **_Say it ugly first!_** where and which don't belong at all. It's also fine to work on this a bit, make some progress, and then let it sit for a few days. Sometimes your Brand Positioning Statement needs to gestate for a while before it galvanizes together.

Rome wasn't built in a day, and neither were any of the biggest personal brands in the world. Most of them, in fact, were built over decades before anyone ever paid any attention to them. Success takes time. We're not the people who promise to teach you how to become an overnight success or instant millionaire. Our process is about setting a firm foundation you can build upon for a lifetime. Our goal is to help you create something that has the ability to spread beyond your physical reach and last long after you are gone. If anything, we are the people who help you do in three to four years what takes most people twenty. Inside of that context, please understand you don't have to get this perfectly right on the first try.

BRAND POSITIONING STATEMENT INTERRELATIONSHIPS

Locking down your own perfectly tight and clarifying Brand Positioning Statement will happen much faster if you understand the interrelationships between each of the components. If you can develop clarity and confidence about any of the individual elements, you can then leverage off that and use the principles of the interrelationships to help you get clear on the other elements. Here is a simple checklist of requirements that each element must embody.

Problem and Uniqueness

First and foremost is understanding the relationship between the **Problem** and your **Uniqueness**. They *must* be—in some way—the opposite of one another. They are two sides of the same coin. The Problem, as we've seen, is the thing that is blocking your Avatar Persona. It's an issue that your Avatar both knows they have and is willing to admit that they have. Your Uniqueness is your unique solution to that Problem. Because of those inherent properties, we know that these two elements *always* have an inverse relationship.

> **Example:**   *Take the Stairs*
> **Uniqueness:**   **Discipline**
> **Problem:**   **Procrastination**

Uniqueness and Message

Next up is the relationship between your **Uniqueness** and your **Message**. As a reminder, your Message is a "solution-oriented one-sentence command statement of exactly what the Avatar must *do* in order to overcome the Problem and change their life." We also know that, by definition, your Uniqueness is a "one-word distillation of the entire Message." Hopefully, then, it's obvious that there is a direct relationship between your Message and your Uniqueness. They are essentially two different expressions of the exact same thing. The Uniqueness is a single word that captures the essence of what your solution to the Problem is, while the Message is a pragmatic instruction of what someone must do to overcome the Problem in one sentence. Once we have confidence that you have clearly identified *either* your Message or your Uniqueness, it's much easier to infer what the other one should be because they are different expressions of the exact same concept.

> **Example:**   *Take the Stairs*
> **Uniqueness:**   **Discipline**
> **Message:**   **Do things you don't want to do**

Message and Problem

Similarly, we know the Message is in some way the inverse of the Problem. However, that doesn't necessarily mean they are the *obvious* opposite. For example, if the Problem your Avatar Persona is facing is fear, that doesn't mean that the Uniqueness must be Courage—which would be a very apparent option. It *could be* Courage, but something like self-talk could also qualify as a satisfactory Uniqueness as long as that's in line with your personal beliefs and life story.

To follow this example further, if self-talk was selected as the Uniqueness, then we would know for certain that the Message would have to be both a literal expression of how to do self-talk and something that cures a person's fear. Therefore, one example of a satisfactory Message in that scenario might be, "Remind yourself of your past accomplishments." There could be an infinite number of ways to express a satisfactory Message in this instance, but we know for sure that whatever the Message is, it *must* be a pragmatic action item that is the full expression of the concept of self-talk (i.e., Uniqueness), *and* it must also be an actual cure for the Problem (i.e., fear in this case).

It's important to note that one of our other clients could address the same Problem of fear by having a Uniqueness of "courage." A different client could propose that the way they moved past fear in their own life was primarily through embracing "action"—which would be their Uniqueness. Yet another client of ours might say that "planning" was the vehicle (Uniqueness) that really remedied their fears in their own life. And all of them could be right!

Finding your Uniqueness is not about presenting the world with *the* right answer; it's about sharing with the world *your* right answer. And no one can argue with *your* right answer, as long as *your* right answer is what actually worked for you. But you still have to do the work of clarifying and codifying exactly what your Uniqueness is in a way that others can truly benefit from it.

Problem and Cause

Another important fundamental relationship between two elements of the Brand Positioning Statement is the Problem and the Cause.

We discussed the relationship between these two components at length in chapter 5. You'll recall that the Problem is *what* the Avatar Persona is struggling with, but the Cause is *why* they are struggling with it. The Cause, therefore, drives the Problem, which gives the pair a tight interconnection. And, as a reminder, the Avatar Persona will likely be aware of the Problem, but they probably will not know the Cause.

> **Example:**   *Take the Stairs*
> **Problem:**   **Procrastination**
> **Cause:**   **Distraction**

Message, Uniqueness, and Cause

Last, let's look at the relationship between Message, Uniqueness, and Cause. Message and Uniqueness represent the *cure* for the Problem, while the Cause is the *reason* for the Problem. So, there's an obvious underlying connection between these three components.

> **Example:**   *Take the Stairs*
> **Uniqueness:**   **Discipline**
> **Message:**   **Do things you don't want to do**
> **Cause:**   **Distraction**

You'll remember from the previous chapter that you market the Problem to attract customers, but then you actually treat the Cause to change lives. Therefore, the Message and the Uniqueness have to be the real-life solution and antidote to the Cause. The Message and Uniqueness, if executed upon in the proper way, directly rectify the Cause—and thus the Problem would disappear from the Avatar's life as a byproduct.

Visually, these interrelationships would look like this:

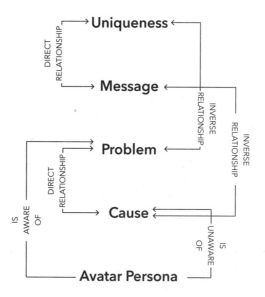

Once you know and understand these interrelational dynamics between each of the components of a Brand Positioning Statement, you can use them to "double back" on themselves as clues and litmus tests to help you lock in your own Brand Positioning Statement.

Here is our internal strategist checklist to help you quickly and clearly draft your Brand Positioning Statement:

Brand Positioning Statement Checklist

- Uniqueness
  - Is it a noun?
  - Is it positive?
  - Is this the Solution to the Cause?
  - Is this the opposite (in some way) of the Problem?
  - Is this (in some way) the distillation of the Message into one word?
  - **Does the Messenger embody this in their own life?**

- Message
  - Is it a command statement?
  - Is it actionable?
    - Keep asking "how" until it becomes a literal behavior.
    - Does it pass the "stand up and do it right now" test? Can you actually "do" what the Message is telling you to do?
  - Is it free from fanciness (jargon, cute language, slogans, etc.)?
  - Is it an affirmative? (never a "don't do")
  - Is it singular in focus? (never includes "and" or "so that")
  - Is it the opposite (in some way) of the Problem?
  - Is it (in some way) an extrapolation of the Uniqueness?
  - **Is this what the Messenger actually did to solve the Problem for themselves?**
- Problem
  - Is it a noun?
  - Is it negative?
  - Is the Avatar aware that this obstacle is blocking them?
  - Is the Avatar willing to admit that they have this issue?
  - Is it (in some way) the opposite of the Message and Uniqueness?
  - If the Avatar were to follow the instruction of the Message, would this issue disappear?
  - **Has the Messenger (or someone very close to them) personally overcome this issue?**
- Cause
  - Is this something the Avatar is unaware of?
  - Is this the underlying issue that is responsible for the creation of the Problem?

- Do the Uniqueness and Message treat this?
- **Is this something the Messenger was at some point unaware of that they later became aware of—and then solved it and their life improved?**

- Avatar Persona
  - Is this a clearly identifiable group of people that you can see in your mind?
  - Is the Messenger able to state places where these people gather? (e.g., media outlets, conferences, etc.)
  - Is this an audience that the Messenger deeply understands?
  - Is this an audience that the Messenger can develop a suite of tools for to help them in their journey?
  - Is this an audience that the Messenger is willing to dedicate their life to serving?
  - **Is this "the person you once were" or someone close to them?**

Here also are examples of Brand Positioning Statements from my three books:

TITLE	TAKE THE STAIRS	PROCRASTINATE ON PURPOSE	WEALTHY AND WELL-KNOWN
UNIQUENESS	Self-Discipline	Significance	Service
MESSAGE	Do things you don't want to do.	Spend time on things today that give you more time tomorrow.	Teach what you know to the person you once were.
PROBLEM	Procrastination	Stress	Obscurity
CAUSE	Distraction	Distraction	Distraction

YOUR ONE-SENTENCE COMMAND

If you are a communicator of any kind, I believe it is your duty and obligation to show your audience how to solve the Problem with a one-sentence command Message and a one-word Uniqueness. Every single person who engages with your Message has given you the gift of their time and attention, and that comes with a high responsibility. You *owe* it to your audience to make each and every moment with them as powerful and impactful on their lives as it can possibly be. In order for you to maximize the impact of your wisdom and give them the highest return on the time they have invested, you *must* communicate your message succinctly, clearly, and with concentrated power. Do it with a one-sentence command statement that can be boiled down all the way to one single word.

Is it easy? Not at all! It's extremely difficult. But that's what makes it valuable and great. Achieving anything great is never easy, and excellence is never an accident. Very few communicators will do the work of consolidating their Message into one sentence and even to one word, and that is because it's very challenging to do. But this work is what separates the master communicators from the average ones. This is the work that almost nobody else will ever do. This work is worth doing *because* it is difficult. Your audience benefits

> **Solve the Problem with a one-sentence command.**

greatly when you take the time and put in the effort to concentrate your entire philosophy and expertise down into its essence—and you will benefit too.

The clearer your Uniqueness, the more likely you are to be remembered. And the more you are remembered, the more you will be rewarded.

Let's talk about how to monetize next!

CHAPTER 7

MONETIZATION STRATEGY

BY AJ VADEN

Have you ever wondered about the connection between the number of followers you have online and the number of dollars you have in your bank account?

With the amount of focus, money, and effort so many people spend on growing their social media following, you may assume that there is some tangible and universal connection between followers and dollars. I have not found that to be consistent nor true.

Now, there are exceptions.

In fact, at the time of writing this chapter, Cristiano Ronaldo still holds the top spot on Instagram with 642 million followers[16] (please note that is roughly twice the population of the United States) and is also the highest-paid athlete in the world, earning some $200 million in on-field earnings alone.[17] Do I think his online following has helped with contract negotiations, brand deals, sponsorships, fan gear, and plenty more? Yes, I do. But I also know he was making plenty of money, based on talent and skill, before the rise of his social following.

LeBron James is the highest-paid athlete in the US with projected earnings of $120 million-plus as of 2024. This includes $48 million in salary and $75 million in endorsements.[18] He currently has 159 million Instagram followers.[19]

Dak Prescott, quarterback for the Cowboys, was the highest-paid NFL player in 2024 with an annual salary of $60 million.[20] He has approximately 2.2 million Instagram followers.[21]

Yes, these are all professional athletes who are all over mainstream media. So, how does this apply from a business standpoint? Let's compare the Facebook follower count to net worth (at the time of this writing) of the current top ten richest people in the world and see what we find.[22] I am choosing Facebook as the comparative platform of choice, as it remains the most widespread and most commonly used social media platform with nearly 3.1 billion users.[23]

1. **Elon Musk:** CEO of Tesla and SpaceX, with a net worth of approximately $432 billion. Musk does not maintain an official personal Facebook account. However, he clearly found lots of value in Twitter (now X) when he acquired it in 2022 for $44 billion![24]

2. **Jeff Bezos:** Founder of Amazon, holding a net worth around $238 billion. Bezos does not have a public personal Facebook account.

3. **Mark Zuckerberg:** Co-founder and CEO of Meta Platforms (formerly Facebook), with a net worth of $207 billion. Zuckerberg has an official Facebook page with approximately 119 million followers.

4. **Larry Ellison:** Co-founder and CTO of Oracle Corporation, with a net worth of $192 billion. Ellison does not have a public personal Facebook account.

5. **Bernard Arnault and Family:** Chairman and CEO of LVMH (Moët Hennessy Louis Vuitton), with a net

worth estimated at $176 billion. Arnault does not have a public personal Facebook presence.

6. **Larry Page:** Co-founder of Google, possessing a net worth of $168 billion. Page does not have a public personal Facebook presence.

7. **Bill Gates:** Co-founder of Microsoft, possessing a net worth of $158 billion. Gates has an official Facebook page with approximately forty million followers.

8. **Sergey Brin:** Co-founder of Google, with a net worth of $158 billion. Brin does not maintain a personal Facebook account.

9. **Steve Ballmer:** Former CEO of Microsoft, holding a net worth of $146 billion. Ballmer does not have a public personal Facebook account.

10. **Warren Buffett:** CEO of Berkshire Hathaway, holding a net worth of $142 billion. Buffett does not maintain a personal Facebook account.

Only two of the top ten richest people in the world have and use a public-facing Facebook account. And for what it's worth, only three of these people have active Instagram accounts (Jeff Bezos with five million followers, Bill Gates with eight million followers, and Mark Zuckerberg with twelve million followers).

Now, I am no billionaire, and I am not on any richest people lists nor any top charts for the most followers. In fact, at this very moment, I have a total of twenty thousand online followers (ten thousand on Instagram, @aj_vaden; five thousand on LinkedIn, @ajvaden; and five thousand on Facebook). I'm not breaking any records over here, y'all. But with the help of my husband and business partner, mentors, coaches, friends, and an amazing team of employees, I have figured out how to build a successful and sustainable business that provides an abundant life for me and our family, gives opportunities to our

team, serves our clients in a deep and meaningful way, and contrib-
utes to the world as a whole.

Here's my point:

You don't have to have millions of followers to make millions
of dollars!

And you don't have to make millions of dollars to make an
eternal impact.

So many of us are impressed by people who have lots of followers.
We bestow a lot of clout on them, assuming they must know what
they are talking about—look at how many people follow them. We
trust them with health advice, relation-
ship advice, financial advice, and/or
business advice hugely on the basis of a
follower count. What we often fail to
realize, however, is that many online
accounts with lots of followers are

> *You don't have to
> have millions of
> followers to make
> millions of dollars!*

(unfortunately) "follower rich and dollar broke." They do not have
the expertise or experience to give out the advice they market, promote, and sell! I don't say that to be harsh or throw shade, as it's
definitely not easy to make money in general and running a business
of any size is not for the faint of heart. I point it out because it's a
prime example of how so many personal brands are focused on the
wrong things and why it's so important that true experts step up and
teach what they know.

These days I find it way more impressive to meet someone who
has made *lots of money* from only very *few* followers, versus someone
who primarily just has lots of followers. Making a large amount of
money from a smaller reach is a stronger measure of a person's efficacy
and capabilities as well as their entrepreneurial prowess.

It's also worth mentioning that a much more scalable and repeatable type of business to create is not one that is dependent on having
lots of followers (which belong to the platforms) but rather one that

could teach anyone with a relatively small following to actually make *lots of money*! Even though we focus the core of our strategies on helping our clients make a bigger difference in the world, a big part of what we do is also to help people monetize their personal brand.

We like making money; it's just that making money is subservient to advancing the mission. We like generating revenue, but generating revenue is subservient to building reputation. We like creating income, but creating income is subservient to making impact.

If nothing else, the primary reason that making money is important for a personal brand is because it fuels the opportunities necessary for you to make a difference—and that matters a whole lot more than just making a dollar.

THE P.A.I.D.S.

After working with thousands of personal brands, we've realized there are five primary ways to monetize a personal brand—five essential vehicles or mechanisms to convert a pile of followers into a pile of cash.

We call these the P.A.I.DS.:

Let's break down the five components of the P.A.I.D.S. model.

Products

If you have a following of any kind, one thing you can sell them is a physical Product. Products are great because they tend to provide a consistent customer experience every time. People can see exactly what it is, use it, and hopefully get clear value from it. If a product works great, it can propagate quickly because it's easy for people to understand.

The downside of developing Products, however, is that they tend to be expensive to produce initially, they are often easy to copy, and they typically have thin margins, so they require mass volume to make really significant money. They also require a true supply chain where you have to source vendors and materials, possibly manage a manufacturing process, and deal with the logistics of shipping and inventory.

☑	**P**roducts	• Clothing • Shoes • Day Planners • Equipment • Inventions	• Self-Published Books • Software • Workbooks

☑	**A**ds/
	ffiliates
		• Podcasting
		• Blogging
		• Radio
		• TV
		• YouTube
			• App
			• Social Media
			  Network
			• Event
			  Sponsorships

☑	**I**nformation	• Video course • Membership site • Certifications • Assessments	• Challenges • Self-published E-books
☑	**D**eals	• Book • Brand • Spokesperson • Television	• Movie • Licensing • Royalties
☑	**S**ervices	• Coaching • Consulting • Speaking • Training • Live Events	• Masterminds • Your current job or business

Ads and Affiliates

This is a super interesting business model because you actually don't sell *anything* to your audience; rather, you sell other people *access* to your audience. Ads and Affiliates can be a high margin business at scale because often what you are selling is attention—which is really just *air*. And there will always be businesses who are willing to pay for the chance to get their brand or message in front of the eyeballs of your fans and followers.

If you are good at "grabbing and holding attention" and can get a lot of people to show up in your audience, then your COGs (cost of goods sold) is producing the media. And with that you can sell other people the chance to get impressions for their brand. Advertisers pay an agreed-upon set fee for a preset amount of exposure. Meanwhile, Affiliates pay a percentage of revenue based on what they make from being introduced to your audience. They are the same model, however, in that your job is helping other businesses grow by curating an audience of relevant prospects for them.

The creator economy and the explosion of social media, YouTube, and podcasting have contributed greatly to the adoption of this business model. For skilled creators it can be a lifechanging opportunity, because many times the media platforms themselves are giving creators a built-in chance to monetize the audiences they've grown. The challenging part is that because this is so popular, you are literally competing with millions of other content creators in your niche from around the world. Plus, from a monetization perspective, bestselling author and international speaker Jay Baer said it best: "You're not just competing against other people who do what you do, you're competing against anything and everything that competes for people's attention."[25]

Information

Information-based products are mostly digital and are typically centered around your expertise. Online courses, monthly memberships, certifications, assessments, online challenges, and e-books are some of the most common business models that come to mind in this arena. This is one of our personal favorites because it carries so many incredible advantages:

- Low barrier to entry
- Low cost to create and set up
- Based around expertise rather than fame or notoriety
- Zero to low manufacturing, shipping, and storage costs
- Can scale to a large audience without having a large team
- Make a massively positive difference in the world and for the lives of others!

On the flipside, because of these and other advantages, there are often higher degrees of noise and competition. Also, a bit of "technological savvy" is required for the initial creation of some of these information products. However, in our experience the main reason why people fail with Information business models is that they don't know how to differentiate their brand, communicate their value, and most of all, they don't know how to sell!

Many of the online marketing tactics that people *think* will work to sell these products only work if you already have a large audience or if you have the ability to run paid advertising. However, teaching experts to make a significant amount of money by selling organically to a very small audience is perhaps the thing we specialize in most at Brand Builders Group. Again, we've figured out—perhaps as good as anyone else in the world—how to generate a large amount of revenue from a relatively small audience.

Deals

The fourth way to get paid is through Deals. Deals are made when a third party pays you up front some moderate fee for the creation of an artistic work or brand-building initiative, and you have an established partnership on how well that piece of work performs in the long-term. The easiest way to spot a "Deal" is typically when there is some sort of cash advance coupled with an ongoing royalty arrangement. Actors get movie and television deals. Writers get book deals. Musicians get record deals. Content creators get brand deals. Investors sometimes get revenue-share deals. Celebrities and athletes get licensing deals to have their name, image, and likeness associated with a product.

To understand the true power that is available through this monetization method, we love to point to global soccer icon Lionel Messi's historic deal that he negotiated when he joined Major League Soccer (MLS) in the US in 2023. Messi turned down a three-year, $1.6 billion contract from the Saudi Pro League to instead join Inter Miami's MLS club for "only" $20.4 million guaranteed per year.[26]

Why would he turn down $1.6 billion for $20.4 million a year? Great question. He did this because he was able to negotiate a future equity stake in the team, which creates a stream of income from his ownership that will continue long after he's done playing. Also, due to his huge online following (500 million on Instagram[27] alone), his profile and influence gave him a massive opportunity to raise the profile of the team and the entire MLS. Thus he was able to secure profit-sharing deals with two of the league's biggest partners, Apple and Adidas. Messi now receives a portion of every dollar of revenue that comes from Apple TV customers who buy an MLS Season Pass—for which 110,000 people signed up the day it was announced, and another 65,000 the day Messi scored two goals in the first thirty minutes of his second game.

On top of that, Adidas inked a *lifetime sponsorship* deal with him and then agreed to pay Messi a portion of *all* increased profits resulting from MLS-related income (his jersey became the top selling of the entire year just forty-five minutes after being announced). All told, Messi's projected earnings were $1.6 billion by the end of 2025, with additional multi-year and lifelong perpetuities still to come.[28] Now, *that's* how a personal brand deal is done!

If it isn't already obvious, one thing to note is that Deals generally come later in a personal brand's career journey when they have already proven their ability to create and provide value. This book teaches you how to build a personal brand from scratch to build the kind of momentum that can get you noticed in significant ways down the road.

Services

The last business model in the P.A.I.D.S. listing is perhaps the most common—Services. Services are most identifiable as a time-for-money exchange in which you provide some level of expertise or direct application of your knowledge or trait for an end customer. For some reason, whenever talking about personal brand Services, people immediately think of being paid as a coach, consultant, speaker, trainer, or advisor. And while those are all models we are intimately acquainted with, that is a very limiting view of what is available through Services.

In fact, a large portion of our clients at Brand Builders Group are professional service providers like doctors, lawyers, accountants, financial advisors, real estate agents, mortgage brokers, insurance agents, chiropractors, counselors, therapists, nutritionists, and so on. We also have a large contingent of all types of entrepreneurs, small business owners, direct salespeople, and solopreneurs. This is not surprising to us because we know the fastest path to cash is to use your personal brand to drive awareness to the thing you are already doing!

People mistake having a personal brand with a certain type of business model. They errantly think that "building a personal brand" means writing a book, creating a course, identifying as a coach, or becoming a speaker. But remember, a personal brand is not what you do; it's who you are. As we've seen, a personal brand is simply the formalization, digitization, and monetization of your reputation. A business model therefore is not your personal brand. Rather, a business model is simply a selection of how you are going to engage in the monetization of your reputation.

The fastest path to cash is to use your personal brand to drive awareness to the thing you are already doing!

Perhaps the most common and straightforward path to making money from a personal brand is through offering Services. By the way, if you are an executive or an employee of any kind, you are benefitting from the Services business model of monetization. The only difference is that you are selling your time and expertise as a personal brand to an organization—rather than the public marketplace—in exchange for compensation. And anyone who has a desire to advance their own career inside of an industry, or even get a raise or a promotion inside of a single company, is *still* building and monetizing their personal brand. The projects you are part of and the body of work you produce as an employee all still contribute and equate to establishing your reputation.

As it relates to selecting a business model to monetize, one of the most common questions we get asked is, "What's the best business model for personal brands?" The truth is that a lot of money can be made from any of them!

The big mistake is usually not in choosing the wrong business model; it's in choosing *too many* business models! When someone comes to us who is struggling financially, it's usually because they are trying to do *too many* different things and monetize in *too many* different ways, and/or they have *too many* ideas for things they want to sell. You can be successful doing *any* of the five core business models; you just can't be successful doing *all* of them. Remember one of our most core fundamental beliefs, "If you have diluted focus, you get diluted results."

D.A.R.E.S.

The last part of our Brand DNA Helix speaks to this exact issue. It's another "chromosome pair" of questions designed to help you get clear on exactly what type of business model is the right one for you.

The fifth question in the Brand DNA Helix is, "What are people willing to buy from you?" Go back and review the options in the P.A.I.D.S. acronym for a quick mental refresh. However, **just because you *can* do something doesn't mean you *should***. Again, the main enemy when it comes to monetization is not a lack of options; it's too many options.

Thus, the sixth and final question of the Brand DNA Helix is, "What type of business do you want to be in?" It counterbalances the fifth question in that it helps you narrow down what the *right* business model is for you.

The framework we use for this is the acronym **D.A.R.E.S.** If there was such a thing as a *perfect* business model, we believe it would contain the following five elements. It would be:

- **Digital**—There is no physical product, which frees you from manufacturing costs and supply chain complications. Think of information products.
- **Automated**—It is completely self-servicing by your customers. Think of a vending machine.
- **Recurring**—This is the financial holy grail—something a customer doesn't just pay for once but instead buys again and again. Think physical products like toothpaste or services like Verizon.
- **Evergreen**—The offering rarely (if ever) has to be revised, edited, updated, or changed. Think of timeless personal development content or something like a home appliance that doesn't update much between models. Evergreen means the product mostly stays the same and can be sold again and again to virtually everyone on the planet.
- **Scalable**—The company is able to grow its revenues without having to grow its expenses at the same rate. Think of things like software: There is usually an initial investment required to create the product, but after that the incremental cost of an additional user is seismically small compared to the number of users who could benefit from the tool.

The concept of D.A.R.E.S. becomes increasingly important when you consider the difference between *growth* and *scale*. The fastest way to *grow* a company is to spend. For example, if you spend more money on ads and hire more salespeople, you are highly likely to grow your revenues. However, if bringing on more customers means you also have to bring on more staff to service those customers, then all your expenses as a company are likely to grow at some rate that is fairly in line with your overall revenue.

If you have a company that does $1 million in revenue and spends $900,000 to acquire and service that revenue, that's $100,000 in profit (10 percent). Let's say you double the business. Now you bring in $2 million in revenue, but if it requires you to spend an additional $900,000 to acquire and service that additional million in revenue, you still only made a 10 percent profit: $1.8 million in expenses, which leaves you $200,000 in profit. While you have doubled both the revenue and total profit, you also have doubled the expenses—and likely doubled the stress, complexity, and people required to run the business. That's *growth*.

	Growth		Scale	
	Year 1	Year 2	Year 1	Year 2
Revenue	$ 1,000,000	$ 2,000,000	$ 1,000,000	$ 2,000,000
Expenses	$ 900,000	$ 1,800,000	$ 900,000	$ 1,500,000
Profit	$ 100,000	$ 200,000	$ 100,000	$ 500,000
Profit Margin	10%	10%	10%	25%

Scale is different. Scale is when you can grow the revenues of a business disproportionately higher than the rate at which the expenses grow. To use that same example, let's say you were able to grow the revenue of the business to $2 million but you only had to invest another $600,000 in expenses to do it. Now, you've spent $1.5 million ($900,000 of expenses from the first year plus $600,000 of new expenses) to generate $2 million in revenue. But instead of making a $200,000 profit, you're clearing $500,000. In this scenario, you've moved from making a 10 percent ($100,000) profit margin the first year to now making a 25 percent ($500,000) profit margin in the second year. You've doubled the revenue from

$1 million to $2 million, but you've quintupled the profits from $100,000 to $500,000!

Visually, the difference between these two concepts looks like this:

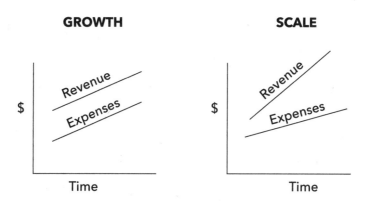

You should note that it is difficult to select a business model that perfectly meets all of the D.A.R.E.S. criteria. In fact, some of the characteristics can work against themselves. For example, Recurring and Evergreen tend to be natural competitors. That's because for something to generate Recurring revenue, people have to be willing to pay for it again and again and again. But for a business model to truly be Evergreen, it means the thing they are providing should never be updated. Since people are rarely willing to pay for something multiple times when the item never needs to be updated or changed, they are natural counterbalancing forces.

The closest example of the perfect D.A.R.E.S. business model we can think of is Netflix. While they used to mail DVDs to people, Netflix wisely adapted into an entirely digital product offering. It's a subscription service that people pay for on an ongoing basis (Recurring) where the customers self-serve in both how they sign up and in what movies they select when utilizing the service (Automated). And while there were presumably huge investments made initially into the infrastructure of Netflix, the incremental cost of adding a new customer now that it's established is very low (Scalable). In some ways, Netflix is also *almost* Evergreen because once a movie is uploaded to the service, that movie is never changed again. However, the one challenge to being truly Evergreen is that customers expect to have new content uploaded on a regular basis.

Needless to say, Netflix has about as close to a perfect D.A.R.E.S. business model as we've ever seen. The success of the choices that led to that are well evidenced in the company's financial performance. Netflix made $6.5 million in profit on $272 million in revenue back in 2003 (a 2.3 percent margin). Fast-forward twenty years, and the company has not only grown to $33.7 billion in revenue but has also converted that into $5.4 billion in profit (a 16 percent margin).[29] That's some serious scale!

Netflix's net income from 2000 to 2023
(in million U.S. dollars)

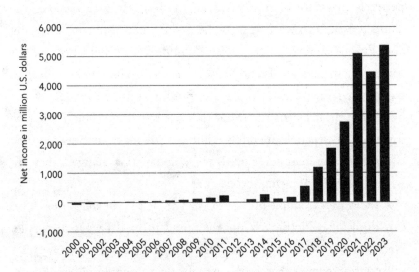

Now, you don't have to be anywhere near the size of Netflix to become ridiculously successful (and wealthy!). But you *should* think through the long-term impacts of what business model you select as early as possible in your journey.

PRIMARY BUSINESS MODEL (PBM)

Just like we've encouraged you throughout this book to select *one* Avatar to serve, *one* Problem to solve, and *one* Message and Uniqueness to advocate for, we also have experienced that the most financially successful personal brands have extreme clarity on their *one* most important revenue stream.

Identifying, codifying, and communicating your Primary Business Model (PBM) is necessary so that everyone inside your company knows exactly which single stream of revenue is the one that gets the most prioritized resources for the business. Your PBM is the one revenue stream that matters above all others, and it's the one you commit whatever resources are required to make sure it succeeds, even if that means other revenue streams have to decrease.

We've learned that it's not so much that personal brands fail as it is that they eventually just give up. The main reason they quit is because they don't make money fast enough. And the primary cause of them not making money fast enough is because they've bought into a pervasive lie that causes massive distraction.

The lie is that success means having "multiple streams of income."

Nobody who got rich, as in *truly wealthy*, got rich from *starting* with multiple streams of income. The way you get rich is not through having multiple streams of marginally performing income. In fact, it's just the opposite. The way you get rich is by having one *amazing* high-performing stream of income that you radically focus on and relentlessly dedicate yourself to. In consistent alignment with the theme of this whole book, we know you are most likely to become wealthy by doing one thing over and over and over again. You become wealthy by mastering *one* skill, perfecting *one* stream of revenue, focusing on *one* business model, providing *one* incredible service, and scaling that

> *The way you get rich is by having one amazing high-performing stream of income.*

one single income stream to a level that will change your life and your entire family tree.

Now, once you get rich, *then* you diversify your income sources. After you have a large sum of money, *then* you can expand and deploy multiple streams of income and invest into new ideas, businesses, or revenue streams. The deception of multiple streams of income comes from the fact that rich people talk about it. And sure, that *is* what rich people do. But creating those multiple streams is what you do *after* you've become rich; that's not how you *get* rich.

Smart personal brands know that the real secret to driving income, growing revenues, and acquiring meaningful wealth comes from concentration, not diversification.

Scan the QR code in the front inside cover of this book to download our Revenue Assessment.

Don't agree with me? Let's use some of the wealthiest people who have ever walked the planet as a litmus test of this concept. We're going to play a game called "How did this person get rich?" I will list the names of some individuals (personal brands) who have become quite wealthy and well-known. Right next to each name I'll list *one single place or skill* that was initially responsible for the vast majority of their wealth creation, and then you can decide if you agree or disagree with me.

- Jeff Bezos: Amazon
- Bill Gates: Microsoft
- Sara Blakely: Spanx
- Elon Musk: PayPal
- Michael Jordan: Basketball
- Oprah Winfrey: Talk show host
- Richard Branson: Virgin Records
- John D. Rockefeller: Standard Oil
- Jennifer Lopez: Actress

- Conor McGregor: UFC
- Mary Kay Ash: Makeup
- Dr. Dre: Rapper
- Wolfgang Puck: Chef
- Warren Buffett: Investor
- Alex Rodriguez: Baseball
- Reese Witherspoon: Actress
- Daymond John: FUBU
- Henry Ford: Cars
- Jamie Kern Lima: It Cosmetics
- Cristiano Ronaldo: Soccer
- Jerry Seinfeld: Comedian
- Cornelius Vanderbilt: Steamships

When you zoom out like this, it becomes glaringly obvious and ridiculously evident that *initially* the path to building your wealth comes not from diversification but from focus. The wealthiest people in the world made the massive majority of their money by mastering one skill or by having one business—not by having many.

Again, the biggest mistake is not in selecting the wrong business model; it's in selecting too many business models. As the ancient Chinese proverb states, "He who chases two rabbits catches neither."

Finding a Short-Term Primary Business Model

D.A.R.E.S. serves as a guide when selecting your long-term business model because you want to think about how that business will take shape over time. But in a more practical and immediate sense, we want you to identify and focus on a "short-term Primary Business Model." Your short-term PBM is the one that matters for paying the bills right now and getting you enough financial lift that you can continue scaling toward bigger things in the future.

So, how do you figure out a short-term model that'll get your business up and running? Let's start with the five criteria you absolutely need for a good start:

Five Criteria of Short-Term Primary Business Model Selection

1. **Time**—Assess how much time you will need in both the early stages and later stages of the business to make it successful. Consider how long it will take you to develop your product and service to earn your first dollar, then break even, then generate real profit. Additionally, consider how many hours of human labor, outside of you, will be necessary over the long haul as the business grows.

2. **Team**—Consider your current team (if you have one yet) and then consider what type of skills (and level of skill) are required to get your business off the ground and ultimately to full scale. Specifically, calculate the current and future expense of hiring and maintaining the team you will need to achieve your vision.

3. **Technology**—Every business will have varying levels of technological needs. Consider on the front end how much and what type of technology it will take to bring your business to life. Typically, the best strategy is to choose a business that (at least initially) lines up with the level of technical competency you either have or have access to.

4. **Capital**—Functionally, the thing that causes most businesses to shut down is that they simply run out of cash. So, consider now, how much cash will you need to get the business launched and then to profitable and beyond? Most importantly, you need a clear plan of where the money is going to come from. Rory and I are debt averse and have a family philosophy that "a business should

grow at the rate that profits show." Our model is always to run customer-financed businesses where reinvestments into the business are only possible if the revenues of the company grow first.

Many entrepreneurs take on debt from banks and lenders and/or bring in investors in exchange for equity to try and grow faster. Be advised: That is risky business with a massive set of added stress and complications. While requiring yourself to make sales first will *feel* like a slower way to build your business, it guarantees that the business is healthy, which means it will grow much faster and more sus-

> *A business should grow at the rate that profits show.*

tainably in the long run. Plus, when you grow the business from revenues, you never have to worry about someone taking control of your business—or your house.

5. **Lifestyle**—Consider the short-term and long-term impacts a successful business will have on you, your family, and your lifestyle. Go ask someone who has done what you want to do. Take the time, ask the questions, do the research. Ask yourself what price you're willing to pay up front to create an ideal lifestyle later.

We've learned it's helpful to think through business model selection with both a short-term and long-term perspective. Short-term allows you to be clear on what you *have* to do right now to earn the right to get to do what you *want* to later. When thinking about the right business model for you, it's important to keep both of these factors in balance:

1. **Short-Term:** Managing the fastest path to cash that will help you pay your bills today.

2. **Long-Term:** The vision of the ideal business and lifestyle that you want to create in the future.

To help you think through this for yourself, let's review what we call the Golden Grid:

	Short Term	Long Term
PRIMARY BUSINESS MODEL (Only 1)		
SECONDARY BUSINESS MODEL (Only 1)		
ANCILLARY REVENUE STREAMS (Multiple)		

Scan the QR code in the front inside cover of this book and download our Golden Grid fillable PDF to complete for yourself.

While the grid is mostly self-explanatory, the key is to force yourself to have only *one* revenue stream in each of the top four boxes. While technically the Ancillary Revenue Stream box allows for you to have more than one stream, we would highly encourage you to limit that as much as possible. You will statistically increase the chances of success of any of your revenue streams by simply focusing your resources on fewer initiatives. In fact, check out some of these data points around this very topic.

- According to 2024 reports, **50 percent of businesses fail within five years**, primarily due to lack of focus and divided attention.[30]
- A study by **CB Insights** found that businesses with a **singular focus** on their main product or service experience **10–20 percent faster revenue growth** compared to diversified businesses in their early stages.[31]
- A **Stanford study** found that start-ups with a single-focused approach and strong execution are **50 percent more likely** to reach profitability within their first five years.[32]
- Research from **McKinsey & Company** highlighted that businesses with a singular focus scale **twice as effectively**, as their teams can concentrate on operational improvements and market penetration.[33]

Clearly articulating and codifying exactly what your Primary Business Model will be is one of the most important strategic decisions a personal brand can make.

Scan the QR code on the front inside cover of this book and schedule a free call with our team to talk through how we can support you with your Primary Business Model.

MONEY MISCONCEPTIONS

It's not only a misconception that the best way to get wealthy is to have multiple businesses that provide multiple streams of income; it's also inaccurate to think that the only way to make a lot of money is to add lots of new customers. Many people think the only way to double a business is to double the number of customers. Not only is that not true, it's also often the most expensive way to grow a business.

For example, let's pretend you had a $30 product that you sold to 1,000 people. That means that you would have generated $30,000 in revenue. Now, imagine I asked you, "What's the best way to double your revenue?" If you're like most people, there's a good chance your first thought would be to go out and get another 1,000 customers. While that's not "wrong," it does require you to reach a lot more people, which means you also probably have to do a lot more advertising and/or selling. It also takes the longest amount of time because you have to find all new people to build trust with, which must always take place before a transaction can occur.

It's these exact reasons why you may have heard that **"the most expensive customer to acquire in any business is a new customer."**

Meanwhile, the most profitable customer in any business is a repeat customer. Repeat customers certainly are wonderful if and when they continue to buy your offer again and again, but the real magic to finding profit inside of a business comes through a different strategy—one we call "Fractal Math."

Fractal Math says that 10 percent of your customers will invest at a level that is 10x what they've already invested. If you apply Fractal Math as a strategy to our example above of a company that generates $30,000 in revenue from 1,000 customers, it looks like this:

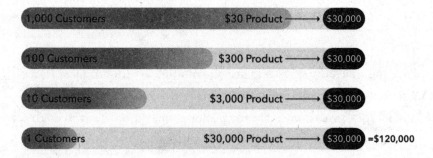

Fractal Math Profit Maximizer

10% of your customers will invest 10X more

1,000 Customers	$30 Product ⟶ $30,000	
100 Customers	$300 Product ⟶ $30,000	
10 Customers	$3,000 Product ⟶ $30,000	
1 Customers	$30,000 Product ⟶ $30,000	=$120,000

If you have 1,000 customers that each spent $30, then 100 of them would spend $300, 10 would spend $3,000, and 1 would spend $30,000. If you applied this in your business, you would not double your revenue—you'd quadruple it! Not to mention that you'd quadruple it without adding a single new customer! Please note that while there isn't anything scientific or guaranteed about this concept, it's a pattern we've experienced for ourselves and have noticed again and again when working behind the scenes with some of our most successful clients.

Notice that Fractal Math is the mathematical expression of two concepts we've already covered earlier in this chapter. First, you may recall that in the opening of the chapter I said you don't need to have millions of followers to make millions of dollars. Also, think back to where I described the difference between "growth" and "scale."

Fractal Math is the pragmatic strategy for why both of those things are true. Most of the world is focused on attracting new customers—but those are the most expensive customers to find! That explains why most companies experience "growth" more than "scale." While growing revenue, they also grow expenses.

Meanwhile, a strategy driven by Fractal Math is radically different because you pursue a path that leads to more profit and more personal peace by serving your current customers in a deeper way.

Again, it's not "wrong" to want to expand your reach. We believe it can be a healthy and divinely inspired calling to want to reach more people. Our advice to you is simply this: Don't be so concerned about the width of your reach

> **Don't be so concerned about the width of your reach that you forget about the depth of your impact.**

that you forget about the depth of your impact. We seem to live in a world where everyone is constantly focused on width. They want more customers, more followers, more downloads, more subscribers, more attention. If that drive comes from wanting to make a deeper impact, then we think it is a beautiful part of what it means to be a Mission-Driven Messenger.

However, while it is true that you can make a really big impact on the world by sharing your content with millions of people on the internet, you also can make a really big impact on the world by adopting a single child. In that scenario, who do you think made the bigger total impact on the world? The answer is debatable, and fortunately they are not mutually exclusive avenues. Answering that question definitively is also completely unnecessary, as they are both beautiful contributions to humanity. The point is not to push you in one direction or another but to help you realize that the entire world is constantly chasing width; meanwhile, they are almost completely overlooking the power (and profitability) available through pursuing depth.

Especially when you are looking to make more money—and specifically *keep* more money—we have found that going deeper with fewer people is not only a much faster method but one with a much higher probability of success.

Think back to chapter 6 when you were working on the "Problem" for your Brand Positioning Statement. You may have noted that people will always pay money to solve problems. And money follows speed—the faster you can solve a problem for someone, the faster they will pay you and the more they will pay you. Thus, the most practical way to help most personal brands make more money quickly is to focus on answering the question, "How can I serve my current clients in a deeper way?"

SERVICES SPECTRUM

Once you buy into the power of Fractal Math, your next question is probably, "How exactly do I apply that to my business as a personal brand?"

The best monetization strategy in the world is to simply *care* about helping your customers succeed, because if you truly care about them succeeding you will always have a clear path to more profit. That is a simple and universal strategy because what *every* customer in *every* industry needs is to succeed *faster.*

Assuming you are truly an expert in your field, chances are the fastest way you could help one of your customers succeed is to simply do the work for them. That's what most of us really want—we want someone to do the work for us. And to some extent, you may be able to offer that as a solution for your audience—a "done for you" service. The challenge with that, however, is not everyone has enough money to pay you the full value of what your time may be worth, and you also don't have an unlimited amount of time to help all the people you want to help. Fortunately, these issues can be remedied by applying The Services Spectrum.

> **The best monetization strategy in the world is to simply care about helping your customers succeed.**

We live in a world stuffed and oversaturated with information. The explosion of the internet has created such a glut of information that many people believe information should be free. Ironically, however, the mass democratization of information has led to a new problem: *infobesity.* There is so much information available that people over-consume but under-apply it. Of the vast array of places we can go to get more information, relatively few of them help us put the information into practice. Within that struggle lies the monetization opportunity available that the Service Spectrum depicts for us visually: People don't pay for information; they pay for organization and application.

While the demand for information has gone down, simultaneously the demand for the organization and application of information has gone up! That is why smart personal brands structure their service offerings in line with that general consumer trend. If you want to make a lot of money, you need to be more than an expert in your field; you need to become an expert at helping people apply that expertise.

For example, much of the information in this book is available for free on the internet. It would just require you to listen to dozens of hours of our podcast, watch hundreds of our YouTube videos, and scroll thousands upon thousands of our social media posts. Plus, after doing all that, you'd have to reorganize all the concepts into their proper sequential order all by yourself. Rather than doing that, you've chosen to invest a few dollars to have the most essential information presented in a concise, cohesive set of properly sequenced instructions. In other words, you've paid for organization.

> **People don't pay for information; they pay for organization and application.**

To apply this information faster, scan the QR code
on the front inside cover and schedule a
free strategy call with our team.

Your customers can't survive on a broad barrage of information alone; they need tools and techniques, systems, and support to help them implement all of the knowledge you have to offer. And while you can't make yourself available to everyone to do it all for them, the great news is that you don't have to! You truly don't need to make millions of people aware of your business. In fact, most of us could have our greatest financial year ever by adding one or two dozen of our perfect customers. That's because of another really important and powerful truth that is explained by The Services Spectrum: As intimacy increases, price increases. You don't only make more money by having more customers; you make more by doing more for the customers you already have.

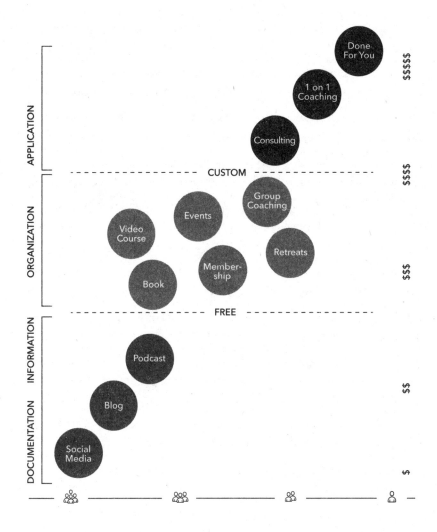

LESSONS FROM CHICK-FIL-A

Chick-fil-A started in 1967[34] and was one of the preeminent early players in the quick-service chicken restaurant space. By 1988, the brand had reached $232 million in sales, and in 1989 its leaders set an audacious goal to more than quadruple the revenues to hit $1 billion by the year 2000.[35]

But in the early nineties a new competitor named Boston Chicken (later renamed Boston Market) came on the scene fast and furious. Boston Market started in 1985, exploded to twelve hundred locations at its peak, and went public in 1993.[36] Even though they had started long after Chick-fil-A, it appeared as if they would be the first to arrive at the $1 billion revenue mark.

The rapid success and steep trajectory of this direct competitor was obviously noticeable and became the subject of at least one Chick-fil-A board meeting. In a story that has been widely reported and recounted by multiple people in proximity to the leadership of the company, apparently heated discussions ensued among the senior executives as to how they would keep up with the growth rate of Boston Market. This rival's mass expansion was creating a natural pressure on the company to grow bigger, faster.

Prior to 1990, the vast majority of Chick-fil-A's revenue came from restaurants inside shopping malls.[37] Now the leadership team, feeling the burden of pacing with their challenger, was focused on how to accelerate the development of more freestanding stores to become bigger and bigger as fast as possible. This went on until, in the middle of the board meeting, Chick-fil-A founder Truett Cathy slammed his fist on the table in a decisive—but uncharacteristic—act to command the attention of everyone in the room.

He then declared sharply to the effect, "I'm tired of all this talk about getting bigger. We don't need to focus on being bigger. We need to focus on being better. If we get better, our customers will demand that we get bigger." This paraphrase was later corroborated on December 11, 2000, when the company announced publicly that it had, for the first time ever, reached its goal of hitting $1 billion in sales. In an interview, Jimmy Collins, president of Chick-fil-A at the time, recounted, "When we set this goal in 1989, we decided our focus had to be on providing quality customer experiences, not on how many stores we could build."[38]

Meanwhile, the "fast-growing" Boston Market had developed a culture of carrying an aggressive amount of debt.[39] That philosophy and practice seems to have been a contributing factor in what led the company to declare bankruptcy in 1998.[40] They were later purchased out of bankruptcy by McDonald's but then sold again, and they reportedly continued to have a troubled financial history, ultimately resulting in millions of dollars in fines and forced store closings by the government, along with more than $10 million in lawsuits from their vendors.[41]

As of this writing, Chick-fil-A operates more than three thousand stores in forty-eight US states, is expanding internationally, and has now crossed over $21 billion in annual sales.[42]

This true story serves as a cautionary tale and illustration for entrepreneurs. So often we become consumed with growing our companies bigger just because that is what everyone else is doing. If we're not careful, we tie our identity into the concept of having more revenue, more followers, and more attention instead of being focused on providing more value, making more profit, and creating more impact.

It is uncommon to find entrepreneurs with the discernment, wisdom, and discipline to focus instead on serving a smaller audience in a deeper way, but when you do, you will see that these businesses are not only making more impact; they are also making more money. Rarely will you find a passionate personal brand who decidedly focuses on being better instead of just trying to be bigger. But when you do find one, you will likely see them winning. It really is true that you don't need millions of followers to make millions of dollars. Just serve your audience in a deeper way.

The question is, will you be one of the few who is deliberately willing to choose *less*? The great Paradox of Profit is that, in the beginning, those who choose to solve more specific problems for fewer groups of people with fewer types of offerings end up making far more money and far greater impact in the world.

If you can bring yourself to make that decision, you are on your way to making more money—as long as you figure out how to properly communicate your value externally to strangers. We're going to teach you how to do that next!

PART 3

HOW TO MONETIZE A PERSONAL BRAND

CHAPTER 8

THE FIVE TITLE TESTS

BY RORY VADEN

The most painful and expensive marketing mistake I've ever made was mistitling my second book. It was a mistake I believe has cost us millions of dollars.

After the success of my first *New York Times* bestselling book, *Take the Stairs*, we quickly got a second book deal. I was excited for two reasons. First, we knew what we were doing this time around, and second, we had stumbled upon a singular idea that I *knew* was going to change the world. We'd figured out how it was *literally* possible to multiply time.

For centuries people have been fed the lie that "time is the one thing you can never get more of." It was that widely held, nearly sacred but errant belief that had set us up to explode onto the scene with fresh insights that not only worked but satisfied the kind of natural marketing hyperbole and sensationalism that was sure to garner us global attention.

You see, it is true that there is nothing anyone can do to get more time inside of one day. We all have the same 24 hours, which is 1,440 minutes or 86,400 seconds. Nothing I can do or say will ever change that or teach you how to have more time within one day.

But that's exactly the problem. Everyone walks around trying to figure out how to squeeze more time into their day—something we call the Urgency Paradigm. The pattern we discovered, however, is that ultra-performers and the top one percenters of the world think differently. They subconsciously make what we now refer to as the Significance Calculation. This calculation is an assessment of how an activity will not just affect today but tomorrow and the next day and the next day on into forever. Therein lies the foundation for how it is *literally* possible to *multiply* time—which is the entire premise of my second book.

In one sentence, the way you multiply time is by spending time on things today that give you more time tomorrow. There are certain activities you can choose to do today that, while they cost you time now, create massively more time for you in the future. When you apply this Significance Calculation to your thinking, along with our proprietary Focus Funnel strategies, they help you create exponentially more time in the future, which helps you alleviate much of the stress and pressure and busyness that most of us feel right now.

We knew we were onto something big, and the timing of my second book (the mid-2010s) was the booming golden era of TED Talks. Thought leaders like Brené Brown, Simon Sinek, Mel Robbins, Adam Grant, and Angela Duckworth were bursting into international renown from the massive exposure they were getting from having their TED Talks viewed online. TED's slogan at the time was "ideas worth spreading," and I knew in my heart that if I could just get on their stage, I would have a chance to do the same.

That part turned out to be much more difficult than I had anticipated. Not only would TED not respond to me, but my application to speak was also rejected by twenty-seven smaller local TEDx events. But then a brand-new local event, TEDx Douglasville, finally gave me a shot! Perhaps they accepted me because it was their very first year and they were just desperate for speakers. Regardless, I was happy to take the slot. It wasn't a glamorous event. With less than a hundred people in an old theater with poor audio quality, this was about to be my "moment." We were going to leverage the success we had laid with *Take the Stairs* and multiply our own impact and reach exponentially with this talk—and it *almost* worked.

The plan was to release my second book right about the time my TEDx talk was released. My talk would go viral and my book sales would go gangbusters right along with it—just as they seemed to for all the thought leaders I mentioned earlier. As I had hoped, the video of my talk took off with lightning speed! People were watching and commenting and loving it and sharing it! That talk has over five *million* views![43]

The problem? My second book has only sold less than fifteen thousand copies post launch. How can that be? How can millions of people love the content, share the message, and write outstanding positive comments on the video, but meanwhile only a few thousand people buy the book that goes with it? How can the same content be released at the same moment in history from the same messenger and have one take off with massive success while the other flatlines into mediocrity at best? What happened? What went wrong? Simple: I picked the right title for my speech but the wrong title for my book.

When TED requested the title of my speech, they simply asked, "What is this talk about?" To which I was able to quickly and clearly reply, "Oh, easy. This presentation is teaching people how to multiply time." They ran with that and titled my soon-to-go-viral video on YouTube "How to Multiply Time." However, I titled my book with a completely different set of logic.

I wanted a title for my second book that was as radical and innovative as I believed the content inside of it was. I wanted something so unique and so clever that people would be blown away with intrigue because they had never heard anything like it before. My goal was to say something fascinating and counterintuitive with the title to suggest the content inside the book would also be new ideas about time management that they had never heard before. And that's how we came to title my second book *Procrastinate on Purpose*.

Of course, the book is not about teaching people how to procrastinate. The idea is that you don't procrastinate on the big, significant, important things at all. Rather, you do learn to procrastinate on the small, trivial, and insignificant things like cleaning your office or checking email (again) or scrolling social media. By learning to "procrastinate on purpose" with the mundane things, you thereby create the extra margin you need in your calendar to reinvest into the things that multiply your time, which are the things you can spend time on today that give you more time tomorrow.

The main problem with the title *Procrastinate on Purpose* is that it takes an entire paragraph to explain what it really means. While the title I selected may in fact be catchy, unusual, clever, counterintuitive, somewhat shocking, and definitely unexpected, its most defining characteristic is also the one that is the most devastating to its success: It's not easily understood! I set a goal to create a title that would be like nothing anyone had ever heard. The good news is I accomplished that goal. The bad news is that nobody buys things they don't understand. Had I simply called the book *How to Multiply Time*, I believe it would have sold hundreds of thousands of copies and driven my demand and corresponding speaking fees through the roof. Thus, the most expensive marketing lesson I've ever learned is: When it comes to titles and headlines, "clear is greater than clever."

> **When it comes to titles and headlines, clear is greater than clever.**

Too many personal brands are failing because they're trying to do exactly what I did. They have amazing content, but they wrap it up in complicated packaging. They're trying to be cutesy, but to the general public it comes out as confusing. They're trying to sound smart, but to the everyday person it just sounds like jargon. They're trying to be fancy, but the message comes out muffled. They are so focused on differentiating that they instead become disorienting. My story is one of a flamboyant and fatal mistake on a book cover for sure, but personal brands die a slow death from making this same mistake again and again, over and over, every single day. They confuse people with what they call their speeches, how they describe what they do, what they put in their email subject lines, and what they write as their website headlines.

You could do all of the work from earlier in this book perfectly in selecting your Avatar as the person you once were, locking in on one Problem to solve, identifying your Uniqueness, codifying your Message, and being disciplined in choosing one focused Primary Business Model. And yet, if you get all of that right but get the external packaging and marketing of those concepts wrong, you will always struggle in an uphill battle—just as I did. On the contrary, if you learn how to nail your titles and headlines right out of the gate, you can move down the path to accelerated success with exponential speed.

THE HOOK VS. THE BOOK

Much of what we have covered so far in this book is what we refer to as *internal* strategy and alignment. The principles and practices we have shared are ways of thinking to properly set your internal strategy. If you don't get the foundational elements of your internal Brand Positioning Statement right, then no matter how good your marketing is, your brand (i.e., business) will eventually fracture as you try to scale. But if you have a strong foundation with clear brand positioning strategy and then combine that with an expert-level external-facing marketing strategy, then you can build a true masterpiece.

Our **Five Title Tests** demarcate an important step in the personal brand building journey, shifting our focus away from internal considerations to external ones. Again, internal strategy work must be done to create clarity, focus, and alignment. But the external work is all about communicating your value to the market in an effective way so they respond and take action. For the rest of your journey through this book—and our other subsequent curriculum topics at Brand Builders Group—we will focus on presenting your Uniqueness to the outside world. Visually, you might think of it like this:

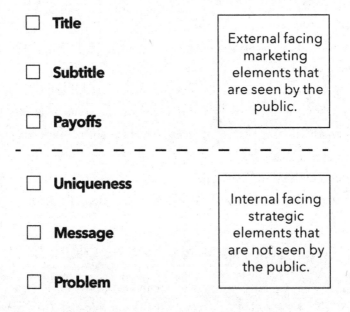

The distinction of the transition from internal to external strategy first clicked for me when another one of my mentors, Hall of Fame speaker and *New York Times* bestselling author Mark Sanborn, shared a concept he called "The Hook vs. The Book." The simplest way to think about this is that The Hook is the cover and, effectively, the outside of the book. Meanwhile, The Book is the words that go on the pages in between the front and back cover. Even though they are related and ultimately are two parts that make up the exact same product, it's critical to understand that the job of The Hook is very different than that of The Book.

The Hook's job is primarily a marketing function meant to attract attention. The Book's job is a teaching function meant is to transform someone's life. The Hook refers to enticing external packaging, while The Book refers to sharing timeless internal principles. The Hook sells, while The Book tells. When you consider what is required to build a bestselling personal brand, you need a powerful Hook (a great title) and a powerful Book (or course or service offering or product) full of life-changing truth.

The Hook	The Book
Markets	Teaches
Attracts	Transforms
Is External Packaging	Is Internal Principles
Sells	Tells
Is the Title	Is the Truth

If you don't understand the difference between The Hook and The Book, then it is very likely that you will make one of the four most common mistakes when titling your next book, business, product, or anything else. For purposes of consistency and continuing the illustration, I'll refer to the following mistakes with book titles, but you should know that these same mistakes apply to titling all sorts of things such as speeches, videos, programs, resources, guides, emails, webpages, and many more.

Title Mistake #1—Telling People What Your Book Is About

Authors have an innate desire to use the title to explain what the book is about. Do not do this! It's very important that you learn to divorce these two concepts of The Hook and The Book. While The Hook should probably be at least loosely related to The Book, it does *not* have to explain what the book is about. Instead, a great title should express what result will show up in the reader's life if they do everything inside The Book.

As a generic and universal example, let's pretend you were using your personal brand to build a landscaping business. You wouldn't want to write a book titled *Everything You Need to Know about Lawncare*. Instead, a much better title would be *How to Get Green Grass*.

Title Mistake #2—Telling People What to Do

The next most common mistake is using the title to try to communicate the internal premise of the book. It's as if authors sometimes feel morally obligated to give the potential reader the message of the whole book right on the cover. But this will usually come out sounding like you are just telling people to do a lot of work. And while a good Book will communicate the truth that being successful in anything in life requires work, it makes a terrible Hook because no one is attracted to something that sounds difficult!

Continuing with our hypothetical landscaping business example, nobody wants to buy a book called *Fertilize Your Front Yard Four Times a Year*. Even though it may be the truth about how to get green grass, and it even has catchy consonance in it, it sounds like too much work to attract anyone. All other things being equal, you'd get a much better response from a title like *Prettiest Yard in the Neighborhood*. Here, I'm not telling people what to *do* on the cover; I'm telling them what they will *get* if they do what I teach them inside the book.

Title Mistake #3—Telling People What You Believe

In general, there is nothing wrong with telling people what you believe, but that typically does not make for a good title. The primary reason is when you put what you believe right on the front cover, it forces me to make a split-second decision of whether or not I agree with you. And you can be certain that if I don't agree with you, I'm not going to buy your book! There is no way I'm spending money and time to read something I already know I don't agree with. This mistake has a double whammy, too, because if I do agree with you, I'm *also* not likely to buy your book!

Use common sense and think about this for a minute. If you title your landscaping book *Pesticides Are Ruining Your Yard*, and I don't agree with you, I'm definitely not buying. But *even if I do* agree with you, I'm likely to just give you a silent head nod along with a "you go, girl" or "amen, dude" and quickly move on without ever pulling out my wallet. Contrast that with a book titled *Best Landscaping on the Block*. Now *that* is a book I might buy, and once I do, then you can tell me all you want inside The Book about how pesticides are the enemy of human health.

Title Mistake #4—Referring to Random Arbitrary Concepts from Inside The Book

One of my first keynote presentations was titled "What's Your Cookie?" It was supposed to refer to the idea that we all have a weak spot for temptation and indulgence, and that if we learn to overcome it, we can achieve anything in our lives. It's not a bad concept—but it's a terrible title! Why? You would have to sit through the entire presentation (i.e., The Book) to ever understand what the title actually meant—and nobody has time for that.

Please don't make the same costly mistakes I've made by titling your next lawn care book *The 2 Percent Rule* as an obscure reference to your belief that if you can keep weeds out of all but 2 percent of the square footage of your beds, you will have a healthy garden. Nobody will buy it, not because they don't want what you're trying to sell but because they have no idea what your title means. Instead, if you want to make more sales, give the title to me straight with something like *Weed-Free Garden.* You'll make more money and keep the stoners away at the same time!

Are there some counterexamples to these? A few bestselling titles that have defied these principles? Sure, there are. But almost every counterexample has one of two explanations: It's either the most original, groundbreaking, well-thought-out, and phenomenally written book the world has ever seen on the subject; or the author has already had some huge platform, network, or wealth. Platform size trumps terrible titles. When you are Oprah or Donald Trump, you can call your book whatever you want, and it will sell. But if you're not already super rich or ridiculously famous, you'd

> *If you don't nail a great title, you'll never get the chance to transform people with your life-changing truths.*

be wise to avoid these common mistakes and realize that if you don't nail a great title, you'll never get the chance to transform people with your life-changing truths.

Over the last several years, we have built a data-science team that does nothing but track the top bestselling books in the US. Every week, we spend hours and hours crunching data and poring over publicly available information as well as our own proprietary reports to track and trend the most salient features and most common characteristics of books that hit the major bestseller lists.

Part of how we have helped more than sixty of our recent clients become national bestselling authors (hitting the major lists such as *USA Today, The Wall Street Journal, Publishers Weekly, SUCCESS* magazine, and/or *The New York Times*) is by triangulating thousands of data points to trace exactly what works in the public domain of selling books. One of the areas we have analyzed where we started to notice statistically significant patterns was related to book titles. Shockingly, we found some repeating patterns in books that consistently sell the most copies that point much more to the way a book is titled than to the way it is written. It was that research that led us to ultimately create what we now teach to our clients as The Five Title Tests.

TITLE TEST #1–THE "I WANT BLANK" TEST

This first test is so magnificently simple that you are likely not going to believe how well it works. However, I *promise* you that this is the single most important of The Five Title Tests. This first test is the most predictable in its performance, the most perfect in its application, and the most powerful in its payoff to you.

We call it the "I want blank" test. If your book (or speech, product, service offering, webpage headline, etc.) title completes the sentence "I want blank" in a way that is coherent and enticing for your Avatar, you have a great title! If it doesn't do that, then chances are your title is no good and you should reconsider.

Here are some examples of books that sell extremely well and consistently over a long period of time. Notice how each of the following titles, when inserted, almost perfectly completes the sentence, "I want _____":

- *Good to Great* (Jim Collins)
- *The 21 Irrefutable Laws of Leadership* (John Maxwell)
- *How to Win Friends and Influence People* (Dale Carnegie)
- *The 7 Habits of Highly Effective People* (Dr. Stephen R. Covey)
- *Profit First* (Mike Michalowicz)
- *Emotional Intelligence* (Travis Bradberry)
- *The Total Money Makeover* (Dave Ramsey)

- *The Secret* (Rhonda Byrne)
- *Money* (Tony Robbins)
- *The 48 Laws of Power* (Robert Greene)
- *Influence* (Dr. Robert Cialdini)
- *12 Rules for Life: An Antidote for Chaos* (Jordan Peterson)

Does following the "I want <u>blank</u>" test guarantee your book will be a bestseller? Of course not. Does that mean *only* books that pass the "I want <u>blank</u>" test will ever become a bestseller? Again, no. But if you look at the number of nonfiction books that have sold more than one million copies and become perennial bestsellers, there is an unusually strong correlation and over-indexing of titles that satisfy this powerful, simple test. And there are many, many more than just the ones I've listed here.

Common sense alone can corroborate this strategy because of how compelling the principle is on its own accord. Consider the long-standing perennial bestselling title *Think & Grow Rich* by Napoleon Hill. What a phenomenal title! Look at the promise the book gives you: I don't even have to *do anything*! I can merely *think* and become rich. Powerful.

Think & Grow Rich is a wonderful book, but I have to say that—in spite of so many people talking about it all the time—I don't find much in it that isn't also written about in dozens of other books about personal development and success.

Similarly, consider the genre of Christian Living. How many books in that category do you think are published every year? It's hard to know for sure, but devotionals alone number at least in the *thousands* according to *Publisher's Weekly*.[44] Think about how hard it might be to stand out in a genre with that many *new* titles coming out every year! And yet, there is one that has sold over fifty million copies and been translated into 137 languages! What's the title? *The Purpose Driven Life* by Rick Warren. Circumstantial? Possibly, but I think not. I mean, who doesn't want a *purpose-driven life*?

I'm certainly not suggesting that the quality of the writing in the book doesn't matter. But I would say that while many of these runaway bestsellers contain quality writing, most of them are not the groundbreaking, Nobel Prize–winning, never-before-heard, completely original tomes articulated with Pulitzer-caliber prose that you might assume would be a prerequisite of legitimate longstanding bestsellers. Is it possible that something else is at play in addition to the writing and the ideas themselves—perhaps something more deeply ingrained into the reader's subconscious? Our data suggests there likely is, and the "I want blank" test captures the very best of it in its most practical expression.

This leads me to what I believe is perhaps the most brilliant book title in recent years. This book has sold millions of copies, been translated into forty languages, and spent four years on the *New York Times* bestsellers list.[45] What book am I talking about? *The 4-Hour Workweek* by Tim Ferriss. Spectacular! I'm pretty sure that every single employed person on the planet would agree, "I want a four-hour workweek."

Let's return to my personal example of my second book title for a moment. How many people do you think want to *multiply time*? It's at least five million, according to the success of my TEDx talk, and my guess is it's a whole lot more than that. On the other hand, how many people want to *procrastinate on purpose*? A quick glance at the low sales will tell you it's far fewer, for sure. Once you fully grasp the "I want blank" concept, you'll start to see these examples all over the place.

TITLE TEST #2–THE CLARITY TEST

The Clarity Test is another tool that helps shape our titles in a way that syncs up with what we know to be true about the human brain from neuroscience. To understand the foundation of why this test is so important, you must remember the role of the brain's reticular activating system (RAS), which we briefly mentioned in chapter 5. As a reminder, the RAS determines what the brain pays attention to and what it ignores, which is extremely relevant when assessing what to title your various works as a content creator. Thus, before you have any chance at capturing someone's attention, you have to structure your title in a way that makes the RAS in their brain "wake up."

Things we don't understand or know anything about are not things we can pay attention to because we don't know that we should. For example, chances are you don't spend much time worrying about advancements in calculus or thinking about the newest technology to perform heart surgery. That's because, unless you work directly in those fields or have some personal experience that intersects with them, you ignore the data. The biological design of other people will cause them to do the exact same thing to your brand if it doesn't clearly and immediately present itself in a way that makes it relevant to them. This is why we started the chapter with one of our most powerful epiphanies, which is that "clear is greater than clever."

The more explanation a title requires, the less effective the title becomes.

As a consumer, a clever title is something I have to stop and try to understand. But beyond that, if your title is even a little obscure and doesn't make a direct, obvious connection to your Avatar, their brains will not take the time to figure it out; in fact, they will deliberately ignore it entirely. The more explanation a title requires, the less effective the title becomes. This is demonstrated in our Clarity Continuum framework. Ask yourself, *Where is my title on this spectrum?*

Title Clarity Continuum

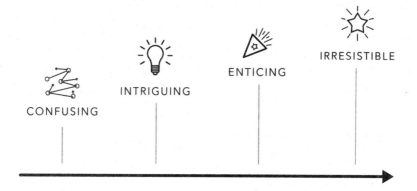

Again, using my second book as a case study, which of these two concepts is clearer in what they are about and what they offer to a potential consumer?

- How to Multiply Time
- Procrastinate on Purpose

One is clear and enticing. The other is convoluted and confusing. One makes someone think, *I need that!* The other makes them think, *I wonder what that means?* You don't want your title to be intriguing; you want it to be enticing! If possible, you want it to be *irresistible*. *Think & Grow Rich*, *The 4-Hour Workweek*, *The Purpose Driven Life*, and *The 48 Laws of Power*—now *those* are irresistible!

TITLE TEST #3—THE POSITIVE ENERGY TEST

When my oldest son was about three and a half years old, he would come barreling into my office every day after he woke up from his afternoon nap and do something very curious. My office is covered in books—all kinds of books with all kinds of covers. Every time Jasper came in, he would grab the exact same book. Even when I would put the book back in a different location, he would come in and find that book the very next time. For a while it baffled me. Out of all of these books in my office, why did he always choose the same one?

The book was called *Never Eat Alone* by Keith Ferrazzi. Considering my son was not yet reading nor looking to consciously build his professional networking skills, I was fascinated by what drew him to this book time and time again. And then it became obvious: It was the *color* of the book jacket! If you've ever seen the book before, you know the jacket is bright orange!

In watching my toddler's behavior, I was awakened to what would later become the third of our Five Title Tests: The Positive Energy Test. Words, colors, and images all have energy, and humans are generally drawn toward positive energy and repelled by negative energy. Further, our RAS is most likely to ignore, overlook, and disregard anything that is neutral energy. This insight reminded me once again about *The 4-Hour Workweek*. Not only is it a phenomenal title, but if you look at the cover of the book, it also has an image on it. What's the image? A man lying in a hammock between two palm trees! And what is right underneath the picture? The subtitle: "Escape 9–5, Live Anywhere, and Join the New Rich." Brilliant!

> *Humans are generally drawn toward positive energy and repelled by negative energy.*

Make no mistake, Timothy Ferriss was either already a marketing genius or he had one on his team. Even more telling is the fact that Tim's original book cover was white and muted gold—somewhat unnoticeable. But guess what color he changed the book jacket to when the "expanded and updated" edition came out a few years later? You guessed it. Bright orange!

In addition to colors and images having energy, so do words in and of themselves. We started analyzing this trait and identified a set of strong correlative examples of bestsellers with the Positive

Energy Test. Notice the intensity and positivity associated with some of these titles:

- *The Miracle Morning* (Hal Elrod; image of an expansive sunrise on the cover)
- *Chicken Soup for the Soul* (Jack Canfield and Mark Victor Hansen)
- *Daring Greatly* (Brené Brown)
- *Heaven Is for Real* (Lynn Vincent and Todd Burpo; bright yellow book jacket)
- *Raving Fans* (Ken Blanchard and Sheldon Bowles)
- *The Happiness Project* (Gretchen Rubin)
- *The Energy Bus* (Jon Gordon; also a bright yellow book jacket)

Does this mean that by using outrageous superlatives in your book titles or only vibrant color palettes, you'll automatically become a bestseller? Surely not. But there is enough evidence here that you should pay attention to it. I am suggesting that you be extremely deliberate about the *energy* that each individual word, color, and image carries in your marketing assets.

For example, a quick online search for "home organization books" returns *hundreds* of options. But what's the title of the one that has sold fourteen million copies worldwide and been translated into forty-four languages?[46] It's none other than *The Life-Changing Magic of Tidying Up*, by Marie Kondo. Marie's title is off the charts on the "I want <u>blank</u>" test, the Clarity Test, and certainly the Positive Energy Test! Who doesn't want "life-changing magic?!" Oh, and by the way, her other book, *Spark Joy*, has also sold nearly a half million copies of just hardcover formats in the US alone . . . but who's counting?[47]

Clearly this wasn't something that a younger Rory Vaden paid any attention to. Do you think the word MULTIPLY has positive or negative energy? *Multiply* is arguably one of the most positively charged words in the English language. It suggests expansive, prom-ising, grand, and abundant. But what about the word PROCRAS-TINATE? Would you say that word has positive or negative energy? It's probably one of the most negative words in the English language! Who would ever think to use that word in big, bold, embossed letters right on a book cover? Oh yeah, this guy right here—or at least his younger, less informed self! Please don't make the same painful and expensive mistakes I have.

TITLE TEST #4–THE NATIVE TONGUE TEST

In our Avatar chapter we talked about the importance of starting with *who*. When selecting your titles and headlines in your marketing, you also want to give special consideration to *who* you are trying to attract. Every psychographic group has a nomenclature of insider terms they use and recognize. Thus, it's important when you choose the words that will be front and center in your various promotions that you select them from a lexicon your ideal receiver will be familiar with.

The Native Tongue Test is powerful because it immediately awakens the RAS of the intended recipient. By using certain and specific words, you can trigger the subconscious to pay attention. A few examples of successful books that have executed this title strategy well are:

- *What to Expect When You're Expecting* (for moms, by Heidi Murkoff and Sharon Mazel)
- *The Lean Startup* (for entrepreneurs, by Eric Ries)
- *Never Split the Difference* (for anyone who negotiates, by Chris Voss)
- *The Happiest Baby on the Block* (for parents with newborns, by Dr. Harvey Karp)
- *The Case for Christ* (for any skeptics of Christianity, by Lee Strobel)

- *Blitzscaling* (for entrepreneurs, by Reid Hoffman and Chris Yeh)
- *Unreasonable Hospitality* (for anyone in a service business, by Will Guidara)

Make a list of all the insider terms your Avatar or target industry uses, and then ask yourself, *When, where, and how can I insert these terms into my titles to immediately grab people's attention?* We believe the future of marketing is about hyper-specificity, and one of the fastest and easiest ways to capitalize upon that is to use the precise language that "your people" are using.

TITLE TEST #5—THE MEMORABILITY TEST

I have been highlighting our mistitling foes with my second book, but what is the explanation for the success of my first book, *Take the Stairs*? I would describe *Take the Stairs* as a book filled with powerful fundamental and foundational principles of personal development. Part of what makes the book appealing is how palatable it is for people of every age, industry, income level, and geographical location. But I'll be the first to admit that, except for a few personal stories and some insightful one-liners, there aren't a lot of *radically unique* concepts in the book. In fact, I would say that *Procrastinate on Purpose* is the much smarter book, with more original thought leadership. Why, then, does *Take the Stairs* continue to sell thousands of copies year after year after well over a decade, in spite of not really passing any of the other Five Title Tests?

The answer is The Memorability Test. **Half the battle of having a successful book (or title of any kind) is simply being remembered.** How many times have you had a conversation in which you were talking about a great book you had just read but you couldn't remember the author's name or the title? It happens a lot. And when it does happen, it radically impacts the author's career. Contrast that with a book title that is easily memorable. That book, along with its corresponding sales, naturally propagates through word-of-mouth. This is what happened with my first book.

If you've ever read *Take the Stairs* or heard my keynote speech on the same topic, you will never, ever look at another escalator for the rest of your life and not think of me. I use *Take the Stairs* as a metaphor for how the most successful people in the world have developed one single habit: doing things they don't want to do. The metaphor, which also serves as a mnemonic anchor—or memory aid—is so strong that it's nearly impossible to forget.

I believe this is the same reason why my friend Brian Tracy's book *Eat That Frog* outsells his other books by more than three times. (Brian has written more than eighty books.) If you've never heard that metaphor before, it won't mean much to you. But if you were to listen to Brian speak, you would likely hear him say something similar to this: "If you eat a frog first thing in the morning, then that is the hardest thing you will do that day. As such, one of the greatest keys to productivity is to do your most difficult task first thing in the morning—and if you do that, the rest of your day will be much easier." After hearing that metaphor just one time, it's almost impossible to forget.

The same concept would be true for Spencer Johnson's legendary book *Who Moved My Cheese?* which has sold millions of copies. His motivational fable is a story of two mice navigating a "maze" (representing life's challenges) to find "cheese" (representing our desires). The book teaches the importance of embracing change. And frequently, when the topic of "change" comes up in a corporate setting, someone references Spencer's metaphor. Rachel Hollis wrote a book in 2018 called *Girl, Wash Your Face*, which also sold millions of copies. That title is also based on a metaphor of self-reliance as if to say, "Pick yourself up by your bootstraps."

Metaphors work as titles when they have clear connections to the message and when they are truly memorable. However, we view metaphors as extremely risky because there is a high chance of violating the Clarity Test, which is much more important. The other issue with metaphors is that they often mean something to people who have been exposed to the explanation, but not much to someone who hasn't. For example, one reason *Take the Stairs* likely sells as well as it does is because it's super memorable for the people who have read it, so they talk about it with their friends. However, one reason it doesn't sell more is because a stranger who sees the book on a shelf is much less likely to pick it up because the title *Take the Stairs* doesn't strongly satisfy any of the other title tests. While being remembered is super important, it's far from the only thing to consider when selecting a title.

SELECTING TOP TITLES

The main reason why most titles are terrible is because so many authors inadvertently believe they must communicate their primary message or instruction from inside the book on the front cover. That's not only unnecessary, but it's basically a recipe for a mediocre (at best) title. Instead, smart authors know that great titles promote the destination and not the journey.

Let's pretend for a moment that I was trying to sell you a vacation. I'm going to present it two different ways and then you ask to decide which seems more appealing.

> *Smart authors know that great titles promote the destination and not the journey.*

Presentation #1

Imagine waking from a deep sleep on a bed that feels like a cloud. You step out onto the balcony of your suite to see an expansive electric-blue ocean just beyond the edge of brilliant white-powder sand. You'll be close enough to smell a hint of the fresh salt water as you notice the gentle warmth of perfect 80-degree weather greeting your skin. A knock on the door delivers your favorite gourmet breakfast prepared by one of our world-class chefs. You'll savor every bite as we use only the freshest ingredients, all grown within twenty-five miles of the resort and handpicked by our team. As you lounge on the deck enjoying your breakfast, you'll look past a row of palm trees and just over our magnificent garden to see the luxurious spa where you'll spend the afternoon getting pampered and refreshed.

Sounds pretty good right? Now how about this one . . .

Presentation #2

Imagine waking up to a blaring alarm at 3:45 a.m. You'll have to fight through exhaustion as you jump up and down on your suitcase trying to slam it shut. You'll load up in the car with your screaming children, who are complaining about how early it is. You'll sit in early morning traffic due to late night construction, causing you to run late so that you arrive to the airport in a panic and a flat-out sprint. After waiting at check-in for an unnecessarily long time, being charged extra fees for your bags, and getting frisked by security because you've been "randomly selected," you finally take your seat on the plane only to find out you are stuck in a middle seat for the next four and a half hours. You'll get terrible coffee on the plane and upon landing at your destination, you'll wait in baggage claim for two hours after discovering that they lost your bag. After that, you'll crawl into the back row of a beat-up van and hold on for dear life as the suspicious-looking driver races like a speed demon through dangerous neighborhoods in what you can only hope is the direction of your hotel and not to some remote part of this island where tourists get stranded and have to pay their way out.

So, what do you think?

If you've ever traveled internationally, you'll realize that those could be two accurate descriptions of the exact same trip! What's the primary difference that is responsible for their stark differentiation? Simple: The first one describes the destination. The second describes the journey it takes to get there. Master marketers and savvy salespeople know that the destination is always the part that is appealing and enticing and attractive. Meanwhile, the journey to get there is often long, arduous, and exhausting.

The difference between the destination and the journey is almost always true in any context. What people *want* is the destination. They want the result. They want the reward that awaits at the end of the rainbow. What they *don't* want is all the work it takes to get there. Now, this doesn't mean you aren't going to be forthright with people about the work it takes to create meaningful change in their lives. It just means that you aren't going to do that on the cover of your book, on the home page of your website, or in the first line of your email. Eventually, you *will* tell people about the work it takes to succeed inside the "Book" (or program or course or service, etc.) because creating any change in your life requires work. But save the work and the description of the journey for inside the book.

On the front cover, in the first sentence of the email, on the main headline of your website is where you share the "Hook." The Hook is the description of the thing they want. It's an explanation of the payoff that results if you do the work that is explained inside the "Book." Your titles should be birthed out of the payoffs that will emerge in someone's life if they follow your advice, complete your program, or execute upon your recommended steps. But don't try and tell them your advice right up front. Rather, if you want people to engage with your offers, you will be wise to center your titles and headlines on describing the destination and not the journey.

So, how do you attract people to see and consider your offers in the first place? That's a good question and what we're going to tackle next!

CHAPTER 9

EXPERT BIO

BY AJ VADEN

C an you imagine spending $750,000 to capture a single photo? According to a former Wynn Resorts senior executive Nehme Abouzeid, that is exactly what the world-renowned hotel did as part of what ultimately created a $20 billion tourism boom for Las Vegas casinos in the early 2000s[48]—in addition to their $6 billion in annual gambling revenue.[49]

During a speech I attended, Abouzeid shared the story about how multiple high-end resorts all contributed to rebranding the image of Las Vegas. Prior to the 2000s, Vegas was not well-known for fine dining and luxury experiences. Together, however, big investors and strategic marketers repositioned an entire city from a desert truck stop to a worldwide entertainment destination.

Part of the strategy, at least for Abouzeid's team, was to strive for meticulous detail, stringently hire the best talent, and relentlessly obsess over lighting to capture the essence of the Wynn nightclub. They engaged in detailed planning, assembled a top creative team, arranged for the perfect shot, and waited until just the right time of day. They then went back into the editing room to perfectly manicure the photo during post-production to create and convey the exact *feeling* they wanted people to experience when looking at it.

This six-figure investment seems to have paid off. That particular picture became one of the most defining images for the Wynn Hotel and Casino. According to Abouzeid, the use of this single photo in advertisements generated millions of dollars in revenue because of its ability to create mass appeal and attract people to the new Vegas lifestyle. (If you search for "Wynn XS Nightclub VIP," you will likely find the photo.)

Why spend so much time and money on a single photo?

Simple: emotions.

Imagery and words create emotions, and emotions play a huge role in people's purchasing decisions. Regardless of whether you personally believe in the value of this type of investment, it points to an important lesson that applies to personal branding: People buy the packaging as much as they buy the product.

> **People buy the packaging as much as they buy the product.**

The packaging matters a lot. The aesthetic, the music, the lighting, the photography, the fonts, the animation, the colors, and so many other factors all contribute to creating an energy and a set of emotions that, when bundled together, communicate the essence of a brand. Now, I'm not going to recommend that you spend hundreds of thousands of dollars on photography; that's not the smartest use of your first dollars. But I am going to invite you to apply the lesson of packaging to a brand asset of yours that is of equal or greater importance to the marketplace—and free for you to create.

FREE $1 MILLION ASSET

I'm going to guide you through creating what I have come to believe is one of the most important marketing assets of your personal brand. It will take only minutes to craft but, if created properly, can make you millions of dollars. Why do I say that? Because it has made our clients millions of dollars—and it has helped Rory and me generate millions of dollars in revenue.

How is that possible?

Because this asset has been an instrumental piece in helping us get invited on the biggest podcasts in the world. It has helped us secure slots on the biggest speaking stages across the globe. It has opened doors to some of the biggest media opportunities in the world. This asset has provided us with introductions to some of the most influential people in the world. It is the asset that led to us getting invited into some of the most powerful boardrooms. And when I got fired and lost my income, team, and contacts, this was the only asset I was left with—from which we rebuilt everything in just five years.

As we've mentioned earlier, when we started Brand Builders Group, we had no website, database, social media followers, technology, flyers or marketing assets, logos, brand guidelines, or fancy photography. We also had no customers. But we did have one thing— something you have, as well, and something *no one can ever take away from any of us.*

What is the asset I am talking about?

It is your Expert Bio.

An Expert Bio is a specific type of bio. It is one paragraph that is deliberately curated to communicate the value and credibility you offer to the world. There is a good chance, if you are like most people, that you highly underestimate the power and importance of your bio. Chances are, you have spent little time crafting it, perhaps overlooking its power and treating it more like an afterthought. Be honest with yourself: When was the last time you updated your bio? And how much care and attention did you really put into it?

Rory updates his bio almost monthly. He is constantly refining it, editing it, tweaking it, and pouring over every single word to create exactly the perception he wants the recipient to have when they read it. In fact, every time Rory gets introduced to a new high-profile relationship, he spends several minutes tailoring his bio in a way that will most resonate with the person he's being connected to. He hand-selects precisely what words and references to use to maximize the speed of the "trust transfer" that will take place from his introducer to his new contact.

Similarly, every time he introduces relationships from his network to one another, he personally writes an uplifting and properly positioned Expert Bio for the two friends that he is connecting so *they* can become quickly acquainted and are both edified right from the beginning.

WHY AN EXPERT BIO

As we defined it earlier, a personal brand is simply the formalization of your reputation. Your Expert Bio is the first material expression of your reputation. Perhaps no other asset aligns more purely with your "reputation" than your Expert Bio. You are going to tell your entire personal and professional life story in just a few sentences. Thus, you are consolidating and codifying everything you've ever done into something that others can digest in a few seconds.

Part of the effectiveness of an Expert Bio is its low-profile ability to go unnoticed. Prospects are typically consciously aware when they are consuming marketing collateral. They *know* when they are on your website, looking at your social media, reviewing your press kit, or watching your media reel or demo video that you have assembled as a highlight reel for them to review. However, when we read about someone, we tend to process it more like a story or a biography than we do as marketing collateral or a pitch deck. It's for these reasons that we help clients create their Expert Bio as their first and most important external facing asset of their personal brand.

LANDSCAPE VS. PORTRAIT VIEW

In order to understand the key strategy to writing a great bio, we're going to once again return to the world of photography. The biggest secret to crafting a persuasive and compelling bio that will open doors for you is understanding the difference between *landscape view* and *portrait view*.

Landscape view is wide and broad and zoomed out. Portrait view, on the other hand, is tight, close, narrow, focused, and zoomed in. All Expert Bios are a recount of a person's past, and the key to writing a great bio is to know when to use landscape view and when to use portrait view.

There are certain elements of your past you'll want to zoom in on. There will be specific things you've done that you'll want to highlight, celebrate, and accentuate. There are parts of your story and specific tidbits of information that you'll want to present so that no one will miss them. Those elements, of course, are the things you've done that are most impressive. We zoom in on those aspects just as you would in portrait view.

But then, we all have parts of our backstory that aren't as impressive or well-known. Perhaps they are newer or underdeveloped or not representative of who we are. Whenever that's the case, we deliberately are *not* going to draw attention to those specifics. We'll let them fade into the distance. For these parts of our past, we're going to use general, broad, and sweeping language. The strategy here is to tell those aspects quickly and to bundle the facts that best position us and our expertise. We will do that without highlighting or zooming in on the places where we may have less experience. This is the landscape view.

These two techniques effectively make up our entire strategy for crafting the perfect Expert Bio. Let's take a closer look at each one.

PORTRAIT VIEW

Portrait View is the most important part of your Expert Bio because those are the primary elements you'll focus on to help establish your credibility. There are two ridiculously easy strategies for reinforcing portrait view: adding names and numbers. While this is incredibly simple, again please do not underestimate its power. The secret to writing a persuasive Expert Bio is to simply add names and numbers whenever possible.

The secret to writing a persuasive Expert Bio is to simply add names and numbers whenever possible.

What exactly do I mean by names and numbers?

Whenever you are writing your bio, you want to look for opportunities to insert specific names of people and/or organizations and exact numbers associated with your experience.

When it comes to sharing names in your bio, there are a few immediate opportunities:

- Names of (recognizable) individual people you have worked with
- Names of (recognizable) individual people who have endorsed you
- Names of companies or associations you have worked with
- Names of media outlets you have been featured in
- Names of organizations where you have spoken
- Names of institutions where you have received training or education
- Names of specific awards or titles you have earned

Take a look at these examples and ask yourself which one is most powerful:

- She has a bachelor's degree from a recognizable university. (Landscape view) OR
- She graduated summa cum laude from Stanford University with a bachelor's in Leadership Communication. (Portrait view)

Which of these two is most influential:

- Rory is an award-winning speaker. (Landscape view) OR
- Rory is a Hall of Fame Speaker and two-time Toastmasters World Champion of Public Speaking Finalist out of over 90,000 contestants. (Portrait view)

And which of these two would make you more likely to book this person on your show:

- She has been interviewed in the media. (Landscape view) OR
- Her insights have been featured in *The Wall Street Journal* and *The New York Times* and on Fox News and ABC's *Good Morning America*. (Portrait view)

Which of these two companies would you hire to coach you on building your personal brand:

- Brand Builders Group is a top personal brand strategy firm. (Landscape view)
- Brand Builders Group has been a part of building the personal brands for people like Lewis Howes, Ed Mylett, Amy Porterfield, Eric "ET Hip Hop Preacher" Thomas, Jasmine Star, John Maxwell, Luvvie Ajayi Jones, Trent Shelton, Natalie Ellis, and more. (Portrait view)

The answer is obvious when looking at it like this, and yet we see clients all the time with terribly generic bios that vastly undersell themselves and the quality of their experience. Notice how this simple technique of zooming in on a particular fact exponentially improves the level of perceived credibility to the reader. It's so simple and so incredibly powerful because you are drafting off the reputation and trust of the specific names you are referencing, many of which will be more recognizable than your own, especially when you are starting out.

By the way, the concept of adding Names to bolster your credibility isn't just my opinion. We have proven this through academic sampling and statistically significant data gathered from our Trends in Personal Branding National Research Study.

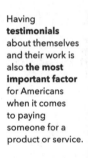

Having **testimonials** about themselves and their work is also **the most important factor** for Americans when it comes to paying someone for a product or service.

Q: How important are each of the following when it comes to paying someone more for a product or a service?

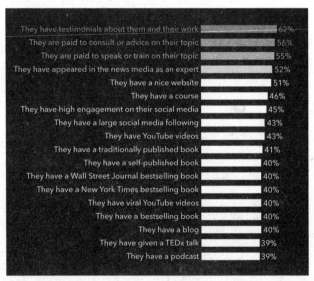

They have testimonials about them and their work	62%
They are paid to consult or advice on their topic	56%
They are paid to speak or train on their topic	55%
They have appeared in the news media as an expert	52%
They have a nice website	51%
They have a course	46%
They have high engagement on their social media	45%
They have a large social media following	43%
They have YouTube videos	43%
They have a traditionally published book	41%
They have a self-published book	40%
They have a Wall Street Journal bestselling book	40%
They have a New York Times bestselling book	40%
They have viral YouTube videos	40%
They have a bestselling book	40%
They have a blog	40%
They have given a TEDx talk	39%
They have a podcast	39%

One of the questions we asked was, "How important are each of the following when it comes to paying someone more for a product or a service?" We listed several options. The top four were:

- They have testimonials about them and their work (62 percent).
- They are paid to consult or advise on their topic (56 percent).

- They are paid to speak or train on their topic (55 percent).
- They have appeared in the news media as an expert (52 percent).

All four relate *specifically* to entities that can be named in your Expert Bio. So, just as we mentioned with your Avatar, Brand Positioning Statement, and Primary Business Model, this is another case where "the more specific, the more terrific!"

People tend to assign more credibility for specificity than generality.

In addition to using Names, you will also want to use Numbers in your Expert Bio to add credibility. People tend to assign more credibility for specificity than generality. Numbers are powerful because while some people may or may not recognize the Names you use, nearly everyone can recognize Numbers in a way that immediately creates context for your credibility. Another benefit of Numbers is that every single one of our clients has Numbers they can use in their Expert Bio, even if they don't have any Names to use.

You might include Numbers such as:

- Number of years you have been in business
- Number of clients you have serviced
- Number of hours/years you have spent on research
- Number of your speaking engagements or states/continents you've spoken in
- Number of times you've been interviewed in the media
- Number of articles you've written
- Number of people on your team
- Number of total online followers or impressions your content has received
- Revenue size of the organization you run
- Any number(s) related to the average results your clients achieve

Would you rather hire:

- A surgeon who is fresh out of med school. (Landscape view) OR
- A surgeon who has successfully conducted more than three hundred operations. (Portrait view)

Would you personally be more compelled by:

- A groundbreaking new fitness fad (Landscape view) OR
- A program that has helped more than 1,000 people lower their cholesterol, improve skeletal muscle, and decrease their chances of life-altering illness by 50 percent (Portrait view)

Who do you think can help you more when it comes to your publishing career:

- An author who has written a book (Landscape view) OR
- A *New York Times* bestselling author with more than one million copies sold (Portrait view)

And which of the following would you be more likely to take business advice from:

- A serial entrepreneur (Landscape view) OR
- An entrepreneur who has generated hundreds of millions in revenue and had four exits with a combined enterprise value of $1 billion (Portrait view)

At first, you might be intimidated by reading some of these and thinking that you don't have such compelling numbers, but I bet you do! All of us have numbers as a part of our business and personal brand. If you're a Realtor, it might be how many homes you've sold, your average sale price, or the total dollar amount of your historical transactions. If you're a financial advisor, it might be how much capital you have under management. If you're a chiropractor, it might be how many patients you've seen in your career. For any of us who create consistent content on social media, even if your follower counts aren't that impressive, if you add up the cumulative number of impressions you've had on all your content, I bet *that* would be impressive! Train your brain to look for numbers in your business that showcase your credibility, and I promise you will find some.

LANDSCAPE VIEW

With Portrait View, you are zooming in on your most credibility-boosting, hyper-specific details. On the other hand, with Landscape View you are going to zoom out from individual details that are not as impressive, then bundle the more general parts of your story using broad brushstrokes that still position you nicely for how you want to be seen.

For example, let's pretend you haven't worked with any publicly recognizable clients, you haven't won any specific awards, and you haven't (yet) spoken on any large stages or been featured in any major media outlets. If that's you, welcome to the party! That's how we all started. What's most important for you to know is that the things we zoom in on in Portrait View are not the things that *actually* make you credible; they are just the things the public leans on for *perceived* credibility.

Just because your bio doesn't include some of those notable items doesn't mean you are not credible. It just means you haven't yet racked up some of the designations the general population assigns credibility to. Your *actual* credibility comes from experience and education, not from media attention and popularity. Please don't cut yourself short by mistaking one for the other.

Now, in the absence of some major "credibility triggers," we're just going to take a more Landscape View approach to your experience.

Instead of specifics, you are going to use more encompassing terms to describe yourself, such as:

- Fastest growing
- Industry leading
- Widely regarded
- Highly recognized
- Tenured and experienced
- Well respected
- Sought after
- Leading expert
- Nationally (or World) renowned

Please don't hear what I'm not saying: I am *not* telling you to lie! You should not say anything that isn't truthful. But these types of terms are incredibly subjective. The only gatekeeper and judge of whether you should use them is you. And if you have some basis and reference point that you can use to justify them (or similar terms), then by all means use them! (*One caveat is that we are **not** advocates of personal brands singling themselves out as "world's greatest" or "#1" or "absolute best" unless you've been given some specific award or title by an objective third party. Even if you have, our advice is to be respectful of your colleagues; you will get much further if you support one another versus compete for ranking*).

More often than not, however, most of us do not tend to have the problem of hubris. Instead, we are so focused on humility that we under-serve ourselves and our market by hiding our accomplishments and dimming the value of our expertise. Remember that confidence is not the opposite of humility; pride is. Confidence is more the opposite of incompetence. If you know you can do the job well and help create a positive result in the lives of others, then you should be moving through the world with lots of confidence. That is completely independent and irrespective of a measure of pride or humility.

Humility is not a measure of how good you do something; it's a measure of who you do it for. Humility comes from a predisposition and orientation that is focused on helping others. Hubris or pride, on the other hand, is predicated on a predisposition and orientation of propping up your own ego or being driven for attention. **Pride is about self. Humility is about service.** That is why it is possible to have both high confidence and high humility at the same time. You can be highly confident and highly service-centered simultaneously.

> *Remember that confidence is not the opposite of humility; pride is.*

In fact, your Expert Bio has nothing to do with you being arrogant. It's simply demonstrating that you have earned the right to talk on this subject. Why have you earned that right? Because you're most powerfully positioned to serve the person you once were. You have lived it. You have gone through it, you've studied it, and you've helped others go on the path, which means you have earned the right to talk about it and teach it.

And if you have not yet walked down the path, helped other people down the path, or at least studied it, then you really shouldn't be selling your expertise on it just yet. If your background lacks any validity for saying the things you are saying, then you're probably not operating in your Uniqueness, which means you need to go back and start the Brand Positioning Statement work over. But I believe you most likely *do* have credibility.

Getting this far into this book almost guarantees that you are feeling called to use your experience and education to improve the lives of others. Otherwise, you wouldn't still be reading this! So, it's likely that you do have expertise. You do have education. You do have experience. You just happen to be one of the world's best-kept secrets. And perhaps the reason you're one of the world's best-kept secrets is because you haven't yet broken through the wall and developed the confidence necessary to promote and celebrate the professional expertise you have to share!

That is why it's possible this Expert Bio is less an academic exercise of properly documenting and displaying your credibility and more a mental exercise of moving past your own limiting beliefs. We never want to lie or even stretch the truth, but we do want to accentuate the high points that hold you up in the best light based on the work you've put in. Landscape View is simply about bundling all those things to equate to subjective terms you can use to describe yourself that are both elevating and fair. You want to be accurate but also accentuate.

One way you can position facts as "accurate but accentuates" is to apply the laws of Portrait View and Landscape View. The chart below demonstrates accurate details on the left (portrait) while showcasing how we can accentuate those facts (landscape) on the right.

It Is Not	It Is
2	Multiple
24	Dozens
Top 200	Top 1%
Canada & US	International

BIO BRAINSTORM

Your Expert Bio starts with a brainstorm of everything you've ever done that could even remotely or possibly contribute to your credibility. Below you will see a list of memory joggers that we hope will help you remember awesome things you have done.

Answer the following fifteen questions for yourself and your own backstory. And remember, don't edit; just write.

1. What are you the author, creator, or host of? (Think books, e-books, articles, research reports, white papers, courses, programs, podcasts, YouTube channels, apps, communities, movements, etc.)
2. What are you the founder of?
3. How long have you been in business or active in your area of expertise?
4. How many businesses have you founded, purchased, owned, spoken to, consulted for, worked with?
5. How much revenue have you sold, produced, generated, managed, raised, or donated?
6. How many people have you served, helped, reached, or spoken to?
7. Who have you worked with (companies or individuals)?
8. What results have you achieved or helped others achieve?
9. What media outlets have you been featured in?
10. What degrees, certifications, or designations do you hold?
11. What are you a member of?
12. What awards have you won?
13. What topics could you or do you speak on?
14. What have you studied or researched?
15. What are you an expert in?

The next step is to go through your answers and circle the top ten most compelling "credibility triggers" relevant to the type of expertise you want to be associated with. As you identify those elements, designate which pieces you are going to focus on with Portrait View and which ones you will broadly group together for Landscape View. After you've done a complete brain dump of every possible credibility-building element of your backstory, you can now decide what to leave out. Or as we like to say, highlight the best and leave out the rest.

One advanced trick for strengthening your positioning is to use a combination of Portrait View and Landscape View. You may find that certain parts of your story are impressive while other accompanying parts aren't. For example, let's say you've spoken at multiple universities, none of which are all that prestigious. But then you get an invitation to speak at Duke University. Now, you can update your bio to say something like, "[Name] is frequently invited to speak for higher-education programs and leading academic institutions such as Duke University." It is fully true and accurate but also accentuates to elevate. Whenever using the technique of combining Portrait View with Landscape View, the key is to include the credibility points of "the greatest common denominator." Mention only the specifics that are most recognizable while leaving out any less reputable instances, and group them together broadly.

Highlight the best and leave out the rest.

EXPERT BIO TEMPLATE

If you are still struggling to get words on a page, we understand, which is why we created a simple tool that any personal brand can use to immediately write a more attention-worthy bio.

We call it the Expert Bio Template, and we modeled it from Mad Libs games—the ones with a story that is purposefully left incomplete for you to fill in the blanks. Each blank comes with a short instruction of what type of word should occupy that slot. As a player, all you must do is follow the instructions to complete each blank with no context, and then you have the fun of going back and reading the story to see how it turned out.

The Expert Bio Template functions in a similar manner. A major difference, however, is that the goal is not to make people laugh but rather to make people buy! You certainly don't have to use this, but if you are struggling to write your own Expert Bio, this template will help you get that first draft complete. Simply fill in each of the following blanks with the relevant information about you and your past experience. Once your draft is complete, you can use a little AI assistance to help you sharpen, soften, or create various versions to get it to where you want.

Expert Bio Template
By Brand Builders Group

_____ is the _____ _____ on _____. S/he has worked with
[Your Name]   [leading credential   [job title]   [topic]
                         adjective]

_____ of _____ _____ from _____ like _____
[x#]   [adjective] [companies/organizations   [geography]   [1-3 recognizable client
                        /etc.]   names]

to _____.
   [insert client payoffs/results]

With _____ on _____ and _____
     [formal education or research   [topic]   [# years of work exp./companies worked]
     credentials]

s/he is _____ _____ by _____.
        [adjective "widely regarded"]   [avatar job titles]

His/her insights have been _____ in _____ _____
                           [featured/mentioned/seen/heard]   [adjective]   [outlets/locations]

like _____.
     [insert most recognizable media outlets]

As a _____ s/he can help any _____ with _____ to experience _____
     [PBM service]   [avatar]   [problem]   [payoff/benefit]

through utilizing his/her _____ _____.
                          [adjective]   [insert branded methodology]

When the template is completed for a legitimate expert who has meaningful industry experience but who is not yet renowned, it might sound something like this:

Susie Jones is one of the world's emerging experts on the topic of menopause health. She has worked with some of the top-ranked hospital networks in the country, like HCA and Ascension Health, to provide more accessible answers to midlife women going through the menopausal transition. With hundreds of hours of professional training on perimenopausal and postmenopausal conditions and over fifteen years of experience as a nurse practitioner, she is widely regarded by healthcare practitioners as a trusted resource. Her insights have been featured in local and national news outlets including Women's Health *magazine. As a certified nutrition counselor, she can help any woman aged forty to sixty who is experiencing mood swings, hot flashes, weight gain, or any other common symptoms to experience improved quality of life through utilizing her proprietary Mid-life Lifestyle Adjustment System.*

Pretty compelling, right? If it works for our fictitious friend Susie Jones, it can work for you too!

HOW TO USE YOUR BIO TO GET BUSINESS

Once you have your newly improved bio, take the time to update it in places like LinkedIn, your website, your media kit, etc., which should help you bring more qualified prospects. But the most powerful way to use your bio is to give it to your friends, family, and past clients anytime you are trying to drum up media interviews, speaking opportunities, or new potential customers. In fact, if you were starting a new business, new revenue stream, or new idea from scratch, and you had no database or online following whatsoever, the simple four-step process detailed below could help you get your first five customers using your Expert Bio.

This is important because everyone thinks the way to launch something is with a massive audience, expensive paid advertising, or unpredictable viral social media campaigns to get those crucial first customers. When we're launching a new business, product, or revenue stream, it's natural to think we need to "go big," broadcast it everywhere, and sell to the masses. In reality, we've not seen that typically as the best way to get early financial traction. It's not that mass marketing is wrong; it's just that very often marketing is slow while selling is fast.

The best way to get quick wins and the fastest way to get your new endeavor off the ground is much simpler and more personal than that. It all starts with *referrals* from people who know you and who are willing to introduce you *via your Expert Bio* to other people they know.

Referrals are the secret sauce that most people either overlook or overcomplicate, so let's walk through exactly how this might work. Instead of selling to strangers on the internet, you're going to focus on working through real-life relationships with people who already know and trust you. But here's an important distinction: Don't try to sell to your friends; just ask them for referrals. If you try and sell to your friends and family, you're likely to make it awkward for everyone. Instead, just follow this four-step process to generate lots of warm leads quickly.

Step 1: Build Your "Fast 50" List

The first step is to create what I call a *Fast 50* list. This is a list of fifty people you know personally—friends, family, colleagues, or anyone with whom you have a genuine, trusting relationship. We're not talking about casual acquaintances. These should be people who know you well enough that they'd do you a small favor, and you'd be willing to do the same for them.

To make this easy, go through your phone contacts and ask yourself, *Who do I have a real connection with?* Write down their names until you have a list of fifty people.

Don't worry, you're not going to be asking any of these fifty people to buy anything from you. Instead, you're going to ask them to help connect you with the right people.

Step 2: Create a "Trust Soldier"

Instead of selling something to your Fast 50 or asking them to sell something for you, you are instead going to give them an asset that they can offer to others on your behalf. What we call a *Trust Soldier* is a free resource that adds value to people's lives while also building credibility for you and your brand.

> **Trust must always take place before there is a transaction.**

The three keys to an effective Trust Solider are that it must be helpful to the end user, it must align with your area of expertise, and it must have a call-to-action baked in that will invite the people who consume it to take the next step with you.

Here are a few examples of Trust Soldiers you could create:

- A PDF checklist or quick-start guide
- A free chapter or section of an e-book
- A copy of a content-rich slide deck, presentation, or report
- A 5–10 minute audio training on a key topic
- A short video series sharing helpful tips or insights
- A free ticket to a live workshop or webinar

- A podcast episode where you were the host or guest on your subject matter

By offering a Trust Soldier, you're providing value and establishing trust right up front—and that matters a lot, because, as we discussed in chapter 7, trust must always take place before there is a transaction.

Step 3: Reach Out to Your Fast 50 List and Ask for Referrals

Once you have your Trust Soldier ready, you simply reach out to your Fast 50 and ask them to help you share it with a few people they know who might benefit from it.

Here's a script you could use to reach out:

Hey [Name], I hope you're doing well! I wanted to share something exciting that's happening in my life—I've recently launched a new [business/product/service].

It's something I'm really passionate about, and I'd love to get it in front of people who might find it useful. As part of that, I've created a free resource on [what your free resource does] that I think could be helpful for anyone who is a [insert Avatar Persona]. I was wondering if you might be open to helping me. Could you think of five people who meet that criteria who might benefit from having this? And if possible, is there any chance that you would be open to sharing this free resource with them? If so, I'll send you something that you can just copy and paste to send to them.

This approach is non-salesy and very low-pressure. You're not asking for a big favor; you're just giving your friend an opportunity to connect you with people who might genuinely need what you're offering. The more focused and specific you are about who you are trying to reach, and the more valuable the tool is that you have created for them, the more effective this step will be.

Step 4: Make It Easy for Your Friends to Share

The last step is to make it ridiculously easy for your friends to help you if they say yes. After they agree to share your Trust Soldier for you, don't make them do the work of writing an email or message from scratch, as that will drastically decrease the likelihood of them ever doing it. Instead, *you* write it for them so they can just copy and paste it and send it to their friend! Here's an example of what you could write for your friend to use to send to their friend:

> *Hey [Name], Hope you are doing great! I wanted to share a free resource I recently came across that I thought might be useful for you. My good friend [Name] created it as s/he helps people to [describe the problem your service solves, e.g., "build their personal brands to grow their reach"].*
>
> *S/he just launched a new [description], and as part of helping to spread the word about it, s/he gave me a few of these free tools to send out. I only got a few to share but I immediately thought of you and wanted you to have it! It's called the [Trust Soldier Name] and it's a simple [modality description]. I genuinely thought you would find the tool useful.*
>
> *Here's a little bit more official information on my friend too: [Insert one paragraph Expert Bio]*
>
> *You can access the tool at this link [insert link]. I hope you find it useful but let me know what you think!*
>
> *PS. After you go through it, if by chance you want to meet my friend [Name] to learn more, just let me know and I'll be happy to connect you!*
>
> *All the best for now!*
>
> *[Signature]*

Once you've customized this, send it to your friends so they can copy, paste, and send it to a few people. In doing so, you're making it as simple as possible for them to help you. Send these messages out to the people on your Fast 50 list. Even if just five of your friends help you and each of them sends it to just five people, that's twenty-five potential warm leads for your business. If just 20 percent of those leads become customers, you'll have your first five customers, all from a simple free process and a new Expert Bio!

Not only that, but you can easily adapt these templates and follow the same process to book your first few media appearances and/or speaking stages. This approach works because it leverages the power of trust and genuine offline human relationships. But it will only work if you have built meaningful real-life friendships, so build relationships before you need them.

ELEVATOR PITCH FORMULA

The more you learn about our sales philosophy at Brand Builders Group, the more you'll see that we advocate for this simple but vital truth: The fastest way to make meaningful money quickly is almost always through real, offline human relationships. As much as we believe in and study digital marketing, we still firmly believe that when it comes to relationships, offline is greater than online. In light of that, it's important for you to be able to quickly communicate what it is that you actually do. If people in your network can quickly and clearly understand what you do, then there is a great chance that they can

> *We still firmly believe that when it comes to relationships, offline is greater than online.*

help introduce you to potential customers. However, if you struggle to verbalize succinctly exactly what your personal brand is all about, you will inevitably struggle to grow your business.

It's inside of that context where the dreaded "elevator pitch" conversation comes into play. If you don't already know, the reason it's called an "elevator pitch" is because you're supposed to have a compelling explanation of your brand and story that can be communicated to a stranger on a short elevator ride while going up or down only a few floors. And it is absolutely shocking to me how many personal brands struggle to consolidate what they do into a single coherent sentence. There is something about the pressure of being put on the spot, combined with the shortening attention span of every audience, that makes it super easy for just about anyone to stutter and stumble when they get an opportunity to share their elevator pitch.

The remedy to that is quite simple: Use our Personal Brand Pitch Formula.

> **I help [who] to [what] by [how].**

The formula is made up of three parts:

1. **[Who]** refers to your Avatar Persona, a one-phrase description of the type of person you serve. Keep in mind that "the more specific, the more terrific."

2. **[What]** refers to the payoff that your service or program provides. Think back to the "I want <u>blank</u>" test from The Five Title Tests. This blank is the one that you populate early on as part of your Elevator Pitch. You are communicating the result you provide to your customers right up front.

3. **[How]** refers to what you do, or how you do it.

For example, I would say, "I help entrepreneurs to become more well-known by teaching them how to build and monetize their personal brand."

If you were a nutritionist you might say, "I help midlife women to lose extra body fat by resetting their hormones."

A financial advisor might say, "I help blue-collar business owners to multiply their money for retirement by connecting them with reliable investment vehicles."

A BIO THAT PEOPLE WILL BUY

The Personal Brand Pitch Formula works for just about any business or personal brand in any location because it is straightforward, easy to understand, and benefit-laden to anyone who hears it. That matters a lot because, as you now know, clear is greater than clever.

Far too many people today struggle to differentiate themselves from one another. So, they look at what all their competitors are doing and orient what they say based off that. Yet that strategy tends to cause people to be overly creative and unnecessarily focused on differentiation.

While we encourage people to find their Uniqueness, that is not the same thing as differentiation. Differentiation is oriented around what other people in the market are doing versus what makes you unique. Differentiation is overrated. You don't have to be different to be helpful; you can just be helpful. Customers don't typically care that much if you are *different* because they aren't looking for someone who is different; they are looking for someone who can solve their problem.

If you've completed all the steps in this book so far, your reputation is fully formalized and ready to be monetized. Now it's time to digitize it so that we can scale your impact globally!

Scan the QR code in the front inside cover of this book and download our Expert Bio template.

CHAPTER 10

ONLINE LEAD GENERATION

BY AJ VADEN

After two years of planning and more than twenty-one hours of travel time, we landed in Tokyo, Japan. We've been to plenty of big cities, including several in other parts of Asia, but nothing quite like Tokyo. The buildings, the crowded streets, the traffic, the lights—so many lights! The city is electric with energy. Oh, and the hospitality. That is what surprised us the most. We were in Tokyo speaking at a conference, and as part of the conference we were assigned a local host to ensure we had a friendly face to greet us at the airport, guide us to our hotel, and generally make sure we had a point of contact for non-conference needs. Our host in Tokyo was a gentleman named Makoto.

Makoto could have arranged a car service for us, considering we were landing at almost 11 p.m. and the drive from the airport would take a couple of hours because of traffic. This was already a big inconvenience, but Makoto insisted he be there in person to greet us. And it wasn't just him. He had invited several other members of the conference committee to stay up late, take a train to the airport, and await our arrival. We had a whole welcome committee standing at baggage claim with gifts, drinks, food, and the genuine excitement that we were there. It was unreal. Then, it got even better. The next morning Makoto called our hotel room to inform us that after the conference he wanted to gift us a two-night stay at his family's nature resort right outside of Kyoto so we could experience another side of Japan. What?!

As we got to spend more time with Makoto, he carried the conversation with questions and topics including my grandmother who had just turned 101, Rory's favorite football team (the Denver Broncos), our financial philosophies (such as our separate "allowance" checking accounts), and more. How could someone we'd just met the previous night, who lived on the other side of the planet, know so much about our personal lives?

Where did this extraordinary hospitality come from? And how did he learn all this stuff about us?

He shared he had read both of Rory's books more than once, had listened to every episode of our podcast, watched all our YouTube videos, and clearly had seen just about every post we'd ever made. But something stuck out to us. Since we don't have millions of followers, we can easily recognize names that show up consistently with any likes and comments in our feeds, but neither of us recognized the name Makoto. Then he shared, "I don't like commenting online. I just love to learn, and I've learned so much from you. I'm so grateful!"

He had spent years following us. He had consumed nearly every single piece of content we had ever created. And yet, he had never, not even once, left a comment or a note to tell us he was enjoying it. Fascinating!

That's when a lightbulb went off for me about the power of building a personal brand. We live in a world in which you can change lives without ever having a conversation with someone. You can serve people without ever seeing them. You can lift people up without even looking at them. And other people can know *you* without you ever knowing *them*. When we talk about the power of online marketing and digital content creation, we might focus on cost per lead, return on ad spend, and conversion percentage. But we often overlook something far more powerful: Content marketing gives you a chance to serve human beings on the other side of the screen.

Makoto wasn't just a follower, or even a fan; he knew more about our lives than most of our friends and family! There was a pre-established relationship before we met. Because of that, he treated us differently. Imagine for a second what that could do for your business. Imagine what would happen if hundreds or even thousands of people developed a strong affinity for you and your work, even if they never talked to you. Imagine the blessings and warm referrals and coincidental customers that would result from people all around you who were learning from you and benefiting from your expertise. It would show up as like-minded clients, abundant profits, and unexplainable growth. You see, something magical happens when people learn from you online: You automate trust at scale.

The goal is to automate trust at scale.

THREE FACTORS FOR BUILDING TRUST

In the last chapter we talked about how differentiation is overrated because people don't care that much about buying from people who are different; they mostly just care about buying from people who can solve their problems. We don't need the world's most innovative Realtor; we need someone who can sell our house. We don't need a CPA with the most advanced technology; we need someone who can properly complete our taxes. We don't need the world's greatest dentist; we need someone who can clean our teeth and keep us from getting cavities. In other words, the main thing we need to buy from someone is *trust* in who they are and *trust* in their ability to do the job.

But have you ever thought about where trust comes from? It's one thing to talk about the importance of trust in garnering consumer transactions, but what are the primary behaviors that lead to trust? What are the actions that you can *do* that create more trust? We know the more trust a personal brand has with their audience, the more transactions will take place. Monetizing your personal brand is learning how to extract some of the trust you have deposited with your followers and convert it into dollars. But we can't extract transactions from an audience where trust hasn't yet been built. Again, reputation precedes revenue, and trust must be established before there's a transaction.

First, **people need to *see* you.** We trust people we see on a regular basis. If you were to make a list of the people you trust the most in your life, there is a good chance it is filled with people you see with your own eyes on a consistent basis. Ironically, this also explains the power of celebrities. Why do celebrity endorsements work? And what makes corporate brands pay so much for celebrity spokespeople? It's obvious: They do it for trust. They are drafting off the trust the general population already has with that celebrity, knowing there will be a trust transfer that extends to their brand or product.

On the surface, it makes no logical sense that we would trust celebrities and their endorsements. After all, we hardly know them, and much of what we *do* know is often based on a character they play rather than who they are in real life. It doesn't compute that we would trust someone we know nothing about in real life and who, in the case of actors and actresses, specializes in pretending to be someone they're not. Crazy, right? So, why do we trust them?

Easy. Because we see them all the time. We trust what we see because we trust what is familiar. Inversely, we distrust things we've never seen because we distrust what is unfamiliar. If I am walking down a dark alley in the middle of the night and notice a person coming my way whom I've never seen before, I don't trust them because I don't recognize them. If you want more people to trust you, then more people simply need to *see* you.

The second factor of building trust is that **people need to *know* you.** We trust those we know things about. Again, if you were to review your list of people you trust most, there is a good chance you know a lot about them. It's also highly likely they know a lot about you. We trust people more when we know intimate details of their life that a typical stranger wouldn't know. Part of why Makoto had a high level of trust with us is because he had learned so many tidbits of personal information from consuming our content. Had we never shared those and/or had he never seen nor heard them, he likely would not have developed the same level of trust.

In fact, we can prove this with data. According to our national research study, 67 percent of Americans said they would be willing to spend *more money* on products and services from the companies of founders whose personal brand aligns with their personal values.

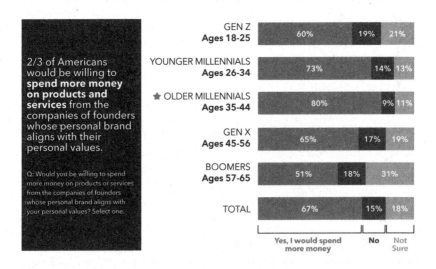

If you haven't yet, you can download a copy of this study by
scanning the QR code listed on the front inside cover of this book.

As one of our favorite leadership authors, Simon Sinek, famously said in his TED talk, "The goal is to do business with people who believe what you believe."[50] When you stratify the data by age, it's easy to spot that this trend is generally increasing and will become even more prevalent in coming years. If you'll notice, while 67 percent of all Americans said this, it was 73 percent of younger millennials and 80 percent of older millennials. Over the next twenty to thirty years, these generations will have the majority of all spending power in the United States. Clearly, people are most interested not just in knowing *what we do* but in knowing *who we are.*

> **People are most interested not just in knowing what we do but in knowing who we are.**

This research is a contributing factor to a decidedly different strategy we have deployed in our own business: **We are sharing more of what we believe with our audience.**

During an era that is rich with offense and cancel culture tendencies, I know many close friends who hold back what they really believe for fear of losing business, losing followers, or losing team members. It's an easy thing to fear when you look at all the crazy that can happen from one post, one speech, or one interview. Almost instantly its context gets lost, twisted, and redistributed in a completely different way than you said or intended. That said, this data remains true. People want to know who they are doing business with, and they want to do business with people who share similar beliefs and values as they do.

As much as you may repel some with what you believe, you will also attract many others. You may lose customers, but you will gain new ones. People will unfollow you, but new people will start following you. Team members may decide this is not the place for them to work, or they may become even more committed simply by knowing who you really are and what you believe. Sharing what you believe is key in helping others opt in or opt out. And you have to be okay with whatever they choose. You cannot be everything to everyone. You do not serve all audiences; you decidedly have to serve *one* audience. **It's better to be the real you to a smaller group of people than to be a neutral, watered-down version of you to a larger group of people.**

The third primary way to build trust with an audience is to help **people *learn* from you**. We trust people we learn from. There is an unspoken law of reciprocity that takes place when someone teaches us something. Each of us extends trust as a subconscious thank-you to people who share information that is useful to us.

> *Don't create marketing collateral that tells people what you do; instead, teach them everything you know about how to do it.*

This fact informs a huge part of our content marketing strategy for personal brands. If we know that trust must take place before there is a transaction, and if we know that trust is given in exchange for sharing knowledge, then we can be confident that one of the most effective marketing strategies on the planet is to **teach people what you know**! Don't create marketing collateral that tells people what you do; instead, teach them everything you know about how to do it.

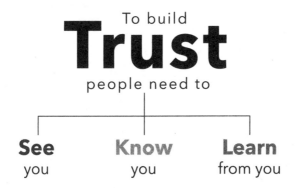

To build
Trust
people need to

| **See** | **Know** | **Learn** |
| you | you | from you |

GIVE IT ALL AWAY

Teach what you know for free but do it in bite-sized chunks and in random miscellaneous order. Initially it may seem counterintuitive to teach everything you know for free, for fear that no one will ever buy anything from you. But remember, "People don't pay for information; they pay for organization and application of the information."

But let's address this very real fear that *if we give away all our best stuff right up front, then no one will have a reason to buy from us.* In reality, that's not the problem; it's actually the opposite. The very real dilemma that most personal brands face is that the content they share is not valuable enough for someone to want to return for more!

Save the best for first!

Understanding the danger of not adding enough value to an audience fast enough leads us to our next content marketing principle: *Save the best for first!* We get asked all the time, "Where should I start?" or "What should I share first?" The answer is **start with what you know best**. Every day you should wake up and ask yourself, *What is the next most helpful or valuable piece of content I can share with my audience?* Not only does this help you maximize the chances that your next piece of content will help generate your next customer, but it also forces you as a content creator to always be leveling up. That's the real race happening across the various media platforms in the world today.

There is a flat-out war for attention. Perhaps that is why the co-founder of Netflix, Reed Hastings, once said his company's real competition is sleep![51] Getting your brand and message in front of customers means you're competing with the highest-end production companies, the most sensationalist news outlets, the most captivating video games, and the most addictive algorithms from social media sites. You had better be ready to bring your A game—and fast!

THE 3 Es OF CONTENT MARKETING

After working with thousands of personal brands, we can confidently say there are three main types of content marketing strategy. We call them "The 3 Es," and they are: Entertainment, Encouragement, and Education. Anyone who is winning in the war for attention is very clear on which of The 3 Es is their predominant strength.

Entertainment is pretty self-explanatory. Under this strategy, you are creating content that is usually based in storytelling with the primary purpose of holding someone's attention. News media, celebrity tabloids, sports, music, and comedy are all examples of Entertainment content. In addition to storytelling, the other strategic element often at play here is generating emotion. Entertainment content is always the most likely to go viral because it is the most likely to trigger emotions. In the words of our good friend and content strategist Hilary Billings, "When people get emotional, they get promotional."[52]

Encouragement is content you create to make people "feel good." In this category, you tend to find things like pastors, proposals, puppies (because, let's be honest, no one really likes cats!), babies, and motivational speakers. For personal brands, this means focusing on content that deliberately inspires and uplifts. When we think of the master of this category, we think of Jay Shetty, who built one of the biggest personal brands in the world by embracing an original motto of "making wisdom go viral."[53]

Education is obviously and quite literally content that is created with a direct focus on informing or teaching people. This is the category we live in, as do most of the people we serve. This space lends itself perfectly to authors, speakers, experts, entrepreneurs, executives, and professional-service providers. Standing out in this space has less to do with production value and more to do with content value.

While Entertainment is most likely to go viral, **Education content is most likely to convert customers**. Research indicates that

educational content can significantly enhance consumer trust and purchasing decisions. In fact, a study by Conductor found that consumers who engage with educational content were **131 percent more likely to purchase** from that brand. Additionally, when presented with multiple brand options, **83.6 percent of consumers** chose the brand offering educational content.[54] This is why you need to be clear on your content strategy from the beginning. If your goal is to convert customers, don't worry about going viral, and don't focus on how many followers or likes you get. Instead, focus on reaching your target audience and helping those people experience value.

THE CONTENT DIAMOND

The Content Diamond is a systematic process for filling an entire social media content calendar by repurposing one main asset into several shorter micro assets. We know that if we have a repeatable strategy for creating a quality version of a longer-form asset, it can be the source to then subdivide and recreate shorter-form micro assets for use across multiple platforms.

Most personal brands fail at using social media to drive leads for their business because their content marketing strategy is complicated and unorganized. Our advice is simple: **Make a list of every question your Avatar has about your area of expertise and answer each question one at a time on video**. Then, edit and cut that main video into smaller assets that you can distribute all around the web.

Step 1: Make a List of 52 Questions

The first step is to create a list of questions that your potential customers have. Start with fifty-two questions to ensure you have one question/answer (i.e., piece of content) for each week of the year. This should be fairly easy and take you less than thirty minutes to complete. You are the expert on this subject matter after all. If you get stumped, ask your team, ask your customers, ask your prospects, or ask AI for some recommendations.

Scan the QR code in the front inside cover of this book and grab our 52 Prompts Guide to a Year's Worth of Content

Step 2: Record the Video

Step two is recording the video. This is where people get hung up, and we know why. Most likely three things will hold you back from doing this:

1. You're self-conscious about what you're going to say or how you will look.
2. You're self-conscious about what other people will think of you or your content.
3. You're self-conscious about the technology, process, or platforms.

Let's tackle each of these objections one at a time. In terms of what you'll say, here's a proven formula adapted from Toastmaster International's formula for effective presentations:

1. Tell them what you're going to tell them.
2. Tell them.
3. Tell them what to do next.[55]

A more practical expression of this is to follow the QAC protocol:

1. Question
2. Answer
3. Call to Action

Let's put the QAC protocol to work in a real-life example. If you were a financial advisor, the opening line of your video might sound like this:

Question: "What is the limit on retirement account contributions?"

Do not say, "Hi, my name is _____," and definitely do not say, "Hey, what's up everybody!" The first words out of your mouth should be a question that is relevant to your business and expertise. This automatically serves as the "tell them what you're going to tell them" section. This is how you will capture people's attention up front (you have about three seconds to do this), so make it short, clear, and to the point. Before you answer the question, spend 1–2 minutes (max) talking about why the question is important, common misconceptions about the subject, and frequent mistakes people make in this area. Give background and context. This is teeing up why your answer is important and significant to the listener.

Answer: Spend 1–3 minutes providing the answer to the question. This is the "tell them" part. It might include defining relevant terms, discussing useful statistics, sharing helpful tips, explaining things in simple terms, and most of all, describing whatever your personal philosophy and beliefs are about the best way to approach this issue. This is your expertise in a monologue version of the Q&A format.

Call to Action: Last, you need to give the audience a call to action (CTA). In other words, tell them what to do next. For their best interest and yours, it's important to condition your audience to engage and do something after listening to you. Here's a list of some of common CTAs that add value both to your listener and to your business, in order of cascading commitment.

- Hit "Like" if you enjoyed this video.
- Let me know your thoughts on this! Leave a comment below.
- If this was useful for you, think of one friend who might benefit from it and hit "Share" to send it to them.
- For more free tips from me, make sure to hit "Follow/ subscribe."
- [Follow these directions] to join my email newsletter.
- To take a deeper dive on this subject, download a copy of my free report by [insert directions].
- Sign up for my free [long-form training] (like a webinar, etc.) over at [URL].
- If you're serious about applying this concept in your own life, request a free call with my team by [insert directions].
- Looking for more on this topic? Check out the product I created to help with this exact problem over at [URL].

Super simple, right? Yes! It should be. Now that you know precisely what you're going to say, the next roadblock is getting past any limiting beliefs about how you're going to look on camera. Here's everything you need to know: You should look the same way on camera as you do in real life! Everyone gets hung up thinking they need to change or upgrade their appearance on camera. You don't! In fact, you *shouldn't*. People want to see the real you. And this may be shocking, but the more "real" you look, the more effective your videos will be. If you dress up in real life, do that on camera, but if you don't, then don't!

The most powerful and effective thing that you can be on camera is exactly who you are in real life!

You're not becoming a news anchor or an actor. The most powerful and effective thing that you can be on camera is *exactly* who you are in real life! Remember the three factors for creating trust from earlier in this chapter:

- People want to *see* the real you.
- People want to *know* the real you.
- People want to *learn* from the real you.

The more you allow yourself to be the real you, the faster they are going to trust you. The fabulous irony of personal brands being on video is that the more you pretend to be something you are not, the less they are going to trust you.

Now let's talk about dealing with technology. A word of warning: Most people wildly overthink the technology aspect of all this. You do not need a recording studio with Hollywood-grade video cameras, lighting, and audio equipment. You can record all these videos right on your phone, which is exactly what we did, and it's what nearly all our clients have done. People don't buy from you because you have cinematic photography; they buy from you because you have useful information. Unless you are a photographer or video editor, don't worry about trying to make the videos look and sound perfect. What matters most is that the viewer can actually see you and can hear you clearly. So, make sure there is light pointing at your face from behind the camera (even if it's just a table lamp) and speak clearly.

CONTENT REPURPOSING MACHINE

Once you have the video recorded, the full power of The Content Diamond kicks into high gear. The process starts with the 3–6 minute video you have recorded at the top of the diamond. We're going to split the creation of the micro assets into two distinct paths: first, text and imagery assets; and second, video and audio assets.

Before I walk you through this, I want to include two disclaimers right up front. First, there is a *high* likelihood that the names of the tools and platforms I list in this section are going to change, because the world of technology is shifting fast. If something here doesn't match up exactly with the digital products and platforms available when you read this, don't assume the technique is out of date. While the names of these companies and the specific tools may change, this process is timeless. What matters is using source content that comes directly from you and then repurposing it in a scalable way across any number of outlets and locations.

The second disclaimer has to do with the platforms listed below—Medium, LinkedIn, Pinterest, Instagram, X (Twitter), Meta (Facebook), YouTube, and Podcasts. You may be looking at this list and already getting frustrated and overwhelmed at the thought of trying to be present and active on every one of these sites. That is not what we are saying. We are going to walk you through this process in its entirety, but you have to discern for yourself which platforms you are going to create content for. That depends entirely on where your audience lives.

Remember, this is not about you; it's about reaching your Avatar and providing value to them. This is also why nailing down the specifics about your "who" is so critical before you get to this stage. The more you know about your Avatar, the easier it is for you to decide where you should be spending time online (and offline). If your Avatar is found on LinkedIn, that is where you direct your attention. If your audience lives on Instagram or Facebook, that is where you go. **You create content on platforms that reach your audience.** If your audience is not present on one of these listed platforms, just skip that part and move on.

That said, let's follow the "text and imagery" path on the left side of the diamond for a moment.

Step 1 is to transcribe the video. This converts the spoken word from video into text. Once we have the content in a text format, we can create several types of text-based assets.

Step 2 is converting the transcription into a full-length article. You can do this yourself, pop it into your favorite AI tool, or hire a basic copywriter to get the transcription edited. You now have an article that can be optimized for online reach and placed throughout the web. This can include posting the article on social media sites that are conducive for longer-form content, as well as submitting it for publication on mainstream media outlets.

Step 3 is to highlight what we refer to as the "Pillar Points" of your article. Pillar Points are your own original phrases that become memorable stand-alone quotes or "one-liners." These catchy Pillar Points make great posts to X (formerly Twitter) and/or Threads, opening headlines for captions, or simple text-message updates to your database. Additionally, if you overlay the Pillar Points onto some royalty-free graphic background images, they can be made into carousel posts on Instagram, Meta, or LinkedIn, or as stand-alone, pinworthy posts on Pinterest.

The other half of The Content Diamond is the "video and audio" path down the right side. Working off the "main" video, your first step is to create an asset for long-form video platforms like YouTube. Pop your content video into an AI video-editing software or hire a basic video editor to take your original video and edit out any flubs or unnecessary words. Then, add "jump cuts." This is where the camera zooms in on you then jumps out or side to side to create variety in the frames. This is not fundamentally necessary, but it does help hold people's attention.

Other optional video edits you can easily make to accentuate the content include highlighting key moments with pull-out quotes, adding "lower-thirds" to show the speaker's name and title, inserting calls to action or section titles, mixing in stock footage or B-roll, adding royalty free music, and/or working in transition effects. The most important thing, however, is that you have value-rich video content. The rest of these editing suggestions can be added as you grow.

With your full-length video ready to go, you can now edit it down into tighter sixty- to ninety-second clips to post on short-form video platforms such as LinkedIn, Meta (Facebook), Instagram, YouTube shorts, and any others that emerge. You can also take the Pillar Points you identified on the text and imagery path and overlay them on stock video footage or your own B-roll and turn them into videos. You can enhance those by adding music, utilizing a text-animation feature, and/or potentially adding your own voiceover from the video on top of them (all of which can be done with AI video-editing software).

The final piece is stripping the audio off the edited full-length video file. And guess what? Now you have a whole new stand-alone asset to use as a short-form audio podcast—welcome to podcasting!

You complete The Content Diamond when you pull all those micro assets you've created into one central location on your blog. Over time, your blog becomes the central headquarters, digital footprint, and a running repository of the most useful information you've created. It gives you a body of work that you can use to build your personal brand, and it all begins with one video asset per week that you repurpose into several smaller ones.

CONVERTING CONTENT INTO CUSTOMERS

As simple and straightforward as The Content Diamond process is, if it still feels like a decent bit of work, you're right—it is! That begs the question, "How is this worth it? How do I know if this is actually growing my business?" That's an important question worth answering on the front end so you can plan for a healthy ROI.

There are three main metrics that indicate trust is being built, thus leading toward increased future revenue. One is long-term, one is mid-term, and one is short-term. To maximize the return on the work you put into this process, you need to both measure these metrics and have a functional plan for how to convert that trust into dollars.

Metric #1: Impressions (Long-Term)

The first metric, impressions, focuses on the long-term. We know now that part of what causes people to trust you is that they actually see your face and know your name. According to the University of Maryland, The Rule of 7 suggests that someone must encounter your brand or message seven times before making a purchasing decision.[56] This rule has been around since the 1930s, when movie studios first measured and realized the importance of multiple exposures to a marketing message. While the exact science of measuring this could be quite difficult, common sense suggests the principle is still very relevant. It matters how often people see you, your brand, and your message. We trust the people we see most often, and in marketing, that is measured as impressions.

While I don't know if seven is the exact number every time, we have regularly seen this concept to be true for us and our clients. We know that many of our clients "followed us online for years" or "heard us on several podcasts" or "saw us speak at multiple events" before they finally decided to buy from us. Recognizing the truth behind this forces each of us to consider, *How can I get my ideal customers to see my content and message faster and more frequently?* We've already established you don't need millions of followers to make millions of dollars, but in order to get new customers, those people each need to see you or hear about you around seven times. That is why gaining someone as a follower still matters.

The goal of the first or second impression is to impress them enough to hit the follow or subscribe button. Not for your vanity's sake but because if they start following you, the likelihood and speed at which they encounter you and your content goes up exponentially. Without getting too far in the weeds, the ratio of impressions to followers matters a lot. You want to optimize not only for impressions but also for a conversion of those impressions.

Metric #2: Leads (Mid-Term)

Next, the mid-term metric is "leads," also known as "email addresses captured." Once you capture a "lead," you have advanced the relationship and are now in control of when you push messages in front of them. Additionally, the intimacy has increased. Impressions start as their first exposure to you, and they see and hear about you on a mostly random basis. Maybe they stumble upon a piece of your content or find themselves at an event or listening to a podcast you're on. This is similar to how traditional advertising has worked for decades, in which you randomly drive past a billboard or get stuck watching a commercial during your favorite show. But once a follower becomes a "lead" by giving you their email address, you are now in charge of the communication rhythm and frequency. This happens through trust—trust that most likely originated through your content.

While the goal of an impression is to convert them to a follower to accelerate the number of impressions they have, the goal of a lead is to get them to participate in some type of accelerated experience with you. You can shorten the sales cycle by speeding up the amount of value you contribute to someone's life. The more time they spend with you and the more value you provide, the more likely they are to buy.

That's why our company offers loads of free training. Visit the resource site listed on the front interior cover of this book to get a feel of how much and how many free value-adds Rory and I offer, both as a company with Brand Builders Group and with each of our personal brands. It's a lot, because we know that if we can get someone to take the time to engage in one or more of those free assets, they are more likely to see us, get to know us, learn from us, and thus trust us more and more through the process.

Metric #3: Free Calls (Short-Term)

The short-term metric for most entrepreneurs is "calls requested" or "appointments set." Closing for free calls or appointments is something we refer to as "soft-offer selling" because you don't share a price or ask for payment in your marketing. You simply offer the chance to talk with you or your team to learn more. This is especially important if you are selling high-dollar offers (north of $2,000) or complex offers (such as professional services or any relationship-based sale). Driving for a free call or appointment with your marketing is the best strategy. Thus, measuring free calls is the critical metric to focus on that lets us know a sale is drawing near.

In fact, free calls are the single most important marketing metric related to new business at Brand Builders Group. Free calls matter because only people who have a legitimate interest in what you're doing are going to make the time to get on the phone with someone from your team. It definitely doesn't mean a sale is guaranteed, but it does mean the relationship and trust level have accelerated to a point where someone is at least open-minded about creating a specific result in their life, and they genuinely believe you may be the one to help them with it.

Another reason why driving for free calls is such a great strategy is because it is one of the easiest to implement. You can start offering this *right now* in all your content marketing, during any live presentation, in emails, social media posts, networking meetings, and more. It's a low-barrier-to-entry call to action to help people take the next step with you. Over time, you can get more advanced with this by posting forms for people to fill out and landing pages for them to visit, but today, for now, you can just tell people to email you, DM you, or text you to set up their free call. Don't let technology hold you back. Don't overcomplicate the process. Show up. Provide value. Tell them what to do next. Repeat.

To learn more about working with Brand Builders Group, scan the QR code in the front of this book and request a call with our team.

SURVIVING THE STARTING POINT

These principles are not rocket science. They are simple, proven, and time-tested. And sooner or later, they will work—*if* you deploy them properly. The only question is how big and how fast the results will be.

Is there any reason why this would not work for you? Only if you give up too early.

It's easy to get discouraged and frustrated when you don't see the impressions, the likes, the followers, the leads, the free calls, and/or the sales piling up. We have seen that 99.9 percent of the time when a Messenger fails, it is because they *felt* like they weren't succeeding fast enough, so they quit. The reality, though, is that it's almost never that they were *actually* failing; it was only that they *felt* like they were failing. They quit because the negative voices inside their head convinced them it wasn't working and that it was a waste of time, money, and resources. **Frustration happens when you don't have perspective.** And unfortunately, our perspective is often shaped by inaccurate or untimely comparison.

For example, if you *only* had forty views on one of the videos you posted online, you might feel like it was a waste of time. But if you were speaking to a group of forty people in a room right now, I know for certain that it would not feel like a waste of time. Why is it that forty people in a room feels like a lot, while forty people online doesn't feel like that many? I know why. It's because you are comparing your forty views to people getting four hundred or four thousand views, and you feel insignificant. But when you are in a room with forty human beings you can see, meet, and shake hands with, it becomes real. Comparison fades away when you realize these are forty lives, *Think of your online audience as an offline room.* forty dreams, forty people with families and goals and fears that you can help. Come on! Forty people is forty people! Think of your online audience as an offline room.

When you envision your audience as real people, you start to treat them differently because you value them differently. You stop comparing yourself to the people who get millions of views, and you instead focus on serving the people you have access to in a deeper way. You focus on providing for them, appreciating them, and being continually committed to them. Something magical happens when you don't think of them as a "like" or a "follow" or an "email" or a "contact in your database" but rather as actual *people*. When you connect to their humanity, you disconnect from your vanity. That's exactly what happened with Makoto.

We mattered to Makoto because—even though we didn't "know" him—he could tell he mattered to us. He had a strong desire to serve us because, for years, we had been serving him. Your audience will do the same for you. They will care for you . . . if you first care for them. They will provide for you . . . if you first provide for them. They will love you . . . if you first love them. But you have to go first.

Encourage them.

Entertain them.

Educate them.

And commit to do it for them *even if* they never do it back. Isn't that why you got into your business in the first place? Didn't you start in your profession because you wanted to help people? Didn't you choose this line of work because you wanted to make the world a better place? Nobody can stop you from doing that except you! With the amount of technology available to all of us today, you are one button-push away from turning on your camera and teaching people what you know. You are one moment away from hitting record and sharing life-changing insights with people. So, what are you waiting for?

Don't just focus on making dollars; instead, stay focused on making a difference. If you do that, you can never lose.

PART 4

PERSONAL BRAND ACTION PLAN

CHAPTER 11

CLARIFY YOUR CALLING

BY RORY VADEN

There can be a variety of different reasons why a personal brand might not succeed, but there is really only one reason why your personal brand would never *start*: It's because you don't think you're good enough.

Most people never embark on the journey of trying to formally build their personal brand because they have convinced themselves that they don't have anything worth sharing or saying. Or perhaps it's because they don't believe there is anything unique about them or their message that would add value to anyone's life. In any case, the sole reason why someone would silence the calling they feel on their heart to share their story with the world is *imposter syndrome*.

People get in their own way and give in to the fear-driven thoughts that pop into their heads. They worry that:

- *I won't look good on camera.*
- *I won't be sharing anything that hasn't already been said before.*

- *I don't understand how to use the technology.*
- *No one will show up or care about anything I'm sharing.*
- *I won't be able to support myself financially.*
- *Former friends and colleagues will make fun of me for "trying to become an influencer."*
- *People I love will question my motive as "running after fame."*

But here's something to know about fear that you may have never noticed before: Fear is an entirely self-centered concept. You only experience fear when you are thinking about yourself. You tend not to experience fear when you are thinking about others.

For example, let's pretend you are driving down the road and witness a car accident, and you see someone in an overturned car who is yelling for help. As you rush to assist, chances are you're not worried about how cute your outfit is or whether your breath stinks. Why? Because you've suspended your concern about what other people think of you. That doesn't matter right now. All that matters is that another person desperately needs your help. Notice that nothing has changed about your self-confidence or self-esteem or self-worth. You are the exact same person, and so are they.

The only thing that has changed is the context of the situation and your own mindset. You've shifted from thinking about yourself to thinking about others. Therein lies one of the most powerful truths we've ever discovered for personal brands: There is no fear when the mission to serve becomes clear.

Isn't that incredible? Isn't that powerful? Isn't that true?

In fact, we often recognize servicemen and servicewomen and first responders for

> **There is no fear when the mission to serve becomes clear.**

their tremendous bravery. We admire them for their courage. And yet, our team has come to realize that the antidote to fear is not courage; it's service. What seems to give these incredible people the extraordinary power of running headfirst into danger is not bulletproof bravery or confident courage, but rather a willingness to heed the call to become a humble helper.

Many of these soldiers and first responders do experience fear and trepidation, but they act anyway because they know there are lives at stake. It is their care and concern for others that gives them the decisive willingness to act. It is not so much that they have a character trait of superhuman strength but one of superhuman service.

This leads us back to dismantling one of the most destructive limiting beliefs about personal branding. Ironically, a personal brand is not about *you*; it's about the people you were created to help. Building a great personal brand should not be a self-centered pursuit but a service-centered one. The personal brands that stand the test of time and survive the increasingly competitive landscape do so because they're not just building a business; they are leading a crusade. As my friend and bestselling author Sally Hogshead says, "The world is not changed by people who 'sort of' care."

A Mission-Driven Messenger is called to create something that will reshape the world in a positive way, not just get themselves more attention. True Messengers have realized that their highest self is to be their highest value to others. They know there is far more at stake than simply making money or growing in notoriety. On the contrary, they realize their own lives have meaning in the context of their desire and ability to serve. While other people might be chasing fame, fortune, followers, and personal freedom, a Mission-Driven Messenger has discovered their purpose can only be achieved by using their life in a way that makes others' lives better.

> *True Messengers have realized that their highest self is to be their highest value to others.*

To be a true Mission-Driven Messenger is to have a stark counter-culture orientation. In a world that tells you to pursue achievement—or materialism, or accumulating money, or recognition—Mission-Driven Messengers know intuitively that while none of those things are necessarily bad in and of themselves, they are ultimately empty and unsatisfying. Because when you are achieving, there are wins and losses; but when you are serving, there are only wins.

That perspective frees you from imposter syndrome because you aren't competing against other people; you're competing *for* other people. And you aren't trying to win the approval of other people who don't need you. Instead, you are relentlessly focused on reaching the people in the world who need help in a way that only *you* can uniquely provide!

The goal of a Mission-Driven Messenger is to eradicate a specific problem from the lives of others. Usually, we are driven by our own past pain—when we

> *When you are achieving, there are wins and losses; but when you are serving, there are only wins.*

or someone we love suffered from (or through) something—that we don't want other people to face. While pain is difficult to live through in the moment, it is something to be grateful for because it is the very core of what shapes you for your destiny. It's one of the reasons why we share with our clients something that our pastor Kevin Queen shared with us, which is that "Your influence will never grow wider than your character runs deep." The pain you experienced in your past is what has given birth to the purpose of your future. It has prepared you for something. Perhaps, more importantly, it has prepared you for some*one*. This, again, is why we so often say, "You are most powerfully positioned to serve the person you once were."

> *"Your influence will never grow wider than your character runs deep."*

We've been able to help our clients win in business largely because we identified a simple pattern that connected them to a transcendent and deeper personal purpose. And if you want to find yours, remember, you must ask yourself:

- *What challenge have I conquered?*
- *What obstacle have I overcome?*
- *What setback have I survived?*
- *What tragedy have I triumphed over?*

Or, you might simply look out in the world and ask yourself:

- *What problems exist that make me mad? What pisses me off?*
- *What problems exist that make me sad? What breaks my heart?*

What is the problem you see in the world that makes you say, "I'm not okay with that! I'm not comfortable with that! I won't allow that to happen to other people! Not on my watch!" As we said earlier, we believe it is God's divine design of your humanity that whatever breaks your heart, breaks your heart for a reason, because you were created to do something about it!

That is what a calling feels like, and we believe that the calling you feel on your heart is the result of a signal being sent out by someone else that needs you. Not only does that person need you; they likely need *you* much more than you need *them*. For you, it might just be a matter of another follower or a few more dollars in your bank account. But think about how many people need you and your message. It's very possible that there are people out there right now, all over the world, who are seeking and searching, begging and pleading, and quite literally on their hands and knees praying for answers you know like the back of your hand!

We believe it is God's divine design of your humanity that whatever breaks your heart, breaks your heart for a reason, because you were created to do something about it!

And the only reason you wouldn't help those people is because you're scared. You are scared that you might not say the right thing. You're scared that you might not do the right thing. You're scared that you might not *be* the right thing. But you only feel fear when you are thinking about yourself. There is no fear when the mission to serve is clear. So, kick imposter syndrome to the curb. Stop thinking about yourself. Start thinking about the people you're trying to help.

Go out today and find someone to serve and teach everything you know to the person you once were. That is how you find your purpose. That is how you clarify your calling. And that is the truth of how you build a world-renowned, *Wealthy, and Well-Known* personal brand.

CHAPTER 12

BRAND BUILDER JOURNEY

BY RORY AND AJ VADEN

Congratulations! You now have a clear understanding of what a personal brand is and exactly what it takes to lay the foundation for one that changes the world. If you've finished this book and completed the exercises we've suggested, you should have a clear understanding of your Brand Positioning Statement, which includes the following elements:

- **Uniqueness:** a one-word distillation of your Message that captures the core essence of your proposed solution to the Problem.
- **Message:** a solution-oriented one-sentence through-line statement that distills your entire body of work into a single actionable command, instruction, or order.
- **Problem:** a one-word identification of the core issue you are going to solve for your audience.

- **Cause:** a one-word clarification of the underlying root issue that is responsible for creating the Problem.
- **Avatar Persona:** a one-phrase description of the audience you are going to serve.

Additionally, you are now fully educated on the myth of multiple streams of income and, instead, should have identified your Primary Business Model, "the one revenue stream that matters above all others in your business."

Your Brand Positioning Statement and your Primary Business Model make up your internal-facing brand strategy and create the alignment for you and your team to operate by. We have also helped you start the journey of building some of your first external-facing assets.

By now, you should have new or revised working titles for all of your products, programs, and services (as well as your email subject lines, webpage headlines, etc.) that meet The Five Title Tests. You also should have an updated and fresh one-paragraph Expert Bio to use in conjunction with the templates we provided in chapter 9 to help you go out and land your next five customers. Beyond that, you should have some directional idea of your go-forward content marketing strategy by selecting one of The 3 Es and narrowing in on either entertainment, encouragement, or educational content.

Most of all, you have edified your pre-existing natural intuition that building a personal brand is not self-centered but service-centered, and you know there are people out in the world who need what you have. You've also solidified that the real reason you are doing all of this is not for fame or fortune but rather to be of service to the person you once were.

Wow! You've come a long way!

We know there's probably a part of you that wants to feel like you're *done*, but the truth is, this is only the very beginning. Making a massive impact on the world does not happen overnight. It takes years and really is something that the most dedicated Mission-Driven Messengers commit their entire lives to.

The good news is that we have a plan to help you accelerate your impact. It starts by asking, "Where do we go from here?"

BRAND BUILDER JOURNEY

We are not a company that teaches people how to make millions overnight. Rather, we have lent our resources toward helping people find practical and legitimate strategies to help accomplish in a few years what takes most people decades. The reason so many of our clients spend years working with us is because we have a well-planned and methodical system for delivering proven results to personal brands over the long-term.

It's a proprietary process we've developed called The Brand Builder Journey, and it walks you through the precise steps required to breakthrough Sheahan's Wall. One of the most important things we've discovered on our own path is that too many people do the right things but in the wrong order. They start building their personal brand by trying to launch a website, developing a large social media following, chasing publicity, or running paid ads. Those are all really important things to do, but it's critical that you do them at the right time. We have heard *countless* stories of clients who have literally wasted tens of thousands of dollars by not building their personal brand in the right succession.

Through our personal experience, and having worked with thousands of personal brands, we've developed a four-

> *Too many people do the right things but in the wrong order.*

phase process to help personal brands go from a person with an idea all the way to an eight-figure entrepreneur. Each phase in the process includes three courses that are dedicated to teaching the most advanced and actionable strategies available in specific topical areas that are essential education for successful personal brands. The set of deliverables and outputs of each course become the inputs for the next steps in your journey. Visually, the journey looks like this:

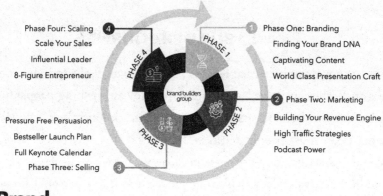

**Brand
Builder**
JOURNEY

PHASE 1: BRANDING

Phase one is the **Branding** and identity phase. What you have experienced in this book is the first of our twelve formal courses in the Brand Builder Journey. Specifically, the content in this book comes from Finding Your Brand DNA, the first course of the first phase of our curriculum.

The next step in phase one is Captivating Content. Here we help you extrapolate your Brand Positioning Statement into pioneering original intellectual property and innovative thought leadership that is unique to you. We guide you through a systematic step-by-step process to extract the expertise in your head into a set of codified visual frameworks, strategic stories, and practical exercises. We even help you write your own catchphrases while making sure to reinforce a singular central message throughout your content. The output of this time together produces a detailed outline of a brand-new body of work that can expand and contract to fit as your next TED Talk, keynote, half-day training, full-day training, two-day training, online course, year-long consulting program, and/or full-length book manuscript *all* at the same time.

Once we have helped you create your fresh content, we then help prepare you to deliver it via the spoken word in our next course, World Class Presentation Craft. We believe the fastest way to take an absolute stranger and convert them into a lifelong fan is to deliver a one-hour *world-class* presentation. Thus, we not only help you write out your entire speech and plan out your slides, but we also teach you mastery-level presentation mechanics. This includes learning the psychology of laughter and how to write jokes, advanced storytelling formulas and character development, tactics for increasing your personal charisma, insights for how to move the audience emotionally, and how to sell from the stage and capture leads gracefully.

> *We believe the fastest way to take an absolute stranger and convert them into a lifelong fan is to deliver a one-hour world-class presentation.*

PHASE 2: MARKETING

After your content and messaging are established, you enter the **Marketing** phase. Phase 2 starts with our flagship course, Building Your Revenue Engine. This is our deep dive into what is typically associated with personal branding: visual identity, websites, social media, and working with the news media. However, the real secret is teaching you how to create a digital automated ecosystem that works 24/7 to nurture trust on your behalf and drive warm pre-qualified leads to your front door. During this training we share a behind-the-scenes look at our top converting funnels and unveil a powerful accelerator for your business called The 15Ps of Copywriting.

Once the digital footprint is in place for your personal brand, you'll enter our High-Traffic Strategies training. This is where we teach you how to optimize all your online assets and how to "force growth." We show you how we can guarantee traffic to any web properties by simply buying it with intelligent paid media. This life-changing strategy shows you and your team how to maximize lifetime customer value and track everything, which ensures you recover your ad spend and can therefore scale your message ad infinitum. In addition to self-liquidating funnels, you'll learn about search engine optimization, affiliate marketing, paid ads, and other expert strategies for driving massive awareness for your personal brand.

This life-changing strategy shows you and your team how to maximize lifetime customer value and track everything, which ensures you recover your ad spend and can therefore scale your message ad infinitum.

We round out phase 2 by taking you through Podcast Power. After advising several of the biggest podcasters in the world and building two of our own to millions of downloads, we've learned a number of practical tips to help anyone launch or grow a successful podcast. You'll go through exercises that help you create the premise, content outline, lead capture, and monetization plan for your entire show. In addition to helping you understand the business model and content production sides of podcasting, we will walk you through technology requirements, sharing our favorite equipment recommendations for multiple budgets. Plus, we will walk you through some of the most effective ways to use your podcast to build key relationships.

PHASE 3: SELLING

Selling is the primary focus of our phase 3 curriculum. It starts with one of our most requested topics, Pressure-Free Persuasion. Based on our proprietary service-centered sales training methodology, we focus on teaching non-salespeople how to comfortably and casually close more leads. Not only that, but we walk you through pragmatic templates you can use to generate warm referrals to keep your pipelines full. Most of all, we give you explicit talk tracks to help you navigate customer objections and sell higher-dollar offers so that you can grow your income quickly.

Then, we lead you through one of our best trainings for generating massive income, Full Keynote Calendar. This course is all about the business of speaking. You'll learn where to find speaking opportunities, what to send when you contact them, and how to develop the marketing materials you need to get booked. This is your go-to training to attract more opportunities, negotiate higher fees, and be on your way to doing what many of our clients do—speak on the world's biggest stages!

Finally, Bestseller Launch Plan is our capstone phase 3 training because it draws upon tactics and strategies from everything in our curriculum up to this point. The only difference is that we take all of those assets and skills that you've learned to build along the way and show you how to focus them into your very own book launch. You get behind-the-scenes access to the exact mechanisms we've used to help launch dozens of our clients to the top of the charts as national and *New York Times* bestselling authors. You'll learn all about the technicalities of how bestseller lists work, different avenues for publishing, and seven key strategies to help you sell a huge number of books! Brace yourself, because this is a big part of the moment we've been building for, when most people finally "break through the wall" and establish themselves as truly renowned thought leaders.

PHASE 4: SCALING

Turning your personal brand into an eight-figure business is what our **Scaling** phase is all about. It starts with one of our most elite-level trainings, 8-Figure Entrepreneur. In this curriculum we teach the nuts and bolts of managing cash flow, creating operational efficiency, understanding financial statements, enhancing business valuation, and building systems that scale. Think of this as a high-speed MBA as we teach you the components that lead to a highly valuable personal brand business. You'll get an insider look at the philosophies and practices we utilized to build two completely different eight-figure businesses from scratch. This is where you'll learn to become a true CEO and owner who can turn your business into a lifelong and generational wealth-building machine.

The second course in phase 4 is called Scale Your Sales. It's through this process that we teach you how to recruit, hire, train, manage, and motivate a team of salespeople. The biggest personal brands in the world have a team—or at least a person—who is selling on their behalf on a regular basis. Sales don't happen by accident or luck but rather by time-tested principles and practices that you can systematically deploy in your business. You'll learn some of the best strategies available on the market for building a true proactive sales engine that will grow your business each and every day.

And finally, the last official module in our curriculum is called Influential Leader. In order to scale the impact of your personal brand, you will have to develop leaders in your organization to whom you can delegate some of the day-to-day operations while you focus on creating content, providing vision, and building relationships. This program is where we teach you exactly how to build and develop that leadership team.

This training is designed to teach your team the six core behaviors that leaders must adopt as regular habits. As your team becomes stronger at leadership, you will be freed up to focus more on sharing your message with the world while they take over running the operations of the business and creating more impact and income potential for all of you.

While we do have a few other training courses focused on more of your personal development, these twelve courses make up the foundational and essential education for all personal brands and content creators in the modern era. Each of them is just as comprehensive and actionable as what you have learned so far in this book, which explains why our clients and their teams typically engage with us over the course of several years. Not every client completes every one of these training courses with us, because they may already have expertise in one or more areas on their own. So, we work with each client to create a customized Brand Builder Journey for them to engage in the focused learning and implementation that will help them move the needle fastest.

If you haven't yet, you should request a free brand strategy call with our team by scanning the QR code on the front interior cover of this book. On that call we will want to hear about your vision and your progress so far and, if applicable, share with you what we see for what a customized journey would look like with us. If you're serious about building your personal brand and taking your impact to the next level, then go ahead and request that call now.

WORK WITH US FOR FREE?

At Brand Builders Group (BBG) we offer a variety of formats and environments to gain the knowledge of our entire curriculum, which enables people of all budget levels to be able to work with us. One of the most powerful parts of our community, however, is our referral partner program called BBG4Free.

We call it BBG4Free because we pay all of our customers a 10 percent *lifetime* referral fee (yes, in perpetuity) on anyone they introduce us to who purchases one of our core educational offerings. Here is where the "free" part comes in: If one of our customers refers ten people to us who become clients, at the same membership level as they are, then effectively their membership with us becomes free. And the more clients they refer, the bigger their referral income grows!

The best part? You don't have to sell anything to become a referral partner of BBG. You can go to our portal, register, and become a BBG referral partner in less than five minutes. Upon registering, you get your own unique referral tracking links that you can share to offer a free brand strategy call or a free training with our team. From there, if anyone becomes a paying client using your links, you get a 10 percent referral fee as a big thank-you for introducing us to someone in your sphere. This is an instant income opportunity for you just by talking about BBG with your friends, family, colleagues, or online community.

We call it BBG4Free because we pay all of our customers a 10 percent lifetime referral fee (yes, in perpetuity) on anyone they introduce us to who purchases one of our core educational offerings.

This is our Win/Win scenario in how we partner with the people who believe in what we are doing. It's a win for you because you get to share something of real value (a Trust Soldier) with your audience . . . and you gain financially by being a promoter of what you believe in. It's a win for us because we get to continue to build a community of like-minded, growth-oriented, Mission-Driven Messengers who want to make the world a better place.

People like you!

Hope we get to talk to you soon!

EPILOGUE

TRULY "WEALTHY" AND TRULY "WELL-KNOWN"

What It Means to Be Truly Wealthy

BY RORY VADEN

Throughout this book we have talked a lot about how to make money and become wealthier. We talk about it even more in our subsequent training courses at Brand Builders Group since it is a key component of running a successful business. I love teaching people about financial intelligence because, having been raised early on by a single mom and barely having enough to get by for much of my life, I know the stress of what it's like to live with very little.

You see, when I was young, I used to think that wealth was having an abundance of money. Later, I thought wealth was having an abundance of time. But as I've gotten older, I've come to believe that wealth is simply having an abundance of peace. Peace is the new profit. I know people who have a lot of money but don't have much peace. I also know a lot of people who don't have much money but have a deep sense of peace. Inversely, I know people who have lots of money and also lots of peace; and I know people who have little money and little peace.

The astonishing and unexpected lesson for me has been learning that money is not the source of peace. For so many people, the answer to "How much money do you need?" always seems to be "Just a little bit more than I currently have." I spent a long time on that insatiable treadmill myself.

Peace is the new profit.

Yet, whenever I was focused on money, I never seemed to have quite enough to bring me peace. I eventually realized the whole financial pursuit is somewhat futile anyway because no matter how much money we accumulate or don't accumulate, one day all of us will die and our money will just disappear and pass on to other people.

So, throughout my life, I have tried many other things to see if they would give me the peace, joy, and significance I was searching for. I've pursued success, fame, competition, alcohol, indulgence, materialism, entertainment, and a number of other worldly experiences. Ultimately, they all fell short. Nothing seemed to truly satisfy the longing in my heart for lasting peace. There has only been one steadfast source of genuine peace in my life—and that is faith.

For much of my life, I was a skeptic of faith and specifically Christianity. But as I sampled all that this world had to offer and continued to feel empty, I was eventually confronted with the sobering question, *Is this all there is?* I then realized if there *was* something beyond what this life had to offer, I needed to find it. That is when I bumped into another challenging question: *What is my strategy for defeating death?* It was obvious I didn't have one—at least not a substantive one—and that led me to start exploring Christianity more closely.

After years of putting my nerd brain to work exploring and analyzing the logical, historical, and academic evidence that exists to support the story of Jesus of Nazareth, I became a deeply convicted believer. In fact, I came to personally agree with C.S. Lewis that once you know the historical facts surrounding the life of Jesus, it takes far more faith to believe His story is *not* true than to believe that it *is* true. My own journey and my own assessment of the general population helped me reach the conclusion that nonbelievers don't struggle from a lack of faith; they struggle from a lack of research. If you want to learn more about my findings and research, check out my free podcast, *Eternal Life: 7 Questions Every Intelligent Skeptic Should Ask About Jesus of Nazareth.*

I believe that true wealth is an abundance of peace. This is why I say, "Jesus is my real answer." Obviously, we teach a lot of other things that hopefully help people achieve some sense of peace from growing their income and making a positive impact on the lives of others. But knowing Jesus is the only everlasting, never-changing, deeply satisfying, always forgiving, permanently available and pervasively accessible, real answer. I'm not trying to evangelize or convert people; it's just that a relationship with Him and knowing what He has done for me is my real answer to what has finally given me true peace and thus true wealth.

Nonbelievers don't struggle from a lack of faith; they struggle from a lack of research.

As I mentioned earlier, I've noticed that many people who make a massive worldly impact and who have achieved massive amounts of worldly wealth still struggle to experience peace, and so they continue to work incessantly. There have been seasons in my life when I worked relentlessly too, but I don't believe that is meant to be the standard modus operandi for our entire life. Here's what I've learned: *Overwork* is a sign of *under-faith.*

If you do *nothing* but work you are saying with your actions, "If it's to be, it's *only* up to me." There's certainly a lot to be said about the value and importance of hard work that is healthy. I don't believe God can bless work that was never done in the first place. All throughout the Bible God does big things through people who obediently answer

His call with action. However, if you are working virtually nonstop—or if you are completely consumed with making *more* money—it's likely because you don't believe that God will fill in the gap for you. The absence of peace is the sign of a lack of faith.

Overwork *is a sign of* under-faith.

The irony for me as a hard-driving entrepreneur has been discovering that the true wealth I seek—abundant peace—has been available to me all along. And that is because that peace is available at any given moment to any person anywhere who learns about and receives the gift of eternal life available through knowing who Jesus Christ is and what He has done for you. He's available to all of us, always.

Hall of Fame NFL quarterback Peyton Manning has been very outspoken about his faith. He has been quoted many times discussing his faith and how football pales in comparison to his relationship with God and the confidence he has in the love God has for him. In his book, he writes "I don't think God really cares about who wins football games, except as winning might influence the character of some person or group."[57] Peyton nailed it. Just like a good earthly father, God's love for us doesn't change based on how we perform. He loves us simply because we are His. Once you come to know that, grasp it, and believe it, you will have true peace—and thus true wealth.

What It Really Means to Be Well-Known

BY AJ VADEN

When we think about being "well-known," our minds often jump to images of fame, public recognition, and large social media followings. But I want to challenge that idea. To me, being well-known is not about being known by the masses; it's about being deeply known by the people who matter most, the people who already surround you on a daily basis. Relationships play a critical role in *being known* as we weren't designed to walk through life alone. True connection happens when we allow others to see and know the deepest parts of us, and when we take the time to know others in the same way.

Even more than that, it's about knowing who you are, why you're here, and living a life that reflects the mission and purpose you were created to embody.

You see, the truth is, you already are well-known. You were created by God, and He knows you intimately. Every detail of who you are—your talents, your quirks, your strengths, and even your flaws—were designed with intention and purpose. That means your identity is not something you need to earn; it's something you need to uncover and embrace.

Being well-known starts with recognizing that your life, as it is, has meaning and value, not because of *what you do* but because of *who you are.* And yet, many of us spend so much of our lives trying to prove ourselves to others, chasing external validation, and seeking to be known by more people, rather than focusing on being known by the right people.

Let me share something I believe deeply: It's far better to be intimately well-known by a few than to be casually recognized by many. To be well-known is to have people in your life who truly understand what you stand for, what you believe in, and what you value. It's about trust, depth, and authenticity. This is where your Uniqueness becomes so evident. There is no one else like you. Your experiences, your perspective, your voice—all of it combines into a one-of-a-kind identity no one else can replicate. Honoring that Uniqueness is a vital part of being

> *You see, the truth is, you already are well-known. You were created by God, and He knows you intimately.*

well-known. It's about showing up as your authentic self and allowing others to see the real you.

But here's the thing: Before you can be well-known by others, you have to truly know yourself. That starts with believing some foundational truths: You are worthy, you are enough, and you were created with a unique purpose. You were placed on this earth at this specific moment for a specific reason, and discovering that reason is one of the most important journeys you'll ever take.

Yet discovering your purpose doesn't just happen. It requires intention. You have to pause, listen, and pay attention to the still, small voice guiding you. You have to believe that there is a calling on your life, even if you don't yet know what it is. This is where faith comes in. Faith to believe in what you cannot see and what you cannot understand; a faith that includes believing you are fully known and fully loved, no matter what. That level of faith is what gives you the confidence to build a personal brand that reflects the identity you've already been given.

> *You are worthy, you are enough, and you were created with a unique purpose.*

Now, I know not everyone shares my beliefs, and that's not the point nor the goal. But I believe we all share a desire to feel known and to live a life that matters. The core of being well-known is this: allowing other people to see who you really are. It's about making deliberate choices that align with your values, your identity, and your purpose. It's about being intentional with your words, your actions, and your relationships. It means living a life of purpose and intention, rooted in the truth of who you are and why you're here. It means prioritizing depth over breadth, authenticity over popularity, and connection over recognition.

You are already well-known.

ACKNOWLEDGMENTS

The journey of writing *Wealthy and Well-Known: Build Your Personal Brand and Turn Your Reputation into Revenue* would not have been possible without the countless people who have supported, guided, and believed in us along the way.

First and foremost, we want to express our deepest gratitude to the founding team members of Brand Builders Group: Elle Petrillo, Isla Lake, Thomas Dodson, Jeremy Weber, Jayne Weber, Kristen Hartnagel, Elizabeth Stephens, Jennifer Kerr, Brittany Parker, Kevin Vaden, Nicole Gale, Elyse Archer, and Kristen Cullen. Each of you risked your livelihoods and financial security to join us on this wild and uncertain adventure. You believed in the vision of what could be before there was any proof that it would work. Your courage, dedication, and unwavering faith in this mission laid the foundation for what Brand Builders Group has become. We owe you an immeasurable debt of gratitude for taking a leap of faith with us and helping to turn a dream into reality.

We also want to take a moment to express our deepest gratitude to the many individuals and communities who have shaped and supported us along this journey.

To Lewis Howes, it's pure fact that we would not be where we are or doing what we are doing without you. We are eternally grateful for the divine intervention that brought you into our lives. We cannot possibly begin to express our gratitude for your generosity, belief in us, and willingness to help us when things felt so out of reach. Thank you from the bottom of our hearts.

To the incredible industry professionals who generously mentored, coached, and pulled back the curtain to share their behind-the-scenes wisdom—thank you. Special acknowledgments go to Eric Chester, David Avrin, Nena Madonia, the Andy Andrews team, Jason Dorsey, Jay Baer, Phil Jones, and David Horsager. Your insights and guidance have been invaluable to everything we've built and accomplished.

From AJ to my EO forum, thanks to Dominique, Mark, Aaron, Denis, Ben, and Jonny for walking alongside me during one of the hardest times in my life. Thank you for always calling out the best in me and believing in our potential before we knew what we were doing. Forum 23 for life.

We also want to recognize and thank our team members at Brand Builders Group. You have taken our dreams and helped transform them into something extraordinary. Your dedication and passion have been instrumental in bringing to life the mission we felt uniquely called to pursue.

To our amazing Brand Builders Group community of clients, thank you for believing in us and for allowing us to play a small role in amplifying your voices and helping your messages be heard. We care deeply about your success, and we promise always to strive to bring you the very best possible systems and strategies to help you make an even greater impact!

A special shout-out to our OG clients, Hilary Billings, Keir Weimer, and Anton Gunn, not only for being our very first clients, but also for walking this journey with us for several years. Watching you grow while growing alongside you has been a great privilege.

Thank you to our Referral Partners and Affiliates who have helped promote us, our mission, and our content, and to every podcaster who has ever had us on their show and helped us get our message out to the world. A special thanks to Ed Mylett, Jenna Kutcher, Amy

Porterfield, Donald Miller, Chalene Johnson, Michael Stelzner, Jasmine Star, and Sean Cannell.

To our families, thank you for providing the support, stories, background, context, and foundation of who we are. From AJ to my dad, thank you for pulling me out of the wreckage all those years ago and for your generous provision over the years. To my mom, thank you for giving me a firm foundation in Jesus and showing me what it means to have real faith. To my brothers, I honor you for all you have been through, for who you are, and I love you dearly. From Rory to my mom, thank you for always believing in me and for being my first booking agent; and to my dad, thank you for walking with me from the *very* beginning of my personal brand and through decades as my "IT guy" who has provided steadfast support in every way possible to me, my family, and our dreams. I love you both so much! To my brother Randy, thank you for building the toughness in me that has helped shape my character and my career.

To our children, Jasper and Liam, you are the heartbeat behind so much of what we do. Being your parents is the most challenging and rewarding journey we've ever taken, and you inspire us to be better every single day. We strive to be role models you can look up to, knowing that our greatest legacy is the one we leave through you. We love you with everything we have.

Finally, we want to acknowledge the eternal and incomparable role that God and Jesus play in our lives. We are fully aware that none of this would exist without the saving grace, protection, and providential calling of God. Everything we are and everything we have is a direct result of His love and guidance, and we owe it all to Jesus. To Him be all the glory, always.

NOTES

1. "Cortés Burns His Boats," *The Fall of the Aztecs*, PBS, accessed January 15, 2025, https://www.pbs.org/conquistadors/cortes/cortes_d00.html.

2. Amy Tikkanen, "List of Athletes with the Most Olympic Medals," Britannica, last updated January 16, 2025, https://www.britannica.com/topic/list-of-athletes-with-the-most-Olympic-medals.

3. Peggy Shinn, "With Nine Olympic Gold Medals and 14 Total, Katie Ledecky Becomes the Most Decorated U.S. Female Olympian," Team USA, August 3, 2024, https://www.teamusa.com/news/2024/august/03/with-nine-olympic-gold-medals-and-14-total-katie-ledecky-becomes-the-most-decorated-u-s-female-olympian.

4. World Aquatics, "Katie Ledecky: Personal Best Results," https://www.worldaquatics.com/athletes/1002483/katie-ledecky; World Aquatics, "Michael Phelps: Personal Best Results," https://www.worldaquatics.com/athletes/1001621/michael-phelps.

5. Simon Sinek, *Start with Why: How Great Leaders Inspire Everyone to Take Action* (Portfolio, 2009); Simon Sinek, "Start with Why—How Great Leaders Inspire Action," TEDx Talk, YouTube, September 28, 2009, https://www.youtube.com/watch?v=u4ZoJKF_VuA.

6. Peter Sheahan, *Making It Happen: Turning Good Ideas into Great Results* (BenBella Books, 2010).

7. "This Day in History: Jan. 12, 1951: Radio Legend Rush Limbaugh Born in Missouri," *Fox News*, last modified January 12, 2024, https://www.foxnews.com/lifestyle/this-day-history-jan-12-1951-radio-legend-rush-limbaugh-born-broadcaster-missouri.

8. "pendulum, n." sense 2, Merriam-Webster, 2025, https://www
   .merriam-webster.com/dictionary/pendulum.

9. Adam Hayes, "Demographics: How to Collect, Analyze, and Use
   Demographic Data," Investopedia, last updated June 18 2024, https://
   www.investopedia.com/terms/d/demographics.asp.

10. "psychographics, n.," Oxford Reference, 2025, https://www.oxford
    reference.com/display/10.1093/oi/authority.20110803100352698.

11. Dave Ramsey (@DaveRamsey), "Debt is dumb, cash is king, and the
    paid-off home mortgage has taken the place of the BMW as the status
    symbol of choice," Twitter (now X), March 25, 2002, https://x.com
    /DaveRamsey/status/1507359648952823813.

12. "Reticular Activating System," ScienceDirect, https://www.science
    direct.com/topics/veterinary-science-and-veterinary-medicine
    /reticular-activating-system.

13. "goose bumps, pl. n.," Merriam-Webster, 2025, https://www.merriam
    -webster.com/dictionary/goosebumps.

14. Josephus Daniels, *The Wilson Era: Years of War and After, 1917–1923*
    (Chapel Hill: University of North Carolina Press, 1946), 624.

15. Sally Hogshead, *Fascinate: Your 7 Triggers to Persuasion and Captiva-
    tion* (HarperBusiness, 2010).

16. "Top 10 People With Highest Followers on Instagram in 2025: Cris-
    tiano Ronaldo Tops the List," *Forbes India*, last modified February
    2025, https://www.forbesindia.com/article/explainers/most-followed
    -instagram-accounts-world/85649/1.

17. Brett Knight and Justin Birnbaum, eds., "The World's Highest-Paid
    Athletes," *Forbes*, May 16, 2024, https://www.forbes.com/lists/athletes
    /?sh=5f2633205b7e.

18. "LeBron James," Spotrac, https://www.spotrac.com/nba/player/_/id
    /2257/lebron-james?utm_source=chatgpt.com.

19. "LeBron James Quits Social Media Amid Lakers' Struggles," *The
    Sun*, last modified November 2024, https://www.the-sun.com/sport
    /12939180/lebron-james-quits-social-media-lakers/.

20. Jacob Camenker, "The NFL's Highest-Paid Players in 2024," *The Sporting News*, September 8, 2024, https://www.sportingnews.com/us/nfl/news/nfl-25-highest-paid-players-2024/694fb43f95a9784f4724647d.

21. "Dak Prescott Instagram Followers Statistics / Analytics," *SPEAKRJ*, https://www.speakrj.com/audit/report/_4dak/instagram.

22. *Bloomberg Billionaires Index, Bloomberg*, accessed March 11, 2025, https://www.bloomberg.com/billionaires.

23. "Facebook Statistics 2025: Users, Revenue, Growth & Trends," *Demand Sage*, last modified January 2025, https://www.demandsage.com/facebook-statistics.

24. George Stahl, "Musk-Twitter Deal Values Company at Around $44 Billion," *The Wall Street Journal*, April 25, 2022, https://www.wsj.com/livecoverage/twitter-elon-musk-latest-news/card/musk-twitter-deal-values-company-at-around-44-billion-MdEXkyNxU0GbJ1kqBc1M?utm.

25. Jay Baer, *Youtility: Why Smart Marketing Is about Help not Hype* (Portfolio, 2013).

26. Feargal Brennan, "Lionel Messi Salary, Contract at Inter Miami: Argentina Star Earns More than 25 MLS Rosters," *The Sporting News*, October 26, 2024, https://www.sportingnews.com/us/soccer/news/lionel-messi-salary-inter-miami-contract-mls/hwhug6sxxh4p8kwym9d7sfwv?utm.

27. William Gittins, "Lionel Messi Hits 500 Million Instagram Followers: How Many Does Cristiano Ronaldo Have?" *AS*, last modified February 27, 2024, https://en.as.com/soccer/lionel-messi-hits-500-million-instagram-followers-how-many-does-cristiano-ronaldo-have-n.

28. Paul Mueller, "Here's Why Lionel Messi's Inter Miami Contract Will Change the Way the World's Best Athletes Are Paid," *Fast Company*, February 17. 2024, https://www.fastcompany.com/91030230/breaking-down-lionel-messi-inter-miami-contract.

29. Julia Stoll, "Net Income of Netflix from 2000 to 2023," Statista, November 8, 2024, https://www.statista.com/statistics/272561/netflix-net-income/.

30. Dr. Gabriel O'Neill, Esq., "50% of Businesses Fail Within the First 5 Years—Guide 2024," *Manage Business,* last modified September 24, 2024, https://managebusiness.org/50-of-businesses-fail-within-the -first-5-years/.

31. CB Insights study citation needed

32. *Launching a Startup,* Stanford Executive Education, accessed March 11, 2025, https://em-execed.stanford.edu/launching-a-startup.

33. Laura Furstenthal, Jon McClain, Brian Quinn, and Erik Roth, *Committed Innovators: How Masters of Essentials Outperform, McKinsey & Company,* accessed March 11, 2025, https://www.mckinsey.com /capabilities/strategy-and-corporate-finance/our-insights/committed -innovators-how-masters-of-essentials-outperform.

34. "How Did Chick-fil-A Get Its Start?" *Chick-fil-A,* accessed March 11, 2025, https://www.chick-fil-a.com/customer-support/who-we-are/our -culture-and-values/how-did-chick-fil-a-get-its-start.

35. "Chick-fil-A Reaches Billion in Sales Milestone," QSR, December 11, 2000, https://www.qsrmagazine.com/news/chick-fil-reaches-billion -sales-milestone/.

36. Jonathan Maze, "New Jersey Orders the Closure of 27 Boston Market Restaurants," *Restaurant Business,* August 15, 2023, https://www .restaurantbusinessonline.com/financing/new-jersey-orders-closure-27 -boston-market-restaurants.

37. "Chick-fil-A Reaches Billion in Sales Milestone," QSR.

38. "Chick-fil-A Reaches Billion in Sales Milestone," QSR.

39. Dan Daszkowski, "The Storied History of Boston Market," Live-About, last updated December 24, 2018, https://www.liveabout.com /history-of-boston-market-1350952.

40. Kate Taylor, "The Church of Chicken," *Business Insider,* August 8, 2019, https://www.businessinsider.com/how-chick-fil-a-took-over -america-2019-8.

41. Maze, "New Jersey Orders the Closure of 27 Boston Market Restaurants."

42. "Chick-fil-A Reaches Billion in Sales Milestone," QSR.

43. Rory Vaden, "How to Multiply Your Time," TEDxDouglasville, June 1, 2015, https://www.youtube.com/watch?v=y2X7c9TUQJ8.

44. Emma Wenner, "Faith-Based Publishers Depend on Devotionals, *Publishers Weekly*, August 2, 2023, https://www.publishersweekly.com /pw/by-topic/industry-news/religion/article/93027-books-for-blessed -days.html.

45. "*The 4-Hour Workweek*," *Wikipedia: The Free Encyclopedia*, last modified March 11, 2025, https://en.wikipedia.org/wiki/The_4-Hour _Workweek.

46. "Marie Kondo," KonMari, https://konmari.com/about-marie-kondo.

47. Marie Kondo *Spark Joy* sales 6 million source?

48. "Las Vegas," Encyclopedia.com, last updated May 11, 2018, https:// www.encyclopedia.com/places/united-states-and-canada/us-political -geography/las-vegas.

49. David Barboza, Macao Surpasses Las Vegas as Gambling Center," *The New York Times*, January 23, 2007, https://www.nytimes.com/2007 /01/23/business/worldbusiness/23cnd-macao.html.

50. Simon Sinek, "Start with Why—How Great Leaders Inspire Action," TEDx Talk, YouTube, September 28, 2009, https://www.youtube .com/watch?v=u4ZoJKF_VuA.

51. Emily Gaudette, "Netflix Declares War on Sleep, Its Biggest 'Competitor,'" *Newsweek*, November 6, 2017, https://www.newsweek.com /netflix-binge-watch-sleep-deprivation-703029?utm.

52. Christine Serlin, "11 Takeaways From the 2024 MFE Conference," *Multifamily Executive*, last modified October 9, 2024, https://www .multifamilyexecutive.com/news/11-takeaways-from-the-2024-mfe -conference_o.

53. Lu Parker, "Lu Parker Talks to Motivational Speaker Jay Shetty, Whose Goal Is to Make Wisdom Go Viral," *Maria Shriver*, accessed March 11, 2025, https://mariashriver.com/lu-parker-talks-to-motivational -speaker-jay-shetty-whose-goal-is-to-make-wisdom-go-viral/.

54. "Educational Content Makes Consumers 13% More Likely to Buy," Conductor, last updated April 6, 2022, https://www.conductor.com/academy/winning-customers-educational-content/?utm.

55. *Speechcraft Support Guide for Speeches, Toastmasters International District 90*, accessed March 11, 2025, https://www.d90toastmasters.org.au/downloads/SpeechcraftSupportGuideforSpeeches.pdf.

56. "Marketing Rule of Seven," University of Maryland, Communications and Public Affairs, https://www.umaryland.edu/cpa/rule-of-seven/.

57. Peyton Manning and Archie Manning, *Manning*, with John Underwood (New York: HarperEntertainment, 2001)